The Future of Work

Richard Donkin

First published 2010 by
PALGRAVE MACMILLAN

Palgrave Macmillan in the UK is an imprint of Macmillan Publishers Limited, registered in England, company number 785998, of Houndmills, Basingstoke, Hampshire RG21 6XS.

Palgrave Macmillan in the US is a division of St Martin's Press LLC, 175 Fifth Avenue, New York, NY 10010.

Palgrave Macmillan is the global academic imprint of the above companies and has companies and representatives throughout the world.

Palgrave® and Macmillan® are registered trademarks in the United States, the United Kingdom, Europe and other countries

ISBN 978–0–230–57638–4

This book is printed on paper suitable for recycling and made from fully managed and sustained forest sources. Logging, pulping and manufacturing processes are expected to conform to the environmental regulations of the country of origin.

A catalogue record for this book is available from the British Library.

A catalog record for this book is available from the Library of Congress.

10   9   8   7   6   5   4   3   2   1
19   18   17   16   15   14   13   12   11   10

Printed and bound in Great Britain by
CPI Antony Rowe, Chippenham and Eastbourne

For Gillian

CONTENTS

List of Figures   vi

Acknowledgments   vii

Introduction   1

Chapter 1   A Watershed in Life and Work   16

Chapter 2   Demographics—an Underlying
              Force for Change   41

Chapter 3   Goodbye Retirement, Hello Living   56

Chapter 4   Whatever Happened to Lunch?   77

Chapter 5   Women or Children First?   92

Chapter 6   Technology—Scourge or Savior of Work?   110

Chapter 7   Making Sense of Social Networking   125

Chapter 8   The Inheritors   141

Chapter 9   Leadership, Teamwork and Collaboration   162

Chapter 10   No Accounting for People   184

Chapter 11   Time for Reflection   210

Chapter 12   The Day Work Ended   220

Chapter 13   Toward a Better Society   237

Notes   254

Index   263

Figures

I.1	Circle of influences	12
2.1	Broadband speeds	43
2.2	Labor force change projection	48
5.1	A more feminized workforce	95
10.1	SuccessFactors stack ranker	186

Box

7.1	Networks in history	136

Acknowledgments

Putting together a book like this was always going to be a big undertaking, not least because events that change our future are happening all the time. It meant that, while much of the thinking in these pages was drawn from working and writing for 14 years on the changing workplace, findings and statistics were being added right up to the day I submitted the manuscript (and sometimes beyond). Fourteen years is a long time to be working in this space, and over that time I have consulted and quoted from the research of thousands of people working in the field of employment and management. Some of them, like the late Peter Drucker, who I interviewed at his home in 1996, or Warren Bennis, who became a personal friend and mentor, need no introduction. Neither do the countless management writers, some mentioned in the text, whose work has fed the thinking outlined here. I can't mention all of them by name but must acknowledge their influence. A few others, however, have given regular advice and help and encouragement over the months and years and I would like to mention them now. Stephen Overell at the Work Foundation has been consulted at various stages and some of the research I carried out for the foundation's Good Work Commission is recalled here. Duncan Brown, director of Human Resources at the Institute of Employment Studies, suggested after I had completed my earlier book that I should write something more in the line of a polemic and I have tried to reflect some of that in these pages. Ruth Spellman, chief executive of the Chartered Management Institute, persuaded me to launch the human capital standards group which Tim Melville-Ross kindly chaired during its short lifetime. Stephen Jones at Investors In People was another big help. The librarians at the *Financial Times* have always been good to me and I thank them once again. At the British Library Sally Halper was a real help, guiding part of my research. Over the years numerous public relations specialists have helped me, passing on references, pointing out new studies and contacts. I would like to thank Caroline

Hole-Jones, Colette Hill and Simon Brocklebank-Fowler for their assistance. The book had been on my wish list from the day I finished writing my history of work nearly 10 years ago, but it took some prodding from Stephen Rutt at Palgrave Macmillan to get it moving. Thanks must also go to Eleanor Davey-Corrigan, Suzanne Fowler and Abigail Coften at Palgrave Macmillan. I would like to thank my family, the boys (young men now), John, Rob and George, who have suffered the grumpy old man for too long. I don't know how to start thanking my wife, Gill, who has been supportive in so many ways—reading the text, holding the home together and making endless cups of tea.

Others such as Peter Starbuck, Dave Sellick, Sian Harrington, Andrew Mayo, Chris Bones, Robert Taylor, Harriet Arnold, Seb Morton Clark, Bill Butcher, Peter Siderman, John Dubois, John Ingham, Andrew McNeilis, Nick Isles, Lesley Muir, Andy Austin, Richard Wilkie and the late John Mason have all been helpful in one way or another. Some organizations have also supported my work during this period: Cass Business School (thanks to Caleb Hulme-Moir, Amanda Chick and David Simms), The Adecco Institute, PricewaterhouseCoopers, The Recruitment and Employment Confederation, Earthwatch Institute, The Royal Society for the Arts, Henley Management College, HR Society, Human Resources Magazine and SuccessFactors. I am indebted to all of them. I must also thank John Fey and his company SFL for supporting my website, RichardDonkin.com, where many of the ideas in this book have taken shape.

Shaping a Path for Tomorrow

The future ain't what it used to be

Yogi Berra (1925–)

On a bleak November day in 2008 I was sitting alongside some former colleagues in an East Sussex church. We had gathered for the funeral of an old friend. Before the service the vicar had asked us to ensure that our mobile phones were either turned off or silent.

The memorial tributes were overrunning and I noticed a colleague next to me look at his watch. A few seconds later he was scrolling down the glowing screen of his BlackBerry hand-held communicator and a few seconds after that he excused himself and disappeared outside.

I know that work is changing. It is, after all, the subject of this book. But I hadn't realized before that incident quite how much these changes have penetrated every facet of our lives— and deaths. Or perhaps I had, in that the incident aroused nothing more than curiosity coupled with a mild sense of irritation. Can nothing be free anymore from the intrusion of working life? Not even our funerals?

The BlackBerry has come to symbolize the "work anywhere" culture of our times. This pocket-sized device that can tell us our precise location on the planet, that can access information and communicate in a roll and click of a finger, is a triumph of primate evolution, combining the advantages of bipedalism, the opposable thumb and an enlarged brain to create the ultimate in flexible, mobile living.

Living or working? It's a taxing question—literally, if your expertise is revenue gathering—but the question is just as tough for the rest of us. The fusion of work, rest and leisure has become an underlying source of tension in our lives. Our gradual liberation from offices and factories is forcing us to reshape our understanding of work. What is work today?

For years during speaking engagements I have felt comfortable in defining work to audiences as "something we would rather not be doing." It usually draws some knowing smiles. In spite of those who claim that they love their work, this more negative definition still seems to resonate with many people.

It is the definition that holds for those who drag themselves out of bed on a morning, stand bleary-eyed in front of the mirror, rush out of the door, then struggle for a seat in the daily commute or grumble with frustration in traffic jams. It is the definition that holds for those who watch the minute hand on its slow but resolute journey around the dial, who dread the arrival of their boss and feel they are slowly crumbling under the strain of what the poet, Philip Larkin, called the "toad work."

Larkin resented what he called in his poem, "Toads," the "sickening poison" of office work and its grip on his life, yet in a later poem, "Toads Revisited," he acknowledged it suited him more than a walk in the park. "Give me my in-tray, my loaf-haired secretary," he wrote, acknowledging for all of us the sense of duty that regulates our responses. Work, he knew, would accompany him to the grave: "Give me your arm, old toad; help me down Cemetery Road," he wrote.

Larkin's view of work was depressing but recognizable. He understood that work was more than a means of earning a living; it was part of his identity, "for something sufficiently toad-like squats in me, too," he wrote.

My last book, exploring the history of work, began life as an investigation of the protestant work ethic that underpins such sentiments. This earlier book, written almost a decade ago, was also inspired by feelings that the workplace was undergoing some fundamental changes.

It seemed to me that the way we lived and worked was approaching one of the great watersheds in human history as significant as the agrarian and industrial revolutions. But, if this is the case—and much of this book will be devoted to exploring the evidence—where did it start and where will it end?

Both of these questions are a matter of debate. With previous watersheds it is quite possible to put forward an argument for gradual change. While the agrarian revolution is usually dated at around 10,000 years ago, grindstones for milling grain have been dated as far back as 40,000 years.

Equally the industrial revolution was very much a Western European development. In the US, large-scale industrial change did not happen for nearly 100 years after the textile industry began to transform working life in Europe.

But we talk and write about these events under convenient headings because they help us to understand the dynamics of change. This understanding is broader when change is viewed in context with other developments in history.

Sometimes, however, changes are tangible. People certainly sat up and noticed the changes at the Ford Motor Company in 1913 when it switched to the moving assembly of cars. But perceptions of such changes would have differed, depending on individual perspectives.

Industrial workers would have been aware of the changing shift patterns and pay rates. Those with savings would have noticed the growing affordability, reliability and range of cars as metaled roads extended beyond city boundaries.

Artists, politicians and revolutionaries noticed the impact of these developments on social habits and power structures. The same is happening today. Late in 2008 I went to the first screening of a film called *Us Now* examining the potential of social networks and their associated technologies for changing democratic governance.[1]

It was screened not long after the US presidential election, won by Barack Obama, whose campaign had relied heavily on an army of activists, often organized through web-based social networks, extending practical and financial support to the campaign in ways that emphasized personal involvement.

US Now was highlighting the power of the Internet for changing the nature of representative democracy and governance. How does the manager relate to his job at a football team such as Ebsfleet United, wholly owned by its supporters, who can outline their team choices online before every match? The answer is that he can consult their opinions, even if he chooses to ignore them. The film also illustrated the power of self-organization on the Internet in a web-based bank called Zopa, where everyone is the manager, making individual lending decisions over their own savings.[2]

Much of the Internet's social and information-sharing structure has arisen from the ground up. It does not belong to some grand strategy devised by a corporate chief executive or political power broker. Instead it relies on sparks of innovation and the cumulative endeavors of mass collaboration. While part of this structure is supported by corporate organizations, significant chunks of Internet knowledge are founded on collaborative principles.

The full-time workforces of Wikipedia—the online encyclopedia—can be counted on two hands. The Wikipedia business card is a collector's item. Supporting the sprinkling of full-time staff, however, are 75,000 active contributors and 1200 moderators. With this decentralized, voluntary army of knowledge, Wikipedia has grown rapidly into one of the largest reference sites on the Internet, attracting 684m visitors a year by 2008, reading and sometimes adding to some 10m articles in more than 260 languages.

Has there ever been such collective volunteerism on a comparable scale? Yes there has. Historically we might point to the spread of religions, but for speed of uptake we could look at a last century example—the scouting movement, established by Lord Robert Baden Powell in 1907. Scouting spread rapidly through book distribution, a sound set of values and strong organizational support at a time that radio and telephony were in their infancy. *Scouting for Boys* went on to sell 150m copies, the fourth most successful book of the twentieth century, and today there are some 28m scouts and guides around the world.

It is worth recalling the dimensions of the scouting movement when comparing the penetration of the Internet. While there is no doubting the transformational power of the World Wide Web, we should maintain a sense of perspective over the nature and range of its influence.

No matter how successful it becomes in replicating our everyday existence, the virtual world of the Internet will never replace the vital, living, breathing sensory experience of human interaction. A screen-kiss can melt our hearts but the visual experience is no substitute for reality. We do not and shall never choose to kiss a screen.

We shall, nevertheless, allow the screen to substitute more expensive face-to-face meetings with colleagues, customers and clients in different parts of the world. What once required a time-consuming flight and complex itinerary can now be staged in face-to-screen meetings over conferencing links that have ironed out the technical limitations of the past.

At the same time we are learning new levels of communications etiquette presented with an ever more bewildering menu of individual preferences. Once we simply dictated a letter or picked up the phone and dialled. Today we might text a message, engage in instant messaging, send an e-mail, construct a podcast or broadcast a thought in a blog or over a social network, depending on either the specific aims or the tastes and preferences of the intended recipient. Such relatively new tools are not only testing our collaborative skills but also the personal boundaries we choose to impose on our privacy at work and in the home.

If the computer screen is not yet the Big Brother of George Orwell's dystopian 1984, along with invasive accomplices such as the BlackBerry and the iPhone, it may be seen as a kind of tolerated little brother ever tugging at our sleeves for attention. Are these devices indispensable labor-saving aids or are they technological accelerators of ADHD (attention deficit/hyperactivity disorder), or possibly both in a perpetual state of conflict, from which we seek some equilibrium?

Like Aki Maita's tamagotchi toy pet that enjoyed a cult influence among children in 1996, computers, whether hand-held, laptop or deskbound, demand and get—but do not always earn— levels of devotion that can border on obsession, promoting addictive behavior.

Not since television dominated the lives of post–Second World War families, has a communications technology taken such a grip on people's lives. The difference between this and previous technologies, however, is the degree of interaction and creativity enabled by digital technology and the Internet.

Take an example from my own life. One Sunday morning last winter we had the only snowfall of the year. It was heavy but short-lived. Our two youngest boys, Robert and George, went out on to the grassy hill outside our home and did what youngsters have done for hundreds of years—they made a snowman.

I could see it from my office window. It had the obligatory carrot nose, cinder eyes and black hat. The next time I looked it had been demolished. I felt slightly irritated—all that time spent creating something, simply to kick it down. It seemed a waste and so uncharacteristic of the boys. Is this what their mother and I had reared them to do?

We needn't have worried. The boys belong to the Internet generation. Within half an hour, they were showing us their 30-second video, complete with its surprise ending, music mash up, and YouTube distribution to a growing audience all before lunchtime when the snow had disappeared.

To aid distribution there followed a blog on my website and links to Facebook and various other websites where my children have left their imprints. By the afternoon they were making a remix and counting their viewing figures in the thousands. This wasn't a school project or a piece of homework, but in this short exercise they were demonstrating all kinds of skills expected of those working in the creative industries.

First there was the concept. Then there was building on the idea, use of technology, sampling playlists, matching music to action, editing, then marketing and distribution. The end result was raw but entertaining, a small and amusing product of their imagination that the boys found intrinsically satisfying.

Today they are back at school and university preparing for exams that will give them the certificates on which employers make their judgments about suitability for work. Yet little in these certificates will tell recruiters about a potential job candidate's creative sparkle. Instead the certificates will say more about an individual's willingness to follow a set work pattern—to digest, to analyze, to remember facts, to distil and assemble information. For most employers today those skills are highly prized. But their significance, I believe, is waning.

This is why I wanted to write this book. The world has already changed for our children, but it is changing for all of us just as quickly. Unless my generation—and I belong to the boomer age group (those born between 1945 and 1960)—learns to understand and take advantage of these changes, we are going to create a damaging economic and organizational vacuum for future generations.

It is already happening. The reasons for the credit crunch and its near-catastrophic undermining of the global banking industry were multifaceted and complex. Intrinsically, however, they reflected a society chained to production-led economic growth. There is an apparently virtuous circularity to this society. We are paid to make things which are bought with the money we earn. It is a very simple kind of economic roundabout, oiled by debt, supported by earnings. If one part of this mechanism fails or becomes distorted, the whole machine is placed in jeopardy.

This is what happened when banks and other lending institutions overstretched themselves extending and trading in high-risk mortgage debt, insured, as it was, by rising property prices. As soon as property prices began falling, as people began defaulting on their debts, these policies rebounded, squeezing financial liquidity to such an extent that banks and building societies, relying on an ease of sourcing credit for their daily transactions, became forced increasingly to look to their own resources. Those with few cash reserves were in trouble.

I do not intend this book to be a commentary on the credit crunch. After all, it is not the first time that we have seen failures in the capitalist system. But I do think that this global collapse in confidence is lending even more fuel to generational disillusionment among the young.

Youthful disillusionment is not new either. It helped to bring about the end of the Vietnam War and to ease the rigidities in China's communist system. Much of the youthful unrest in the boomer generation manifested itself in student protest and radicalism. In the 2009 Iranian elections it filtered through in blogs and online messages, outlining dissent in spite of government attempts to block Internet broadcasts.

Today, however, the underground movement that is exposing the threadbare fabric of work is not so much a movement or a protest, but simply the silent endeavor of millions—creating, blogging, uploading, downloading, copying, borrowing, stealing, feeding and expanding creatively on the Internet. This work—if we can call it that—much of it unpaid and unfocused, led to complaints in Andrew Keen's provocative polemic, *The Cult of the Amateur*, that the Internet had equipped the hoi polloi with the means to infest the world's information channels with all kinds of gibberish undermining the work of intellectuals and respected journalists.

He likened the explosion of blogging to T. H. Huxley's "infinite monkey theorem" where Huxley argued that if you provided an infinite number of monkeys with an infinite number of typewriters one of them would one day create a masterpiece to equal Shakespeare.

There must have been similar fears in the Vatican when Gutenberg's printing press made its way across Europe in the late fifteenth-century, allowing mass publications of the Bible in the vernacular for the first time. The Vatican feared, justifiably, that this kind of mass media would challenge its authority, and so came the Reformation. Would we have known Shakespeare without it?

Today we are on the cusp of a new Reformation, but this is a reformation of the workplace from the ground upwards. It is not organized or collectivized, nor is it revolutionary in nature (although it may become so); it is born of a persistent drip-feeding of change fed by diffuse influences that I will explore thematically in the chapters of this book (see Figure I.1).

Robert Peston, the BBC's business editor, has been speaking eloquently about a new kind of capitalism, emerging from the embers of the 2008 banking crisis. The post-2008 business environment may well see a reversion to traditional values in the workplace, placing an emphasis on trust and personal relationships. But I don't see it yet, even though I believe, passionately, that these have always been, and must remain, the fundamental characteristics of the best working arrangements.

Tomorrow's workplace will be defined, not only by a reversion to what we might recognize as old-fashioned values, but also by broader international forces such as those of environmentalism. A growing understanding that the world cannot rely forever on fossil fuels is leading to a backlash against unadulterated economic growth in a resource-hungry world. We don't know when oil will run out but it is just possible that we have already reached the point known as Peak Oil, after which the rate of oil extraction and refinement will begin to reduce. The influence of this decline and the transitions that must accompany reducing oil supplies and diminishing mineral stocks will very likely ensure that sustainable living will be the prime economic concern at some stage within the next two generations, quite possibly even in mine.

These are the underpinnings of disquiet among all generations, but particularly those who are about to inherit the workplace. Employers will find they can no longer rely on the unconditional support of employees and potential employees in the headlong pursuit of material wealth. But they should not interpret changing attitudes solely as a reaction to the events of 2008. The sea change began some years earlier.

In 1997 McKinsey & Co, the management consultant, published a study called *The War for Talent* that heralded an increasingly competitive marketplace in recruitment and leadership development. No longer could employers sit back and cherry-pick their future leaders from thousands of willing candidates. No longer could they assume a craving for long-term institutional employment. McKinsey & Co consultants Ed Michaels, Helen Handfield-Jones and Beth Axelrod argued that if companies were serious about retaining and developing the best leaders, they would need to recognize the strategic value of human capital.

I shall return to the idea of human capital in Chapter 10 as it is often misunderstood or simply dismissed as a trendy term for human resources management, just as HR itself was regarded as a fancier term for personnel management (an argument with which I have some sympathy).

Suffice to say that companies have needed to change their thinking and approaches to recruitment and development radically since the 1990s when the old social contract disappeared and with it any sense of loyalty and long-term career expectations.

What created this transformation? We can look, perhaps, to the changing political landscape of the 1980s when the Thatcher and Reagan governments in the UK and the US introduced sharper, more market-driven approaches to their economic policies. The result was a wholesale clear out among unprofitable industries and a drastic paring down among others, encouraging tighter, leaner, systems of management.

The harsher climate of monetarism provided a fresh canvas for the ideas of Michael Hammer and James Champy whose *Harvard Business Review* article of 1990 and subsequent book, *Reengineering the Corporation: A Manifesto for Business*

Revolution in 1993 heralded unprecedented white-collar job-shedding in the private sector.

New service industries were born overnight. One of these was outplacement—a service that provided support for outgoing executives in job-searching, organizing curriculum vitae, interviewing approaches and networking skills. Another one was interim management. Interims are contracting executives who work, either by choice or circumstance, outside the traditional jobs market. They find work through their networks or using agencies that sprang up, offering skilled executives to undertake temporary managerial roles on a day-rate basis.

Typically these individuals are overqualified for the jobs they are expected to undertake. But their willingness to work at short notice for limited periods of a few weeks or months, combined with the gaps in leadership that resulted from overzealous pruning, enabled them to attract a premium for their services.

When Charles Handy, the management writer, interviewed some of these executives in the early days of the industry he observed that their work was no longer a single job but a collection or portfolio of jobs, hence his subsequent description of this kind of work as the "portfolio career."

Business writing was abuzz with these concepts during the 1990s. Bill Bridges wrote *Jobshift* in which he predicted that the job as we knew it would disappear. So, he predicted, would middle management. Daniel Pink's book, *Free Agent Nation*, envisaged an army of freelance workers replacing the institution of the permanent job. But the reality of free agency, while not a myth, turned out to be something less than representative of working life. As the world moved in to a new millennium, salaried or waged employment remained and continues to remain the predominant model of employment.

But it can't claim to be a happy model. If one kind of workplace epitomized the late twentieth-century job it had to be the office. The jargon-riddled language of office administration has been savaged in print by *Dilbert*, the Scott Adams cartoon strip and on television in *The Office*, a pastiche of everything that is bland and unedifying about office work. Ricky Gervais's David Brent character is the nightmare manager, larger than life, but only just. We watched *The Office*, cringing with a knowing curiosity because Gervais was reflecting a recognizable caricature of sterile working relationships, underpinned by the ubiquitous appraisal form and so-called performance management.

Performance management was the alter ego of collective bargaining. As trade union influence declined during the 1980s it was replaced by a new individualism, particularly in management ranks, where each individual was accountable for their own success or failure. This focus on the individual reached its zenith in General Electric under Jack Welch during the 1990s after the introduction of what Welch called "Session C" appraisals.[3] Managers were required each year to grade the members of their teams as As, Bs, or Cs. The As were the star performers, the anointed ones, destined for promotion; the Bs, the solid, dependable types; and the Cs? Well the Cs could either shape up or ship out.

The system was described by consultants, transferring it across the US workplace, as "forced ranking". It heralded a harsher, more Darwinian style of corporate management that was translated into television entertainment on the *The Apprentice*, a realty business–based TV show launched in 2004 and headed by property tycoon, Donald Trump. Those who failed to make the grade were shown the door and told "You're fired!"

The format was repeated in the UK, this time headed by Sir Alan Sugar, the founder of Amstrad, the computer company. By this time, however, the television schedules were accustomed to harsher-edged rejection formats. The audience-participation "vote off" was pioneered in the Dutch TV creation, *Big Brother*, where the audience played a voyeuristic role, viewing so-called housemates gathered together in sealed living quarters. Members of the TV audience chose who they wished to leave the house. The format was later repeated in dozens of TV shows. In the TV quiz show, *The Weakest Link*, the humiliation of rejection was emphasized when contestants were told by presenter Anne Robinson: "You are the weakest link, goodbye!" and asked to take the "walk of shame."

So who was copying who? Were the television stations simply reflecting a tougher workplace, or was the "vote off" simply a reflection of our baser characteristics, only concealed by otherwise polite behavior? Is there something more honest about the blunt appraisal? After all, no one forces us to enter a talent show.

I want to investigate these issues in the forthcoming chapters while examining what I believe are some of the most significant themes influencing the changing workplace (see Figure I.1). Some of these themes, including forced ranking, perhaps, may prove to be nothing more than short-lived fashion.

Some, like the current interest in healthy workplaces, may flourish briefly as they did during the 1920s and 1930s when progressive large companies made space for playing fields and organized sports and social clubs for employees.

FIGURE I.1   Circle of influences

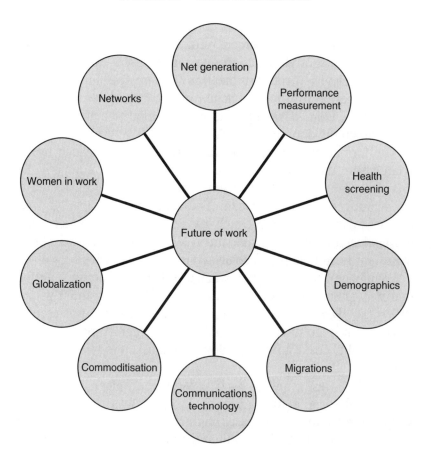

But other influences, such as the Internet, appear to be here to stay and workplaces must learn to exploit the possibilities of the new information and communications media and the way they are shaping behaviors among what the Canadian management writer, Don Tapscott, in his book, *Growing Up Digital*, calls the "net generation."

Yet other influences, such as human capital, deserve greater scrutiny and demand broader understanding if employers are to develop meaningful, reliable and useful ways of measuring and stimulating excellent, rewarding work. After all, that's what really matters about work isn't it—that it's good work?[4]

How can work be improved? On the eve of his presidential inauguration, Barack Obama visited a shelter for homeless teenagers and quoted Martin Luther King's advice urging young people, whatever their talents, to give of their best. King said, "If a man is called to be a street sweeper, he should sweep streets even as Michelangelo painted, or Beethoven composed music, or Shakespeare wrote poetry. He should sweep streets so well that all the hosts of Heaven and Earth will pause to say, here lived a great street sweeper who did his job well."

On the day of the inauguration some 1.8m people crammed into Washington's National Mall as Obama took his oath of office, leaving behind them 100 tons of litter swept up by 300 street cleaners and 20 cleaning machines. Other workers set about disposing of the contents of 7000 portaloos. Somebody has to do this work and it won't go away, at least not in the near future. While there may have been relatively few Beethovens and Michelangelos among the cleaners, the challenge to make such work intrinsically rewarding remains.

Job content matters. So does our experience of work. Don't we deserve to be happy in work? Is it acceptable today simply to tolerate work as the source of our earnings, to accept with a sense of resignation that it will ever be something we would rather avoid? Or can work be something better, something finer, something uplifting and purposeful? It seemed to feel that way to Jim Webber, who died in late 2008 at the age of 105 after working the land for 93 years in his native Dorset, latterly as a gardener before arthritis enforced his retirement at the age of 104.[5]

When work defines a life, including the "triumphs and disasters," from Kipling's memorable poem, *If*, it becomes inseparable from who we are and what we do. In these circumstances, terms such as retirement lose their meaning. Neither might we care about that ghastly, meaningless neologism, "work-life balance" as if the two are somehow separable, as if to work is not to live. In a perfect world the two would be one and the same and, though we may never achieve perfection, it behoves of us to try.

That's what this book is about. It is my own attempt, drawn from a lifetime of work and some 15 years specializing in work and management, much of it in the pages of the *Financial Times*, to make some sense of what we do and what we should be doing in our approach to work and the management of work.

Not all of this is theoretical. For the past seven years I have pursued my own living experiment, mixing work and leisure, seeking opportunities to "learn and earn" from the things I enjoy such as walking, fishing and sailing. Plowing this independent furrow I have learned the importance of fitness and health in work, of organization, learning and the power of the network. I wouldn't portray this kind of working and living as an ideal or, indeed, the future of work. It can be lonely, disheartening and confusing at times. But it does feel like living rather than working. On the other hand it is not always easy to identify the things I might have once viewed as leisure. Of one thing I am certain, the leisure society is a myth.

Work will be as important tomorrow as it has always been but we must find better ways to learn and prepare for working lives, better ways to exploit and make the best of talent, better reward systems and better forms of management. Here's a confession at the outset: I don't know, any more than anyone else what the future has in store for us. Any trend is subject to unforeseen variables. So this isn't intended as a book of predictions with visions of wizzy technology, although in Chapter 13, *The Day Work Ended*, I do include a somewhat tongue-in-cheek vision of 50 years hence as food for thought. Do I think the more egalitarian world portrayed at the end of the book will come to pass? I doubt it, but I do retain a sense of optimism about the future. Capitalism and corporatism are so strong that I think it would take a destabilizing financial meltdown much more severe than happened in 2008 for the world's power brokers to accept more democratic systems of governance, even where technology exists to make it possible. I hope I am wrong in this conclusion, however, and would love to see some of our biggest institutions dragged kicking and screaming, if it has to be that way, to more democratic forms of management.

Also, socially, I do not think there is any great desire among most people to adopt the isolating atmosphere of home-working on a grand scale. People like to congregate in big cities. You need only cross Hungerford footbridge in London on an early summer evening, savoring the buzz of people on the south and north banks of the Thames to understand the lure of city-working and city-living. People will still need to feel a sense of permanence in their lives, so either a full-time job, or the promise of continued work will remain important in anchoring people emotionally, not to mention financially. Without safeguards, free agency, for most people, cannot offer such security. But the future may introduce catalysts for radical change: climate change, oil shortages, insurgency, the need for more sustainable lifestyles, each or all of these forces could lead to rapidly transitioning societies.

The bulk of this book, however, is not attempting to ask the question "what if?" Instead it is attempting to outline and interpret significant existing trends and to offer some thoughts and ideas for policymakers, leaders and individuals trying to make sense of work. The shape of tomorrow is fashioned today.

CHAPTER 1

A Watershed in Life and Work

Change is the law of life. And those who look only to the
past or present are certain to miss the future.

John F. Kennedy (1917–63)

It's a sunny day in late February 2009 and I'm looking out over the back garden of our Surrey suburban home. The snowdrops and crocuses are out, the heather is blooming and the strong waxy shoots of tulips are poking through the soil. A blue tit is examining the nesting box as it always does at this time of year.

There's a reassuring permanence about the seasons as they come and go. They herald change, yet they represent a familiar sequence in the cycle of life. We know what's coming and we learn how to handle the gales, the storms and the snowfalls and how to make the best of fine, clear weather. But we don't seem to do quite so well in the way we manage our lives.

It is as if the whole of humanity is swept along by events as ever-increasing demands on our attention leave few opportunities to find the time and space for reflection. Before we know it, whole years have passed; the years run into decades and suddenly we find ourselves looking back, nostalgically, rather than forward with anything other than a sense of fear and insecurity.

Yet it is today and in the years ahead, where changing attitudes and knowledge, interwoven with events, will be shaping not only the quality of life for future generations but the future life of our planet. The theories of James Lovelock, author of the Gaia hypothesis, suggest that planetary life will prevail, with or without the human race, but we cannot leave our environmental future to chance if we seek to be part of that future rather than authors of our own downfall.

This book is about work and the way it is evolving and must evolve to meet these grand challenges. I don't think it is a conceit to suggest that the way we approach and think about work is fundamental to the way we extract meaning and purpose in life. It's difficult to connect the way we serve hamburgers to the future of the planet, but there are connections and the better we understand these connections, the better we will be equipped to instigate change rather than allowing external changes to determine the pattern of our lives.

Much of the book, therefore, is devoted to examining evidence of change, sometimes through an analysis of statistics, sometimes through anecdotes, stories, comments and observations, and sometimes through what the late Sumantra Ghoshal, the management writer, called "smelling the air." I'm attempting to do something that approximates to Ghoshal's suggestion right now, over breakfast with my newspaper on Saturday, February 21, 2009.

A SNAPSHOT IN TIME

There is nothing special about this day. I'm consulting the newspaper, merely in order to record a snapshot in time. In a *Daily Telegraph*, layered with stories of financial gloom, the front-page lead story is headlined: "Middle classes lose out in school lotteries." But only the first part of the sentence registers: middle classes lose out.

Some would argue that social class—as much as it exists—is less a reflection of economic circumstances and more an attitude of mind, buttressed by hundreds of subliminal features—the names we call our children, our postcode, the clothes we wear, the newspapers we read, the food we eat, the way we speak, the people we know.

One of the most striking features of the recession in 2009 was that it undermined confidence among the middle classes. Today I know middle-class people who feel poor and most of them still have their jobs. The sentiment is as irrational as that of the exuberance which intermittently overtakes the financial markets. Poverty is a dirty, threadbare tent, without sanitation in a Mumbai slum. On the front page of my newspaper is a photograph of Ayush Mahesh Khedekar, one of the child stars of the film of the moment, *Slumdog Millionaire*. He is waiting to board a flight to Hollywood for the following night's Oscar ceremony. *Slumdog* will go on to win the Oscar for best film.

Ayush must be experiencing a sharp understanding of change in the stark contrast between Hollywood and Mumbai. I notice that he is not wearing a Rolex watch. Neither am I. There is still time for Ayush to buy his Rolex but, at 51, I am too late if I want to consider myself a success, according to a story that day on the inside news pages. It says that French President Nicholas Sarkozy's closest friend, Jacques Séguéla, has described anyone who does not own a Rolex watch by the age of 50 as "a failure." Mr Sarkozy owns a Rolex watch but has been advised not to wear it in public.

Most of our emotions and experiences are registered in a relative sense each day as we are confronted with differing definitions of poverty, wealth, success and failure. Elsewhere on the inside pages there is a story about "reality TV star" Jade Goody who is getting married this weekend. The marriage has been arranged hastily since doctors have given her weeks to live after a diagnosis of advanced cervical cancer. She dies four weeks later. The newspapers are struggling with the attention extended toward Goody since she has achieved little against the conventional measures of achievement, other than fame and wealth enough to buy her own Rolex watch should she desire one.

A few days later the *Daily Mail*, a newspaper that understands the best and worst traits of its middle-class readership, contrasted the positive press afforded Goody with various negative blog-community comments leveled at Gail Trimble, The Corpus Christi, Oxford University student who achieved a record points score in the popular BBC TV quiz show, University Challenge. Harry Mount, who authored the *Daily Mail* article, wrote: "In 1960, a university professor earned as much as a Liverpool footballer. If Gail Trimble, now studying for a doctorate in Latin literature, becomes a professor, she is unlikely to earn in a lifetime what a Premier League footballer gets paid in a single season—or, indeed, what Jade Goody earned over the course of the weekend."

The tenor of his argument was that society's values in relation to achievement and success had become warped. Whether or not we agree with those sentiments, it does seem that values have undergone some kind of a sea change. In the US this became apparent in the popularity of *Forrest Gump*, the 1994 film, which challenged long-cherished understandings of achievement. While an earlier film, *Being There*, starring Peter Sellers, had satirized the fragility of the power elite and its self-sustaining confidence, the Tom Hanks character Gump, is suggesting that anyone, no matter what their social or educational background, or, indeed, their physical appearance, can achieve success in life.

Goody's success embodied that message, discomforting those who believe in achievement through a combination of hard work, diligence and talent. Here was Britain's real life slumdog millionaire, proving that it is possible to extract yourself from a disadvantaged background and to achieve the kind of success that would register with the likes of Jacques Séguéla. But Goody's story had the hammer-blow ending of the classic morality tale. No amount of fame and wealth could compensate for the tragedy of untimely death.

Throughout history, people have taken heart from fairy tale success, be it stories such as Cinderella, Pygmalion or the rags-to-riches stories of Horatio Alger. The Alger stories differed, however, in that in each of them success was a reward for hard work.

So have our values changed in that we no longer believe in the merits of hard work? Are the feckless inheriting the Earth? More to the point, do any of these questions matter to employers? I can almost hear the human resources professional asking what any of this has to do with employee engagement, workplace dynamics, motivation theory and reward systems? The answer is everything and nothing.

Social attitudes and value systems have always been integral to our relationship with work. It is vital that employers understand this if they are to build businesses that are embodied in the people who work for the company. Moreover, work can no longer be divorced from life as a separate entity, something that is left behind when we leave the office or factory gate. Nor does it make sense that we should seek some kind of work-life balance. This jaded concept presents work and life as two distinct experiences. They are not. We don't stop living when we go to work and, very often today, we don't stop working when we arrive home.

For thousands of home workers and millions who work for part of their time at home, work has assumed a domestic environment. I have a tiny upstairs office in my home, but just now I'm working on my laptop, sitting at the dining table, for no other reason than I sought a change of scenery.

While part of this book will indeed discuss the mechanics of employment, I think it is important that any analysis of the way we work—or in this case, the way we will work—must consider also the way we live. It must be grounded in the present, it must have an appreciation of context and it needs to have a sense of how we have changed—not simply the way that work has changed, but how our attitudes, understandings and perspectives have changed from those of our parents.

Without this understanding it is impossible to look ahead. It explains why part of the journey leading to this work was to research and write a history book. "The further back you can look, the further forward you can see," Winston Churchill once said.

Most of the historical investigation involved a search for definitions. That search delved back as far as the first tool that we know about, dated nearly 3m years ago. Those ancient hand axes found in Tanzania's Olduvai Gorge tell us two important things: first, that, since work emerged before homo sapiens became identifiable as a species, its role in shaping human evolution has been profound. Second, while work may be defined partly by the objective of the task, it is also defined by the tools that we use, extending our ambition and stimulating creativity.

Sometimes those tools or technologies inspire fundamental changes in the way we live. It happened more than 10,000 years ago when inventions enabling the production, storage and refinement of wheat created an agrarian revolution and a radical shift from the hunter–gatherer lifestyle that had supported our ancestors for thousands of years.

It happened again during the eighteenth and nineteenth centuries when mechanization founded on water and steam power hastened an industrialized society that fundamentally changed the rhythm of working life.

In his great novel *Anna Karenina* Leo Tolstoy reminds us of those rhythms that enabled laboring harvesters to shift a prodigious amount of work when it was needed.[1] Industrial society, in contrast, became focused on ever more efficient production in a system governed by flows of capital and cycles of demand. Adam Smith observed and explained this system in his theory of capital, but it was pioneering industrialists such as Richard Arkwright, Andrew Carnegie and Henry Ford who confirmed its triumph as the second great watershed in human evolution.

Today our society, I believe, is witnessing a third watershed just as profound in its significance for the way we live and work. If so, when did it start? Was it in 1956, as the futurist Alvin Toffler once argued, when the number of white-collar workers overtook that of blue-collar workers in the US for the first time?

I doubt if many people noticed these first faltering steps as working people stumbled into a period of workplace transformation. Change creeps up on us like the dawn. Not long after Toffler's milestone Peter Drucker began to explore the concept of knowledge workers in his 1959 book, *Landmarks of Tomorrow*, although he did not use the term until 1969, drawing the reference from Princeton professor Fritz Machlup's description of knowledge industries. These knowledge workers—"people who get paid for putting to work what one learns in school rather than for their physical strength or manual skill," to quote Drucker—would become the gatekeepers to a digital future.

In 1973 the sociologist Daniel Bell suggested in his book *The Coming of Post-Industrial Society* that we were entering an information age. At that time the personal computer had yet to be invented. But scientists and mathematicians were becoming aware of the computer's potential. "We'll have to think up bigger problems if we want to keep them busy," said computer pioneer Howard Aiken.

The spread of computing, however, would be defined not only by problem solving but by a love of technology. People like technology for its own sake, delighting in the vision of change it represents. They bought cars before there were adequate roads on which to drive them and they flew aeroplanes before they built airports. Infrastructure follows on the heels of invention.

We can now clearly see how the personal computer and its operating system preceded the infrastructure and systems that would characterize computing in the twenty-first century. What was initially feted for its information storage and processing power achieved universal utility in accessing and communicating information cheaply, worldwide and across most levels of economic society.

Cheapness, ubiquity and availability of innovation were significant characteristics of those earlier great watersheds in the delivery and organization of work. The Model T Ford succeeded because it was bought in large numbers by ordinary working families. Another characteristic is the tiered and overlapping way that these societal changes occur. The agrarian revolution did not wipe out nomadic lifestyles, just as industry did not supplant agriculture. In the same way the information revolution will not replace industry although its influence is undeniable—in the online availability of books, for example.

We shall still need to make tangible products in future but the future of work that we have yet to understand is the way that we exploit, reward and organize the production and dissemination of intangibles, and the chief among those is knowledge, devoured by hungry consumers demanding ever more manageable chunks.

More critically still we shall need to understand the way this new tier is influencing attitudes to work and pay. Drucker did not divorce work from pay, but for many people working within digital networks, bridging what is left of the division between home and office life, there is no real distinction between working for a living and living for work. This is not a dystopian interpretation of work but one which envisions work and a fulfilling life as one and the same.

The suggestion that "work can be done any place" is a soundbite of the information revolution. The idea is supported by late twentieth-century developments such as the Internet, hot-desking, tele-working, mobile phones, memory sticks and palm-computing, and multiplied by newer concepts in information access, such as cloud computing. The speed and shelf life of these developments is bewildering. A hundred years from now will anyone remember the fax machine?

The way that some of these more modern technologies occupied no more than a fleeting presence in our psyche can be recalled by many of us in our mid-twenties and beyond in memories of the two-tone electronic screeching that accompanied a successful modem link in the days before broadband communications. The sound lives on in my head, a distinctive imprint from the technological archive that was never heard by my father and will not have been heard by my children. It's like the crunching of a gear stick shifting from one great epoch to another.

Whole new technological languages have stampeded into our lives, falling over themselves in a jumble of acronyms. I know what a USB socket looks like and what it does, after a fashion. Will my children's children? I doubt it, any more than my own children need to know much about spark plugs in cars. Spark plugs were tangible things that we could install with a spanner. There is nothing tangible, however, about the digital code that translates music, pictures, text and film into combinations of 1 and 0. In a few short years the fast transfer and pliability of information, accessed cheaply or at no cost, has led to a worldwide free-for-all of unprecedented proportions.

Millions of people are working with these developments today, either as part of their paid work or in their domestic lives. This new work, no longer confined to the traditional organizational frameworks of most companies and public administrations, is outside the control of the boardroom, eating away at managements' and sometimes governments' best-made strategies. If work were a religion—and it sometimes seems so—the new work would be akin to the non-conformism of the Reformation.

No sooner has a company established its e-mailing system than employees are overloaded by its very popularity. Independent of managements, people are developing etiquettes for communications technologies. New forms of communication are seeping like floodwater underneath and over the tightest corporate barriers, even influencing the working habits of those charged with maintaining discipline in the existing order. Company directors are reading their text messages and e-mails in the boardroom. Instant messaging is aiding collaboration; and relatively recent developments in social networking such as Twitter.com are offering potential in project work, customer communications and team organization.

One of the biggest shifts in many of these new Internet developments is the collective consciousness governing their use and distribution that is rooted not in the profit motive but in ubiquity. This is the toughest nut for established business, comfortable, as it has been hitherto with Milton Friedman's assurance that "the business of business is business."

This is not to say that people are eschewing the profit motive when working within the Internet, but profit very often has been a by-product rather than the primary goal of developments such as Facebook (begun as a distraction from thinking about a girlfriend) and Google (started as a dissertation theme). In the communications revolution work is rediscovering the intrinsic value of a job well done. Moreover, through broadband connections the work is accessible, bounded only by the limitations of an individual's capacity and willingness to learn.

This has not always been the reality of the organized workplace. However many companies represent themselves as learning organizations, their systems of working—hierarchies, reporting systems, shift patterns, management expectations, rewards and strategies—are sanctioned from the top.

While progressive managers, such as William McKnight, the founder of 3M, stressed the need for delegation and freedom among employees to experiment and make mistakes, large employers have struggled to reproduce the fluidity of work that characterizes collaborative Internet enterprise. Facebook is an open system, a publishing platform that enables the delivery of so-called applications where success is measured in their popularity. Most large companies today operate closed systems, expecting their employees to work within rigid corporate policies, accessing organizational-based information from the company intranet.

Traditional businesses are wrestling with the more open styles of collaboration ushered in by social networks. Bill Gates, the founder of Microsoft, said that in business "you have to be able to hear the grass grow." But business has been deaf and sometimes hostile to some Internet developments. In 2007 when Indian brothers, Rajat and Jayant Agarwalla, created a word game called Scrabulous on Facebook—a blatant reproduction of Scrabble—the makers and distributors of Scrabble enforced their copyright in spite of a big increase in sales on the back of a resurgence in the game's popularity.

Today a slightly altered version of the game has reappeared called Lexulous. The speed of mutation in web-based enterprise has so far bedeviled attempts to restrict copying of artistic productions. But while royalties have been lost, performers have benefited from a wider distribution of their work. The rules of the game have changed.

The subversive nature of such change is unsettling for business, worried that it could threaten the transactional nature of work. The concept of a fair day's pay for a fair day's work is resilient and enduring, but millions of people today are exchanging work through collaborative effort in a spirit of mutual assistance. The Internet forum and exchanges of instant messages have become the tutorials of choice.

During the privatization of British Gas, one of the UK's biggest public utilities, people were encouraged to buy shares in a campaign that used the slogan: "If you see Sid, tell him."[2] Information has been transmitted for thousands of years through word of mouth. Christianity spread through the spoken word and the Church held on to its power by a strict control over the written word, until translations into the vernacular, coupled with cheap and prolific dissemination through the printing press, enabled widespread distribution of the Bible that would ultimately lead to the Reformation.

Today the workplace itself is facing a reformation through the widespread distribution and availability of information across the Internet. Sid is no longer waiting to be told things any more. He's finding out for himself, using search engines, web forums and Wikipedia.

Within the Internet some work has moved beyond the transactional framework understood by business. Whatever we may think about Wikipedia as a research tool, its collection of some 2.7m pages of information in English has been compiled entirely through voluntary effort. How can business compete with this freely given collaborative power?

People have always given of their time freely in work that engages their need for recognition, respect and learning. Mark Twain recognized as much in the boys who paid Tom Sawyer for the opportunity to paint Aunt Polly's fence, such was their desire to be involved. Business must learn to stimulate this kind of engagement in those who work on their behalf. But are they doing so?

In the companies I have visited over the past 20 years I have seen numerous examples of workplace processes, learning initiatives, on-the-job training and systems designed to ensure continuous quality improvements. Occasionally I have come across companies celebrating discretionary behavior, but much of today's work has removed the discretion that allows people either to use their initiative or to impose their personalities and style on a job.

THE MARCH OF PROCESS

In human resources management there is an obsession with so-called best practice and benchmarking in order to refine jobs to an extent that even many professional roles are becoming commoditized. "We are going through a phase now where white collar workers will have to realise they are the blue collar workers of the 21st century," said Carsten Sorensen, senior lecturer in information systems at the London School of Economics, speaking in 2004.[3]

Commoditization has been one of the most significant influences on the development of working practices for two centuries. It helped to establish the industrial revolution as factory-based machines, operated by semi-skilled workers, undermined the relative prosperity that had been enjoyed by craft-based artisan weavers and croppers.

Frederick Taylor and other early exponents of scientific management would dedicate their lives to discovering the "one best way" of working. The processes of refinement they set in train have begun to standardize the once marketable skills and pay rates enjoyed by information technology and other knowledge workers.

The attraction of such standardization is that once a job is replicable in all its forms, then it can be transferred to a part of the world where there are people willing and able to do it more cheaply.

"At one time it had a bit of mystery to it and not everyone could do it. But as soon as the work becomes codified and made more transparent it becomes sensitive to price and pay rates start to fall," says Andrew Holmes, author of *Commoditization and the Strategic Response*, discussing falling pay rates among computer code developers.[4]

His choice of language is interesting because the word "mystery" derives from the Latin word, *misterium*, which referred to a professional skill and was once used as an alternative word for a guild. It was the guild system in medieval times that governed and protected many forms of skilled work.

Some of this protection was condemned as restrictive practices. On the other hand, through long apprenticeships, guilds did ensure a dedicated line of progression from journeyman to craftsman. Excellence was achieved through commitment and through learning passed on by the existing masters of their craft.

Typically these masters differentiated themselves within their craft. If you bought a piece of furniture made by Robert Thompson, a Yorkshire-born woodworker, who specialized in oak furniture and paneling, you would have found a little wooden mouse carved into the finished piece. The Kilburn-based workshop he founded maintains the tradition today, but even here there has been some commoditization because the mouse is now carved by various craftspeople.

The mouse has become a trademark and like all the best trademarks or brands, it is supposed to stand for something. Thompson was part of the English arts and crafts movement that flourished across Europe and the US in the late nineteenth and early twentieth-centuries where practitioners consciously rejected the forces of mass production.

These forces—mechanization, the factory system, the development of interchangeable parts and management processes such as work study, moving assembly and divisional administration—created the mass market for goods underpinning modern economies. But for all that it achieved, commoditization had a negative influence, changing once fulfilling work that had been intrinsically rewarding into cheerless, repetitive jobs in which the very language of work became associated with something no longer desirable.

I have a friend who is a housing developer. When seeking out tradesmen for various building jobs (yes, they are still all men in his world) he talks about finding "skins." He says: "I work out how many skins I need and then ring round the recruiters."

Whether it's a chippy (carpenter), sparky (electrician) or bricky (bricklayer), as far as he is concerned they're all skins who have their price and who are expected to return a certain level of work. In spite of his language he is a good manager and respects those who work for him. In a way I prefer this straight-talking approach to employment to the HR-dominated nonsense that names people "employee of the month," in the assumption that a pat on the back and a certificate with a box of chocolates is an acceptable substitute for a proper wage.

In his book, Holmes fears the influence of what has come to be known as the "China price"—the lowest level of labor price. But, as he points out, internal market forces were driving down relative labor costs well before globalized business fell into the thrall of outsourcing and offshoring—twin strategies for pursuing the cheapest sources of skilled labor.

He writes: "In the late 1960s the biggest employer in the United States was General Motors and they paid their staff on average \$29,000 (in today's terms) together with generous pension contributions, healthcare and other benefits. Today (2008) Wal-Mart is the biggest employer and they pay their staff \$17,000 on average with few if any benefits."[5] General Motors, meanwhile, has been saved from bankruptcy through nationalization, earning the new nickname, "Government Motors."[6]

Holmes envisages a spread of commoditization in work that will not only continue to eliminate low-level jobs but will have soon worked its way through the mid-level tiers and into higher levels of employment. He forecasts "the emergence of the extreme worker at one end and the disenfranchised jobber at the other and the inevitable rise of a wider labour war which will no longer be focused on just the most talented in the workforce."

These forces, he believes, could lead to a widening gap between winners and losers within the workplace, creating implications for health and well-being, even for some apparent winners since their skills will be so much in demand that they will have little time to enjoy the financial rewards attached to their work.

What kinds of jobs will be safe in an increasingly commoditized society? Well, not that many, it seems, and certainly not those in management. Holmes notes that one of India's largest information technology companies, Infosys Technologies, based in Bangalore, pays its chairman and chief executive salaries of about $100,000 each and their highest performing executive about $250,000. He argues provocatively that "There are those that believe that firms such as EDS and Accenture could save as much by sending 100 top management positions to India as by eliminating 10,000 staff."

It's refreshing to read some questioning of the "return on management," and the discussion is timely after the banking crisis of 2008 exposed the limitations of senior bankers whose reckless behaviors lost billions of pounds and destabilized the global financial system. If some of the world's most senior bankers could not be trusted with our money, who could?

JOBS IN RETREAT

Some of these questions seem academic with unemployment rising in many economies in what has become a global recession. No wonder, then, that my old colleague Robert Taylor, former employment editor of the *Financial Times*, has been tempted to make comparisons with the depression years of the 1930s. It's not so much a return to the soup kitchens and the grinding desperation during those years that he fears, but a growing instability arising from unemployment. "What's changing is the expectancy of work. We're looking now at a world of turmoil and insecurity," he says.

Perspectives must change, he argues, just as they did in the 1930s. "It's like moving from the world of F. Scott Fitzgerald to that of John Steinbeck," he says. "It's no longer a case of choosing a job strategy. Simply having a job and keeping it will be enough of a struggle for many people." These are alarming trends that are clouding our vision of tomorrow's society.

As the recession began to bite in the winter of 2008/2009, UK companies responded with pay freezes and cuts in working hours. One in 10 of UK companies had frozen pay rates by the spring of 2009 according to Incomes Data Services, pay information specialists. As trading conditions deteriorated, Jaguar motor company staff opted to work a shorter working week in order to save jobs and pay and working hours were cut by 10 percent at Toyota's UK car plants.

By this time the recession had spread worldwide with little prospect of a speedy end to the economic gloom. As the International Labour Organization pointed out, what had begun as a crisis in financial markets had rapidly become a global job crisis.[7] The ILO was predicting that global job losses in 2009 could be as high as 51m. Juan Somavia, ILO director general, painted a harrowing picture of poverty created by unemployment and inequality. "Progress in poverty reduction is unravelling and middle classes worldwide are weakening," he wrote. But, as Somavia pointed out, unemployment was not the only issue facing regions such as sub-Saharan Africa and South Asia, where harsh labor market conditions meant that four-fifths of those employed in these regions could be classed as "working poor" in 2007, deprived of decent work and a decent living.

Even during the boom years when millions of jobs were created worldwide during the 1990s, income inequality had been growing. The ILO's *World of Work Report 2008: Income Inequalities in the Age of Financial Globalization* that examined wages in 70 developed and developing countries, found that, as global employment rose by 30 percent between the early 1990s and 2007, the income gap between richer and poorer households widened.

"This reflects the impact of financial globalization and a weaker ability of domestic policies to enhance the income position of the middle class and low-income groups. The present global financial crisis is bound to make matters worse unless long-term structural reforms are adopted," said Raymond Torres, director of ILO's International Institute for Labour Studies responsible for the report.

The report acknowledged that a certain degree of income inequality could be useful in rewarding effort, talent and innovation, but it said that the broadening gap between rich and poor could prove counterproductive and damaging for most economies. "Rising income inequality represents a danger to the social fabric as well as economic efficiency when it becomes excessive," said Torres.

The report revealed the extent to which income inequality had widened at an increasing pace between the earnings of senior executives and those of average employees. In the US in 2007, the chief executive officers of the 15 largest companies earned 520 times more than the average worker. In 2003 the top executives earned 360 times more. "Similar patterns, though from lower levels of executive pay, have been registered in Australia, Germany, Hong Kong (China), the Netherlands and South Africa," said the ILO.

The ratchetting up of executive pay continued almost unabated throughout the 1990s and 2000s. Only after the financial crisis of 2008 and subsequent taxpayer-funded bailouts of banks and insurance companies was there a noticeable public and political backlash. When it happened, the senior executives experiencing censure seemed almost shell-shocked by its severity. Yet many appeared remarkably unrepentant.

US President Barack Obama led public outrage at a decision to pay executives of the troubled insurer AIG some $165m in bonus payments even though the company had taken advantage of a $170 bn government bailout. Edward Liddy, AIG's chairman, later accepted before a Congressional hearing that the bonus payments were distasteful and said he had asked those who had received more than $100,000 to return at least half of their bonuses. It was not quite sackcloth and ashes but Liddy at least confessed that "Mistakes were made at AIG on a scale that few could have imagined possible." He added that the company had become "too complex, too unwieldy and too opaque." His gesture was overtaken by legislation to claw back 90 percent in tax of large bonuses paid out in companies that had taken advantage of bailout money. "Excess greed and excess compensation have made us all vulnerable," said Obama.

In the UK there was also contrition of sorts among the former bosses of the Royal Bank of Scotland and HBOS, banks that had been brought to their knees by the financial crisis, only surviving through massive injections of taxpayer capital from the government and, in the case of HBOS, its takeover by Lloyds Bank. Most of the public anger in the UK was focused on generous pension terms and payoffs perceived as "rewards for failure." In such circumstances it is surprising that these events did not create the kind of political unrest and protest experienced in France and Russia during this period as people took to the streets in demonstrations against economic reforms.

But Western governments would be foolish, nevertheless, to ignore the possibility of increasing economic and political instability if the recession persists over several years. Could we witness conditions similar to those of the 1930s? After all, the UK Government is printing money again although this time its policy is dressed up as a sophisticated response to the financial crisis called "quantitative easing" designed to increase liquidity in banks.

In early 2009 it seemed that almost every day was bringing fresh after-shocks from the previous year's financial events. No wonder, then, that Stephen Roach, chairman of Morgan Stanley Asia argued in a McKinsey & Co report that 2008 was "a full stop for the era of excess." It must have seemed like that for those in investment banks. "The next era will be very different from the one we have just left behind," he wrote.[8]

But will it be different from every other era or are their historical parallels? Could Robert Taylor be right in harking back to the 1930s? Politically the climate of the 1930s was quite different from that of today. Although countries had attempted to come together within the League of Nations, formed after the First World War, nationalism was rife. The middle class was small in comparison to the working class where people had little residual wealth to entertain the idea of home ownership.

Today a much broader middle class has built up wealth on the back of home ownership, savings, investments and pensions. If the pain of the 1930s recession was suffered mostly by the working classes, today it is being experienced by the middle classes plus what is left of the working class.

There are, however, some similarities with the 1930s. While Russia is rearming and China's economy is faltering, extremism in the twenty-first century is based less on nationalism and political ideology and more on religious orthodoxy. A whole generation is being raised in Pakistan schooled in radical Islamic beliefs. But such beliefs are being transferred across both Islamic and Western worlds. The Al Qaeda attacks on New York's Twin Towers on September 11, 2001, demonstrated that terror on such a grand scale could happen anywhere.

Historically in conflicts nations have lined up against nations. Today, however, the impact of globalization and widespread migration is challenging the uniformity of allegiance assumed by nationhood. Countries and societies are beginning to be defined as much by their differences as they are by common values and loyalties. This means that diversity must be recognized today in companies but this too can lead to tensions when business leaders are attempting to create a shared culture among their workforces.

Sometimes an individual's beliefs can conflict with corporate policy as Nadia Eweida, a British Airways check-in desk worker, discovered when she was told that a crucifix pendant worn around her neck contravened a dress code that forbade the wearing of visible jewellery with her staff uniform.[9] In the face of mounting criticism from church leaders and MPs, BA was forced to review its policy which, it said, had been designed to present a "professional and consistent image" throughout the 90 countries in which the company operates.

So employers and governments must deal with internal differentiation among people and the labor market must learn to deal with market differentiation. Not everyone wants to work today in the way that their parents did.

SMALL IS BEAUTIFUL

It was partly the need for individual differentiation in the employment market that influenced my own decision to embark on a free agent lifestyle in 2002. It was a style of working that had succeeded beyond my expectations until 2008 when companies began to feel the pinch of the coming recession. The phone rang one summer day and I was told that my weekly column for the *Financial Times* would no longer be required. Yes, it was a blow, but realistically I could look back at what was by any measure a "good innings"—14 years writing in the same pink space with a short interlude for book writing.

But other work was disappearing too. In some ways this thinning of my job portfolio had advantages, allowing me the time I had been seeking for years to work on this book. It was a testing period financially, all the same, and still is, as I write. It does mean, however, that I am writing not from the privileged elevation of tenured academia or during a sabbatical with its in-built safety net, but from the authentic "muck and bullets" experience of working with uncertainty. The constant reminder that paid work keeps the wolf from the door is a useful reality check for the free agency fantasist.

This rickety platform, shared by many who have opted for self-employment, encourages the development of common strategies and behaviors essential for independent working, some of which could benefit those in full-time work and concerned for their long-term employment prospects.

The first and most important of these is to work and live within one's means, a recipe for living that has been ignored and which continues to be overlooked by governments seeking to kick-start their economies using neo-Keynesian spending and borrowing strategies. There are few signs that the UK government is seeking to apply such principles more prudently than hitherto, falling back, as it has, on an economic model that relies for its success on unsustainable growth. Everything in our economic system— even student education—is based on the policy of paying back tomorrow for today's benefit. An education-for-debt-swap seems sensible if you can achieve a high-earning job, but thousands of university leavers are scrambling for any kind of work.

Pay-tomorrow policies have worked in the past but are they sensible for the future in a world of dwindling resources? The limitations of resource-hungry manufacturing were highlighted by Ernst Schumacher's 1973 book, *Small is Beautiful*, which pointed out the risks of relying too heavily on oil wealth concentrated in unstable regimes. His legacy, embraced in what he called "Buddhist Economics," was the promotion of self-reliant economies—what today might be described as sustainable societies—in the developing world.

Schumacher was one of the first economists to question the growth economics pursued by his mentor, John Maynard Keyenes. Ironically Schumacher was a champion of coal mining in the UK. He regarded coal an appropriate resource because of the breadth and availability of worldwide reserves. But that was in a time before noticeable climate change when the mechanics of the greenhouse effect were barely understood. He was also writing in a world that had yet to experience the forces of untrammeled globalization sucking wealth from poorer economies toward richer elites. The way this works can be illustrated in Caribbean societies.

Take Antigua, an island paradise that in the eighteenth century became one point of the triangular trade in sugar, goods and people, where slaves from Africa were exchanged for liquid sugar from the very same plantations that exploited the slave labor. Today the descendants of those former slaves are free to pursue their own aspirations but wages in most sectors of the Antiguan economy remain low and 90 percent of the profits from the tourism industry—the new mainstay of the economy—flows out of the island in to the accounts of its predominantly US hotel owners.

When slavery was abolished in 1833, the first reaction of many former slaves was to rest from their labors and subsist, where they could, on what they could find or farm on the land. Most were driven back to the plantations by economic necessity but not before an apoplectic Thomas Carlyle, the self-styled guardian of Victorian values had railed in his pamphlets against what he considered unforgivable laziness. Here was exposed a clash between the religiously inspired European Protestant work ethic and the subsistence mentality of some tribal societies. When the anthropologist Richard Lee spent 15 months with a tribe of Kalahari bushmen he noted that the adults spent no more than two or three days each week finding food, devoting the rest of their time to conversation and dancing.

Such behavior led Marshall Sahlins, another anthropologist, to describe hunter-gatherers as the "original affluent society."[10] Everything they possessed, they needed. Conversely they had everything they needed and wanted for nothing. Today these same people have been shifted off their lands by a Botswanan government that human rights groups say is more interested in diamond mining interests than those of the indigenous population.[11]

Growth and production-focussed economics deny the simple affluence described by Sahlins in a Western industrialized economic system that venerates hard work as a virtue. Yet the long-hours culture of work has created its own unintended by-product in accumulating levels of stress. A recent *American Journal of Epidemiology* study, based on an analysis of 2214 middle-aged British civil servants, concluded that long hours of work could increase the risk of mental decline, and possibly dementia. The study found that people working more than 55 hours a week had poorer mental skills than those who worked a standard working week.

"The disadvantages of overtime work should be taken seriously," said lead researcher Dr Marianna Virtanen, from the Finnish Institute of Occupational Health. Those taking part in the study undertook five different tests of their mental function, once between 1997 and 1999, and again between 2002 and 2004. Those recording the most overtime achieved lower scores in two of the tests—assessing reasoning and vocabulary. It was noticed that the longer the working week of those undergoing the tests, the worse they performed. Employees with long working hours also registered shorter sleeping hours, reported more symptoms of depression and used more alcohol than those with normal working hours.

Why do Western governments and employers ignore such evidence while persisting with economic policies and productivity-driven regimes that have taken Western capitalism to the brink of collapse?

While Schumacher economics has been ignored in Antigua and Botswana as it is in most other parts of the world, it is thriving within employee-owned ventures such as Mondragon in Spain and John Lewis in the UK. It is no coincidence that Schumacher was a trustee of the Scott Bader Commonwealth, another employee-owned company.

The pursuit of self-interest, accepted by Adam Smith, and encouraged in growth economics, is at odds with joint-ownership based in mutualism, collective endeavor and reward. This probably explains why such ventures have enjoyed little support within market economies since they deny the speculator an opportunity to make a Buck.

THE ECONOMICS OF ENOUGH

In a *Financial Times* column published in the autumn of 2007 I asked whether the Western consumer glut was reaching a stage where it was time to question the tenets of wealth creation. I cannot be convinced that a shopping addiction is part of our natural state. Yet it seems that what was once described by Thorstein Veblen as "conspicuous consumption," a phrase originally aimed at those he identified as part of the "leisure class," has become prolific in society. This very consumption, perennially associated with comfort and enjoyment, is becoming an impediment within households satiated in material possessions. The stockpiling pressure arising from today's shopping spree is relieved only by tomorrow's car boot sale.

The shoe-collecting fixation of Imelda Marcos, widow of the former Philippine dictator, is just one manifestation of a modern addiction to spending that has taken consumption far beyond the satisfaction of need and into a wasteful profligacy fueled by the marketing and sales policies inherent in the capitalist system. It was a system that proved incapable of practicing restraint until economies ran into the 2008 liquidity crisis with the force of a runaway train hitting the buffers.

No wonder that Noreena Hertz, a fellow of the Judge Business School, University of Cambridge, described this past era of excess as "Gucci capitalism." In a *Times* article she wrote: "It was an era in which the fundamental assumptions were that markets could self-regulate, governments should be laissez faire and human beings are nothing more than rational utility maximisers; a time when it was less shameful to be in debt than not to have the latest Nike sneakers or Gucci handbag."[12] Today Hertz is one of a growing band of neo-capitalists advocating more cooperative and collaborative forms of capitalism. She argues that a public backlash, combined with failures in the financial system have created a mandate for state interventions that could lay the framework for what she calls a more "open-sourced" version of capitalism.

Perhaps the aftershock of this reality check will persuade some policymakers of the need for a fundamental correction, not just to markets but in the behavior of consumers. Members of Parliament in the UK should be better equipped than any of us to understand this after being confronted in the spring of 2008 with the evidence of their own expense account spending, featured daily in a series of newspaper revelations.[13] But people have not always worked to spend. In the early part of the industrial revolution when people were encouraged to formalize their working weeks around daily shifts, the recognition of "St Monday"—a day off at the start of the week—was widespread as many chose to match the financial returns from their labor against basic needs for food, clothing and shelter.

Consumerism destroyed that subsistence equation since it created material desires that continue to feed what dominant US thinking translates as the pursuit of happiness. It seems extraordinary in a world exposed to growing environmental threats that this consumerist mindset should prevail without challenge. Where is the "economics of enough?"

Polly Courtice, director of the University of Cambridge Programme for Industry and co-director of the Prince of Wales's Business & the Environment Programme, argues the need for a new approach among companies to the way they grow their businesses. She says:

> I think this is an underlying theme in the whole concept of sustainable consumption and production. I'm not saying that growth is not good but that we need to distinguish between good growth and bad growth. Too often growth is undertaken on the careless assumption that it will benefit others to a significant degree while demonstrating a degree of indifference to whether it actually does. Unfortunately too many companies have been engaged in a kind of reckless growth over the past 100 years characterised by short term concerns.[14]

Fifty years ago such comments might have been viewed with incredulity by the business community. Few businesses today, however, can claim to be immune from environmental messages that have strengthened since the publication of Rachel Carsen's *Silent Spring* in 1962. Environmentalism is emerging as one of the formative themes in the future of work and a driving force of global citizenship. It is probably the strongest of all contemporary concerns in uniting global opinion on a common cause.

As we look forward to mid-century several other significant themes are beginning to overlap in the way they are influencing the direction of work. One of the most immediate is demographics, discussed in the next chapter. This has an obvious impact on attitudes to work among those at entry level, covered in Chapter 8, and later in life discussed in Chapter 3.

Other chapters examine the influence of technology (Chapter 6), the impact of social networks (Chapter 7), the role of women (Chapter 5), the need for better collaboration, more empathetic leadership (Chapter 9) and demands for improved measures in the assessment of human capital (Chapter 10).

But none of these themes will begin to gel in ways that they must without an appreciation of changing human needs and responses at their most basic levels. Some of these traits were explored in Abraham Maslow's Hierarchy of Needs. While Maslow's hierarchy is no more than a theoretical framework, it remains useful in charting some of the motivations that persuade well-trained Polish artisans to up sticks and travel hundreds of miles to pursue opportunities elsewhere.

The five levels in the hierarchy begin with basic needs, such as food and water; the next involves issues such as security of employment; the third, friendship and family and the fourth, self-esteem and achievement. Finally there is the pinnacle of self-actualization expressed in creativity. Sixty years after Maslow first published his hierarchy, I am sure he would have been saddened to discover that for millions of people in the world today their biggest concerns remain with that lowest subsistence level.

While the future of employment will be shaped to a large degree by trends outlined in the forthcoming chapters, part of that future will depend on the social engineering established by employment practice. The next generation of children will be influenced to some degree by their parents' relationship with the workplace. It is vital, therefore, to recognize that work performs a social function just as critical as its economic value.

This is as much an imperative for business as it is for government. Business must make a profit. But profit must be the successful and necessary by-product of the enterprise, not the enterprise itself. Enterprise must align itself with the interests of people. Unless it does this it will find itself in conflict with the very people it should be trying to help. It follows, therefore, that companies should be striving to ensure that the work they expect of employees is intrinsically rewarding, enriching and fulfilling.

In future the work of people must recapture the kind of rhythms that so beguiled Tolstoy all those years ago. Within these rhythms we need to find satisfaction, enjoyment, learning and achievement. The work that cannot be about these intrinsic rewards we must surely leave to machines.

CHAPTER 2

Demographics—an Underlying Force for Change

The master in the art of living makes little distinction between his work and his play, his labor and his leisure, his mind and his body, his information and his recreation, his love and his religion. He hardly knows which is which. He simply pursues his vision of excellence at whatever he does, leaving others to decide whether he is working or playing. To him he's always doing both.

James A. Michener (1907–97)

Who would have thought in the dark days of the late 1980s as AIDS ran rampant through gay communities all over the world that the new century would introduce an era of prosperity and unprecedented freedom for gay people that is helping to enrich the lives of those around them? Richard Florida, a creative consultant and author of *Who's Your City? How the Creative Economy is Making Where You Live the Most Important Decision of Your Life*, has identified pockets of creativity and prosperity in a number of US cities that he attributes to the magnetism of gay, artistic and bohemian living in attracting relatively high-earning, creative people.

In studies of living patterns carried out in 2007, Florida and his collaborator, Charlotta Mellander, identified two overriding factors that were shaping regional house prices. The first and most obvious was income—the wealthy tend to flock together. The second, less obvious factor, was the gathering together in various areas of artists, musicians and designers, including a much higher than average concentration of gay men and lesbian women.[1]

Florida and Mellander created what they called the Bohemian-Gay Index to track these patterns. "Regardless of which variables we applied, what version of the model we used, or which regions we looked at, the concentration of bohemians and gays consistently had a staggering impact on housing values," they wrote. There was a similar impact on incomes.

Their findings are an important addition to the demographic debate because they show that it is unhelpful for policymakers to view wealth and poverty through a national or even regional perspective. They also demonstrate that employers need to think carefully about location when seeking to tap in to available skills. The new work, and the creative skills that support it, is clustering in its nature and the clusters are self-organizing. People flock to areas of their own choosing.

Greater mobility is a strong feature of the new work, made possible not just because of more relaxed interstate working arrangements within the European Union but also because of changing social habits as family and communal ties weaken. In the UK one in ten adults cohabit today and the number is expected to rise by two-thirds to almost 7.5m by 2031 as the number of marriages falls.[2] As the old bonds of our childhood weaken, new bonds of fraternity are emerging through the pull of professional and artistic clusters.

Florida and Mellander theorize that bohemian and gay populations feed off what they call an "aesthetic-amenity premium." They write: "Artists and bohemians not only produce amenities but are attracted to places that have them. As selective buyers with eyes for amenity, authenticity and aesthetics, they tend to concentrate in places where these things abound." Another factor, says Florida, is high levels of tolerance and an openness to different cultures, long recognized in the melting pot atmosphere of cities such as New York, San Francisco and London.

Florida has observed the demographic realignment of well-educated, skilled and well-paid people into what he calls "means metros"—specific city areas that have benefited from this influx, and a corresponding movement away from these areas among the lower-middle and middle classes. The studies do not cover age demographics, but it looks very likely that these thriving urban areas are also dominated by younger creative people, many of whom are either childless by choice or who have yet to embark on raising a family.

Another factor influencing settlement and working patterns, particularly among those exploiting the Internet, is the availability of fast broadband. The Pew Internet & American Life Project which estimates US Internet penetration concluded that 55 percent of all adult Americans were subscribing to broadband in early 2008 but geographical distribution and distribution among socio-economic classes were uneven. Some 38 percent of rural Americans and 25 percent of low-income Americans had signed up to broadband services.[3] Research commissioned by the BBC in 2009 found that three million homes in the UK had broadband speeds of less than two megabits per second. What it called "notspots" (Figure 2.1) with limited broadband reception are spread around the country among areas that are more than 4 kms from a telephone exchange. Not all of these areas are in rural locations. In Basingstoke, for example, 50 percent of homes had limited broadband at the time of the report, although the UK government is committed to ensuring that all homes in Britain have access to at least 2 megabits per second broadband by 2012.[4]

FIGURE 2.1   Broadband speeds

BROADBAND NOTSPOTS AND SPEED ACROSS THE UK
Availability   Speed

Under 0.5 Mbps   ■ Under 2.0 Mbps   ■ Fast ■ Slow

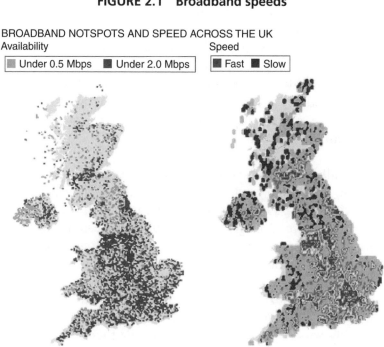

Source: http://news.bbc.co.uk/1/hi/technology/8068676.stm and SamKnows.com.

Could such influences be contributing to the emergence of creative ghettos whose inhabitants are consciously or possibly unconsciously distancing themselves from mainstream or middle-class living and earning patterns? If so, is this a good thing?

Voluntary segregation has been an enduring hallmark of living patterns and almost certainly has its roots in evolutionary species behavior since most species clan together as a survival trait. But there is a fine line between clannishness and what can border on involuntary segregation, sometimes with the best of intentions.

A modern trend toward retirement villages can be seen to have merit in that it can concentrate care workers and facilities among the community that needs them most. But is it healthy for society to divide itself to degrees that can lead to alienation and exclusion? Companies may have needed legislation to encourage diversity policies, but it means that today such issues are taken seriously even if they are often undermined by tokenism. For all our commitment to diversity, the urge to form like-minded groups for mutual benefit will ensure that clustering behaviors persist. It's part of our evolutionary inheritance.

Florida believes the clustering of intelligentsia has a powerful influence on economic growth and innovation. "When large numbers of entrepreneurs, financiers, engineers, designers and other smart, creative people are constantly bumping into one another inside and outside of work, business ideas are formed, sharpened, executed, and—if successful—expanded," he writes. "The more smart people, and the denser the connections between them, the faster it all goes. It is the multiplier effect of the clustering force at work."

It has all happened before, of course. We need look no farther than the Bloomsbury set in London or the Beat generation in Greenwich Village in New York to find twentieth century examples. But is there a danger in such clustering leading to inward-looking behavior among the members of these groups, impervious to the changes going on around them? Decadent bohemian society thrived in Berlin during the 1920s, but it could do nothing to prevent the rise of Nazism that took advantage of widespread disaffection among the much broader working classes. In the same way, the trendy bars of Islington in London, filled with the chattering classes, are a world away in attitudes but just 200 miles of motorway from a suicide bomb factory in Beeston, Leeds.

Today, in Westminster and Washington we can witness unhealthy clusters of political and media professionals who feed so much off each other that they can sometimes become oblivious to the patterns of behavior that exist in other walks of life. This neglect was exposed in the death of David Kelly, a Ministry of Defence weapons expert, who committed suicide in 2003 after divulging information on Iraq's military capabilities to the journalist Andrew Gilligan. Gilligan's subsequent report on BBC Radio Four's Today programme, accusing the government of "sexing up" its claims about the strength of Iraq's weapons of mass destruction, led to Kelly being exposed as a primary source for the story.

Whatever the strength of the story, it became clear during Lord Hutton's inquiry into the affair, that Kelly had been placed under immense emotional strain as a result of his disclosures. The Hutton inquiry revealed the extent to which certain professions adopt levels of conduct within their immediate circles that amount to a kind of game.

The way this game is played can be witnessed in the rituals of protest. In April 2009 as world leaders gathered for the G20 summit in London, The Metropolitan and City of London police forces put in to practice well-rehearsed strategies for isolating the protests. There were clashes between police and protesters recorded by scores of photographers who, while not escaping the jostling, rarely came to harm because their neutrality was advertised in their equipment and behavior.

Ian Tomlinson, a 47-year-old newspaper-seller was not part of the protest but died of a heart attack after he was shoved to the ground by police. He seemed dazed and had his hands in his pockets when the attack was filmed. A policeman was suspended as the Independent Police Complaints Commission launched an inquiry. Whatever the commission concludes, one thing seems clear, the incident involved an individual who was not part of the ritual and did not to conform to type. The set piece rituals of life—whether in the workplace, in the home or at war—demand that we play out our roles in a specific way.

Members of well-defined professions, such as those covering the law and medicine soon learn that they must conform to certain rituals and expectations governing their working practices. For too long the professions have indulged in levels of protectionism, governed by self-interest, which has stifled innovation and creativity. This is a danger inherent in the creation of elites and like-minded groups. When elite clusters become aware of their status they become tempted to introduce the very factors—such as protectionism—that undermine the source of their original success.

The restrictive nature of internal protectionism—including expectations of confidentiality—became apparent in June 2009 when a detective police constable lost a court battle to retain his anonymity in an award-winning blog called Night Jack.[5] The high court threw out an attempt by Richard Horton to stop the *Times* newspaper from naming him as the author of the blog that had attracted a strong following for its realistic rendition of frontline policing. Horton was subsequently disciplined by his employer, the Lancashire Constabulary. While the court ruling was understandable, it effectively brought down the shutters on blogs depicting daily work experiences. Such blogs had become useful windows into the kind of practices that are too often concealed within workplaces. The workplace of the future needs more, not less, openness.

AGE WAVE OR AGE TSUNAMI?

Fluctuating locations of work and other demographic trends, influencing the behaviors and movement of people, are probably the most powerful determining factors shaping working patterns today. While clustering behaviors and migration patterns are going to make a big difference to the way we work and live, the age demographic remains the slumbering giant whose influence can be easily overlooked at a time of rising unemployment.

The danger is that mass unemployment in a global recession will obscure the need to understand how age demographics will transform attitudes to employment and retirement in the coming years. It is this study of lives never lived to which we must refer in outlining our future relationship with work. Late in 2008, for the first time in British history, the number of over 65-year-olds exceeded the number of those aged under 16.[6]

Look at these US statistics: in 2011 the oldest of the baby boomers will turn 65. This will create a retirement wave greater than any experienced in US history, according to Anne Hoolihan, founder of Elevated Leadership International.[7] Some 76m people are in this age group (born between 1946 and 1964), compared with 46m in the next generation, often called Generation X (born between 1965 and 1976). That leaves a shortfall of 30m among those ready to take the boomers' jobs. What about the 100m-strong Generation Y (born between 1977 and 1997)? Some call them the Millenials or net generation or the "baby boom echo" because of the size of the generation. They are not yet experienced enough to take the big corporate jobs, says Hoolihan.

An age wave, yes, and one that demands some forward-thinking policies in employment; we should not, however, be expecting a wave of tsunami proportions resulting in one great dump of retirees. The figures reflected in the labor market are not quite so stark since many from the boomer generation have already left full-time employment. But they do suggest that thousands of older people will stay in or return to the workplace for three reasons—personal need, personal choice and employer demand. Other shortfalls will indeed be met by the younger generations who will simply work differently. Don't imagine sharp-suited fresh-faced executives in the corner seats of power. Think instead of collaborative, inclusive leadership that places less emphasis on power, status and telephone number salaries and more on peer pressure and the sharing of responsibilities.

Similar, if not more acute, demographic statistic are visible in other Western nations and in Japan where the differences are even more striking. By 2050, some 38 percent of the Japanese population will be aged over 60. The trends demonstrate that whatever the stage of the economic cycle, employers across the industrialized nations must begin planning now for an increasingly aging society resulting from a demographic "double whammy." At the very time that the post–Second World War baby boomers and their accompanying population bulge are approaching the age that people enter retirement, improvements in health care and living habits are prolonging people's lives.

FIGURE 2.2   Labor force change projection

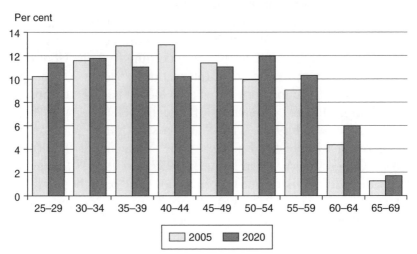

Per cent

Source: *Projections of the UK labor force 2006 to 2020*, Office for National Statistics.

Whether those improvements will be maintained indefinitely in the face of rising obesity levels among the young and reduced pensions is a moot point.[8] Tom Kochan, a professor at the MIT Sloan School of Management, has warned that without a remodeling of the labor market and the institutions that serve it "we (the boomers) will be the first generation in a long time that will leave our kids in a worse position than our parents left us."[9]

Meanwhile birth rates have fallen in many countries leading to a demographic imbalance that could, over the longer term, lead to serious staffing shortfalls if companies rely on traditional channels for their supply of skills and talent.

The way that UK labor supply will dip in the 35 to 45 age cohort is apparent in this graph (Figure 2.2) comparing labor force projections for 2020 with the labor force composition in 2005. This suggests that employers are going to experience shortages in an age group that employers have relied on traditionally for drawing their senior- and middle-management talent. If companies are to look elsewhere for this talent where can they search? One answer, discussed earlier, may be to accelerate promotion among a younger age group. Other alternatives would be to retain experienced older workers or to source more of these roles among women returning to the workforce. If employers are to employ such solutions, however, they need to be thinking now about the best ways to accommodate and retain the best people.

As much of the world moved into recession during late 2008 and unemployment began rising, it was easy to forget these demographic implications. In January 2009 some 600,000 Americans lost their jobs, taking the total jobs lost since the recession began in 2008 to 3.6m and pushing the US unemployment rate up to 7.6 percent. The speed at which jobs were disappearing staggered some commentators. Heidi Shierholz, economist at the Employment Policy Institute, a labor think tank, put the losses into perspective: "Since the start of the recession, the US economy has shed more jobs than the total population of Chicago," she said, "The rug has been pulled out from under working families in this country."[10]

Why worry about a squeeze on jobs and skill shortages, when so many are losing their jobs? It's a reasonable question, given the way industries such as construction in the UK went into reverse, shedding jobs among thousands of central European workers who had taken advantage of free movement of labor within the EU and a vibrant jobs market during the mid-2000s. This was a typical and understandable market response to such a sudden economic shift. But that shift is no more than a temporary mask for a demographic reality that will remain with many Western societies for the longer term. Labor migration, which has eased labor shortages in the past cannot be guaranteed for the future as "feeder" economies such as that of Poland, begin to flourish.

When skill shortages began to bite in the early 2000s employment migration gave countries such as Britain and Spain an economic boost when their construction industries absorbed migrant labor to cover shortfalls in their sectors. While Spain was absorbing thousands of workers from Morocco, some 700,000 Poles are thought to have entered the UK to work since Poland joined the EU in 2004. Builders, plumbers and hotel workers lent their skills in a time of economic prosperity. Once the economy went into reverse, however, many Poles chose to head back home, both to use their improved vocational skills and language skills and to take advantage of an improving Polish economy where the Zloty had risen considerably against the British pound.

Not all of those returning belonged to the manual trades. Teachers, hotel managers, vets and bankers were identified among the 200,000 who had returned in 2008 according to the Federation of Poles in Great Britain.[11] While this might be seen by some as a migrant brain drain, it is more sensible to view the movement as an economic good. Poland lost some of its economic lifeblood in the initial migration but many of those who returned were coming back with enhanced skills of benefit to an improving economy. As the British pound fell against other European currencies, the emergence of more buoyant trading partners was good news for British exporters seeking to find new markets for their products and services.

The reverse migration worked well in other ways for the UK economy. Unlike the native unemployed, those migrant workers who lost their jobs and returned home in the recession were not claiming social security benefits that would otherwise need to have been paid. As the UK government moved to tighten immigration laws, the EU agreed an immigration pact in late 2008, ahead of new laws, to harmonize immigration policy in future. Whether the laws will improve the management of immigration is debatable. An estimated 8m illegal immigrants, mostly from Africa, are living in the EU today. Spain granted an amnesty to some 700,000 mostly North African illegal workers in 2007 in recognition of the contribution they had made to the economy, but other governments, aware of the political sensitivity of immigration policy, have been reluctant to follow suit.

Both Spain and Germany have introduced financial incentives to encourage their nationals to have more children. But is this somewhat nationalistic "grow your own" policy the answer in a world where birth rates globally continue to climb. Malthusian fears of an overpopulated world that can no longer feed itself may have only been postponed by farming efficiencies. Third-world poverty cannot be ignored in labor market planning. Neither should it be exploited for the sake of expediency.

When industrialized economies are doing well it sometimes suits governments to relax immigration controls, tightening them as economic conditions deteriorate. In the exercise of economic policy, however, it is easy to forget that each number in a passport is an individual human being with hopes, desires and needs sometimes bordering on desperation, leaving people vulnerable to the worst excesses of the labor market.

The way that illegal immigrants have been employed to undertake low-wage employment under the radar of the authorities was cruelly exposed in the drowning of 23 cockle pickers in Morecambe Bay, in the northwest of England in 2004. A Chinese gangmaster, Lin Liang Ren, was convicted and sentenced to 14 years in prison for the manslaughter of 21cockle pickers who drowned when they were overtaken by the tide on a notorious stretch of coastline. Two other workers were also believed to have died but their bodies were never recovered. The incident demonstrated that the tightest labor laws can be circumvented when people are willing to exchange a life of poverty in their home countries for the opportunity to start a new life elsewhere. Sadly the future of work for millions born in the developing world will continue to be a future of misery and exploitation.

A MORE FLEXIBLE FUTURE FOR EUROPE

In the meantime, however, labor market reforms in mainland Europe have been expanding the market for temporary workers and breaking down rigidities in employment systems. Research published in 2007 by Eurociett, the European Confederation of Private Employment Agencies, argued that lifting restrictions on temporary work across the European Union could create some 2.1m new jobs and boost the European economy by Euros 12.5bn in the next five years.

This, of course, was before the global recession began to bite when forecasters were forced to back-pedal on predictions. But it is unlikely that recession will reverse the reforms in countries such as Germany, Italy and France that have created significant growth in the European market for temporary agency workers in the past few years. The number of agency workers in the EU more than doubled between 1996 and 2006, from 1.6m to 3.3m full-time equivalent jobs.

But growth could have been stronger still had there been a greater willingness of some European countries to go further in lifting restrictions on temporary work. Restrictions have been retained in the French, Belgian and Spanish public sectors and in the German and Spanish construction industries.

Additionally some countries, such as France, impose maximum time limits for temporary assignments and limit the scope for contract renewals. Tightly drawn labor laws in France, Belgium and Spain, insist that employers seeking to enter agreements with temporary worker agencies must outline "reasons of use" to justify the contracts.

Trade unions must be notified of some of these arrangements, and in a number of countries—Belgium for example—unions have the power to intervene if they object to specified reasons of use.

National variations in labor laws have hampered past attempts to create greater harmonization of European labor laws. Italy, for example, operates a quota system limiting the percentage of agency workers that can be allocated to any one employer. The EU Agency Workers Directive due to be enacted by 2011, should lend some much needed harmonization to the market for temporary workers while ensuring some measure of protection for agency employees.

Whatever the success of the directive, the Eurociett report urged national bodies and governments to speed up specific reforms. "The message in the report is quite simple. If you lift certain restrictions there will be a substantial positive effect in the growth of jobs," says Annemarie Muntz, president of Eurociett and head of public affairs at Vedior, the staffing services and recruitment group.[12]

The use of temporary workers grew as a labor sourcing strategy among manufacturing companies during the 2000s. Typically companies would employ a proportion of temporary workers to give them flexibility during times of fluctuating demand. Airbus Industries, for example, had 11,000 permanent and 4500 temporary workers (30 percent of them engineers) in Germany in 2007 while BMW's futuristic car factory in Leipzig was employing 2500 permanent and 1000 temps in addition to having special production lines focused on employing workers over 40 years of age.

The employment of such "buffer" workforces can work well when companies are thriving, but temporary employees sometimes forget that they will be the first to be sacrificed in a downturn. In

February 2009 when BMW announced it would be cutting 850 temporary jobs at its UK Cowley plant producing Mini cars, workers reacted angrily.

"Sacking an entire shift like this, and targeting agency workers who have no rights to redundancy pay, is blatant opportunism on BMW's part and nothing short of scandalous," said Tony Woodley, joint leader of the Unite union.[13] But this is the reality of twenty-first century flexible working. Companies have introduced these arrangements as a way of responding to peaks and troughs in demand.

The only way such systems can be made fairer for temporary workers is for these employees to be paid a premium for their willingness to work flexibly. Unfortunately where premiums are paid, too often the excess is absorbed by the agencies who act as intermediaries.

In these circumstances it's understandable that temporary work can be viewed negatively. But where temporary work has been used as a conduit into the labor market through the so-called temp to perm route, it has created broader opportunities for the long-term unemployed.

Not all agency work, however, should be seen as a route to full-time working. Eurociett points out that temporary work can prove attractive for disabled workers, older workers and those among ethnic minorities. Full-time working for some of these people may be impractical or undesirable, so the promise of an organized, protected, full-time job can prove unintentionally discriminatory.

The rolling back of labor restrictions across Europe has been a slow, often piecemeal and occasionally turbulent process. In 2002 Marco Biagi, an economist advising the Italian labor ministry, was gunned down and killed in an attack claimed by successors of the Red Brigades, the leftwing terrorist group responsible for killings and bombings during the 1970s and 1980s. Police believed the killing was linked to the assassination three years earlier of Massimo d'Antona, another labor ministry adviser. Both men had been investigating ideas for labor market reforms. Biagi's "crime" was to support reforms, making it easier for companies to dismiss employees.

Protection for workers had been so tight that sometimes employers had resorted to collusion in order to get rid of an individual employee. The way it worked is that the target employee would be offered a better job in another company. Then, after taking the new job, he would be fired by the recruiting company during the trial period the law allowed for a change of mind. This is the kind of realpolitik that can develop when job protection goes too far.

Today, with an expanded European Union, including former communist regimes, the labor markets of individual states are at different stages of maturity. While the European Council continues to debate broader reform, Eurociett has shown that action in just two specific areas could make a substantial economic difference.

Meanwhile employers must continue to adjust their perspectives and recruitment policies to meet the changing composition of society—another feature of demographic change. Martin Tiplady, director of human resources at the Metropolitan Police, London's largest employer with some 53,000 employees and some 2000 volunteer staff, believes that recruiters in future will need to demonstrate a grasp of demographic trends and the ethnic makeup of cities.

The demographic reality facing the Metropolitan police is that London's economically active population is 40 percent black and minority ethnic—30 percent in the population over all. "Some 300 languages are spoken in London. That does not mean we have to speak every one of them but we do need to understand that this kind of demographic informs the way that people relate to their environment," says Tiplady.[14] He adds:

> This does not mean we need a black police officer to look after a black family. But a black family will have more confidence in my organisation if they see that it is reflective of the community in which they live.
>
> Recruiters need to be looking ahead with some foresight. They need to be understanding changing perceptions of careers and career longevity and the way that attitudes are changing among young people. We live in unpredictable times. I don't know what the recruitment market will look like when we finally come out of recession but I do know that it will have changed.

Demographic knowledge is becoming vital to the formulation and administration of labor policy, as significant for employees seeking sources of employment, whether at home or abroad, as it is for governments and economists in the development of labor laws and systems. Emerging nations have historically relied on the movement of people for their future prosperity. Today such movement is becoming as fluid internally as it is between nations. But fluctuations between age groups are just as important in urban planning and development. To an extent, exposed needs will always be met by the forces of supply and demand. But a better understanding of demographic influences will enable more sensitive management of population fluctuations and the public services that will be necessary to guarantee a stable society.

CHAPTER 3

Goodbye Retirement, Hello Living

Retirement at sixty-five is ridiculous. When I was sixty-five I still had pimples.

George Burns (1896–1996)

Shortly after take off on a chilly January day in 2009, an A 320 Airbus on a routine flight from New York to Charlotte in North Carolina collided with a skein of geese that destroyed both of its engines. What happened next would go down in aviation history.

US Airways Flight 1549 from New York's La Guardia airport had reached an altitude of just over 3000 feet when the accident forced a rapid, gliding descent. It was a matter of moments before Captain Chesley Sullenberger realized that he would have no option but to ditch in the icy Hudson River.

He ordered his passengers to brace themselves for impact and turned to his first officer. "Got any ideas?" he asked before executing a perfect emergency ditching, dropping the tail down to hit the water first, and keeping the plane level. Any tipping of the wings could have sent the aircraft in to a catastrophic spin. No one before had pulled off a successful ditching in a commercial aircraft. "Well, that wasn't as bad as I thought," he said, as the plane settled on the water.[1]

Every one of the 155 passengers and crew survived the ordeal and all but one, who suffered two broken legs, escaped with minor cuts or bruising. The last to leave the aircraft after checking that everyone had left was Captain Sullenberger. When passengers thanked him for saving their lives he replied: "You're welcome."

It doesn't take a lifetime of experience to fly an airliner, but sometimes it does when things go wrong. Captain Sullenberger, a former US Air Force fighter pilot, was 57 at the time of the accident, an age at which he may well have been forced into retirement had he occupied a middle-ranking management role in many large corporations.

Ask yourself this: as a passenger on Flight 1549, who would you entrust most with your life: a career veteran like Sullenberger or a younger pilot, whose reactions could be expected to be fractionally faster? I would take accumulated experience over youthful agility every time. Yet there are thousands, no, millions of people around the world with years of hard-earned experience that others who think they understand management have declared redundant. It is one of the gravest scandals of the modern era and a massive economic waste, yet it continues to persist quite openly in our society, as unquestioned as it once was to have owned a slave. How did it happen and what can we do to ensure that every man and woman like Chesley Sullenberger has the opportunity to fulfill a potential that need not fade with age?

It's not as if people have always retired early. So how did we reach a stage where people are living longer while very often ending their working lives at a much earlier stage than their parents?

I never noticed my father growing old. He worked at his physically demanding welding job right up to the age of 65 when he retired on a state pension. That was in 1975, a few months before his employer, a steel fabrication company, went in to administration. My father had 30 years of continuous service with that one employer, but only a meager company pension to show for it. Like many of his generation, whose lives were interrupted by the Second World War, he valued security in the workplace. He valued his job and he valued his retirement, enjoying the opportunity to take life easier.

He wasn't restless or ambitious but he did reflect sometimes about what might have been had his life taken a different path. In that difficult economic period between the two world wars his parents were anxious that their children began earning a living early so that they could contribute to the family income. School was fine, but it didn't pay the bills.

The Second World War disrupted the lives of millions, so people welcomed the opportunity to return to a structured working environment where there were opportunities for advancement as companies built layers of management familiar to those who had served in the armed forces. Officers became managers and non-commissioned officers became foremen, while most servicewomen and women who had undertaken war work returned to household duties and child-rearing.

The rank-and-file workers had trade unions to look after their interests. There was a solidity about the workplace that we no longer recognize today. It's difficult to say exactly when the structure began to erode. It was probably during the 1960s when a new generation, emancipated by the contraceptive pill, worried about nuclear Armageddon and, desperate to break free from postwar austerity, began to challenge the existing order. Guided by Timothy Leary's exhortation to "turn on, tune in, and drop out," this confident generation of baby boomers, swollen in numbers as a result of the postwar rush to start families, began to demand greater freedoms. For women this meant the freedom to move out of the household and into the workplace.

The 1960s restlessness made way for the economic realities of the 1970s as oil shortages and industrial unrest heralded a new wave of industry destruction and regeneration during the 1980s, culminating in James Champy and Michael Hammer's business process reengineering of the early 1990s. Suddenly the old psychological contract understood by my father's generation was ripped to shreds as companies began to experiment with flatter management structures and the concept of "de-layering." Management tiers were stripped out of companies leading to thousands of white-collar redundancies among disillusioned professionals. "If you want loyalty go get a dog," said one US company manager quoted in Charles Heckscher's book, *White Collar Blues*.[2]

This was a new kind of unemployment. The popular image of unemployment at the time was an out-of-work northern man—a miner or a docker with big boots, a thick brown belt, corduroy trousers and a vest.

Such figures were by that time as much a part of history as the Jarrow march. It seemed that not until the last lump of coal had been hewn or the last rivet punched into the last ship's hull could the caricature be laid to rest. George Orwell's legacy had been a long time fading, but by the mid-1990s the road of social hardship no longer led to Wigan Pier but to the suburbs of the Home Counties. Unemployment had reached John Betjeman's Metroland.

The extent of the bitterness in these Tory heartlands could be gauged in a sheaf of letters I received at my desk on the *Financial Times* shortly after taking on my weekly recruitment and employment column in 1994.[3] Most of the letters were from people aged between 40 and 55 who had been working in white-collar managerial and professional jobs before they found themselves too old and too expensive for their employers' needs.

One woman, an export and sales manager, fluent in three European languages, wrote: "Please do not think we do not try; that we do not send out hundreds of finely honed CVs; that we do not know about networking, cold-letters, agencies and all the other methods employed by those out of work." Her job applications, she said, would often receive no replies or a tactful note indicating that her date of birth was a problem.

"For the first time in my life, I have been forced to become conscious of my age," she added. "What employers do not seem to comprehend is that someone who is 45 plus is often more stable, secure, able to take decisions, willing to start early and work late, does not take Mondays off or have small families to cope with, unlike many 25 to 35-year-olds. So why is industry so blinkered?"

The reactions betrayed a sense of shock and grieving as it dawned among the older professional classes that something had changed. If ever there had been a "job for life," that certainty had gone. Attitudes in the private sector had been shifted by the sharp chill of competition underpinned by economic reality. Slowly, brutally, a new understanding emerged, leading to anger among the white-collared ranks. One of the letters began: "I am a chartered accountant, 55 years of age, with an impressive track record of success and achievement in both private and public limited companies as finance director and company secretary."

"Since becoming unemployed last March, for the third time and through no fault of my own I have written countless letters of application without success, in many cases not getting even the courtesy of an acknowledgement". After registering with various specialist recruitment agencies, he was subsequently told by a company recruiter that "virtually every recruitment agency will just push to one side any job application and speculative CV if the age of the applicant is 50 or more."

The bitterness of the accountant was palpable as he wrote: "I truly believe that the majority of agencies and employers think that the over 50s are in wheelchairs or on sticks, are totally bald and toothless, and are too weak and frail even to lift a pen or key into a computer."

I cannot stress the sense of frustration and betrayal that permeated these stories, some of which revealed real hardship. A 50-year-old man from Bath explained how he had been made redundant in 1990 from a job that paid more than £40,000 a year. His house had been repossessed by the building society and sold for less than his mortgage. He had four children and had moved house four times in three years while he had experienced "a total inability to find a job paying any salary at all." In all that time he had claimed no assistance from the state, he said "due to desperate efforts to generate an income by any self-employed means".

He wrote that he had sold insurance and encyclopedias, driven a taxi, written stories, worked as a holding manager in a problem public house, designed promotional schemes for the catering trade, carried out sales training for small businesses and done gardening work. He feared, however, there would be no end to age discrimination. "The discrimination is not going to stop or even diminish— because society has fundamentally changed," he argued. "The corporate bodies we once gave our lives to working for no longer have a social conscience, if indeed they ever had one."

So how was this man coping? "I survive. I look forward, not back. I create a new, completely different lifestyle. I rely on my family and a few close friends. I use all my energies chasing opportunities to make money (not as much as before), rather than trying to find a job, although I still do that as well."

These were letters of despair among good, qualified, able, experienced people who felt, rightly, that they had been dumped on the scrap-heap through, as one of them put it, no fault of their own.

The 1980s and 1990s phenomenon of white-collar unemployment led to new services in employment and new ways of working. Outplacement companies were formed. These go-between services were designed to ease people out of their existing jobs and into new careers. Typically they extended practical advice in CV-design, job search and networking.

Almost overnight early retirement and clearouts among middle-aged managers had become institutionalized. "Employers got used to the idea that people over 50 weren't needed in the workforce," Prof Sarah Harper, director of Oxford University's Institute of Ageing told the Reinventing Retirement Asia Conference in Singapore in January 2009. "And people got used to the idea that you stopped working in your 50s and lived to 90, and someone was going to look after you."[4]

In the early 1990s people had little choice but to get used to this idea. Often there was no chance of stepping back on to the narrowing rungs of the upwards career ladder. But there were temporary openings, allowing experienced managers and executives to earn attractive day rates in stop-gap jobs. Thus was born the interim management industry.

Sometimes people took on a series of part-time or project roles, leading Charles Handy, the management writer to describe what he called "portfolio work." Handy envisaged a new world of temporary work where people would undertake chunks of work. Indeed I bought in to the idea myself, first, taking a year out of work to write a book, then, soon afterwards, negotiating a redundancy package to pursue a freelance career. Very quickly I met others doing the same kind of thing and it became clear that the nature of this new work varied. Many of the interim managers I met were undertaking roles not unlike, although usually less senior than, their previous jobs, only this time for a specified term, typically three to six months.

Increasingly, however, interim roles began to take on the character of project work. Some of my own work could be described as project-oriented too, such as the researching and writing of reports. But the work was very much a portfolio of ever-changing roles. Underpinning these roles I maintained my *FT* identity through my weekly column. It seemed to me that the new work, like any kind of businesses, could benefit from individual brand recognition or, in this case, brand association.

Before leaving full-time work my attitude to the so-called permanent job had begun to change. I don't think I had ever looked forward to retirement but, as an employee, I had been aware of my pension scheme membership that, in return for continuous service to the same employer, promised the annual payment of two-thirds of my final salary on retirement with index-linked increments. The pension scheme worked like an anchor, stifling ambition. I could see the way it was changing people into "timers" intent on keeping their heads down for the home run, seeing out their careers in well-paid jobs, where the salaries had been swollen by annual increments.

A year before leaving I looked at my own salary which I could see was twice that of a qualified, enthusiastic and able colleague, prepared to chase news stories with a hunger that had deserted much of the older cohort. This is not to say that the spark had gone. But my willingness to go the "extra mile," to quote the management-speak of "engagement" was no longer unconditional, if it ever had been. The supplier–client relationship of the workplace that is traditionally but inaccurately described as a manager–employee bargain is founded on mutual respect. In the newspaper industry, in my view, a commissioning editor needs to have pounded the beat, needs to understand the conditions in which contributing journalists are working. The same applies to most line managers. Most of all they need to care about people.

But in the new management of the budget-controlled workplace the first loyalty was to number one. In the harsher workplaces of the 1990s old loyalties deserted the managerial ranks as a culture of dog-eat-dog began to permeate the employment system. When looking at payrolls, there were some significant financial savings to be made by cutting out older, more expensive employees. Many of these people had fewer of the skills associated with the new Internet technologies emerging across businesses during the late 1990s. While most were prepared to learn, there was no squaring the financial equation that balanced the experienced head, trained and reared for an earlier age with the much cheaper, less cynical, bright young thing with readymade skills. No wonder management began to lean on their older employees, dangling carrots of early retirement deals or generous redundancy payouts, while closing the door on career advancement.

I'm not making a case here for the fairness or otherwise of such policies, simply explaining how they happened. You rarely hear human resources directors confirming these approaches. Indeed I would imagine that some would remain in denial to this day, since age remains a sensitive subject in the workplace. But these economic calculations need to be understood and digested by anyone over 40 years of age who has enjoyed steady annual percentage increments throughout their career. Unless they have progressed to senior managerial roles where it is easier—but not necessarily equitable—to justify higher salaries, their earnings will be subject to market comparisons against well-qualified lower-earning younger staff.

Some highly talented people have experienced such scrutiny. When Carol Vorderman, co-host of the popular UK daytime TV quiz show, Countdown, left the program in 2008 it was widely reported that her main reason for leaving was unhappiness with a decision to cut her six-figure salary by 90 percent. The program-makers were not telling her that she lacked the necessary skills or television presence—how could they? But that they were confident in finding a cheaper replacement who they believed would fill her shoes adequately. Their choice was 22-year-old Oxford graduate Rachel Riley. Television executives like to refer to such changes as "refreshing the programme."

Vorderman had joined the show at its inception 26 years earlier. Leaving aside any issues of ageism, a more telling factor in the decision by management to encourage her departure in this way, I believe, was plain economics and a belief, in this case, that the program was bigger than its presenters. In the television ratings game there are risks involved in such moves but the impact on bottom-line savings is sometimes too significant to ignore.

If any of us in our forties and fifties are looking for sympathy in these decisions, we are not going to find it in the younger generation. They view the boomers as the lucky generation with some justification. When Harold Macmillan, the UK's former Conservative prime minister told voters at the 1959 general election that they had "never had it so good" he was speaking not so much for his generation but for a new generation of infants who would escape the world wars that had blighted the lives of their parents and grandparents. Those who benefited from final salary pensions were able to ease themselves into comfortable retirements.

Will today's younger workers enjoy the pension entitlements of their parents? I doubt it. Most of them, particularly in the private sector are looking at longer careers and later retirements as private sector final salary pensions disappear. But that does not have to be interpreted as a retrograde development if the second stages of careers can be engineered to suit the needs and experiences of older workers.

That confident generation that lived through the swinging sixties, Yuppie seventies and the City's prosperous eighties and nineties, may be graying at the temples today, but it has mixed feelings over retirement, partly because of dwindling pensions and partly because its members are keen to pursue longer, more active lives.

We have all moved on from the 1990s. Here at the end of the first decade of the twenty-first century those who survive in work—whether in traditional jobs or in project-based self-employment—must realize that there is no going back to the old understandings.

Yes, the so-called war for talent forced a rethink on employee retention, but there is no sympathy for passengers among the older workforce. The pressure remains on those who reach their fifties. Too often today it is pressure of work as companies increase expectations and load on responsibilities, trying to squeeze quarts in to pint-pot jobs. To take it easy is to invite the tap on the shoulder and the invitation to a friendly discussion about retirement options.

Fast forward a decade to 2009 and people are still being pushed out of work prematurely. In April of that year some 224,000 who had previously held skilled white-collar jobs were drawing unemployment benefits.[5] *Management Today* magazine featured 50-year-old Richard Atkinson, previously a senior manager for a marketing firm, reduced to living on £60 a week jobseekers allowance. "There's a limit to the amount of fresh air and credit cards you can live on," he told the magazine. Some—a lucky few—still have the option of leaving with packages robust enough to finance a future of serial golf sessions. But even for those who do leave on such terms, is that what they really want? Time was when a 60-year-old man's ride off into the sunset would last 10 years or so before he arrived at Boot Hill. Today he might just keep on riding.

In the UK the proportion of the labor force between 50 and the state pension age of 65 (60 for women) is over 25 percent and will rise steadily in the next half century. These trends have emerged as a result of a combination of better health care and the post-Second World War baby boomer "bulge" generation moving into old age. The same trends are apparent in the US. The US Census Bureau reported that there were 193m Americans aged 25 and older in 2005. By 2025 this number will have risen by 22 percent to nearly 236m. During the same period the proportion of people aged 65 and above will have risen from 12.4 percent to 18.2 percent.[6]

According to the UK government Actuary's Department, 65-year-old men alive today in the UK can expect on average to live another 21 years. Women in the same age group will live another 23 years on average. Men born today can expect to make it to the age of 88 and women to 91—and this is an average age that takes account of all those with weak hearts and unhealthy lifestyles. Those who look after themselves can expect to live a whole lot longer.

"That's a long time to be playing golf. I, for one, don't want that," says Chris Ball, chief executive of TAEN, the Age and Employment Network. "What I and many more people like me are seeking today is greater choice about the way we work and how much we work in our later years. I don't want to think about retirement."

A study in 2007 by Aon Consulting, an HR, benefits and pension consultancy, found that more than three quarters of employees surveyed in the UK anticipated working beyond 65. It forecast a trebling of the 1m people working past state pension age by 2017.

These growing pressures, for longer working lives explains why TAEN and other organizations such as Help the Aged have been campaigning strenuously for an end to mandatory retirement ages. The UK government is planning to revise the age of retirement up to 68 by 2048. But that is nearly 40 years in the future. Why do we need formal retirement anyway? Shouldn't the move out of work be a gentler process involving discussion, common sense and a sense of mutual understanding?

In March 2009 the European Court of Justice rejected a claim submitted by Heyday, the campaigning arm of Age Concern, arguing that mandatory retirement ages breached European Union equality provisions. The Confederation of British Industry supported the decision, subsequently upheld in the High Court in the UK, arguing that companies should maintain the right to retire people at a given age.

But evidence from the US, where mandatory retirement ages were abolished in 1986, suggests that the right to work longer will not lead to people hanging around in jobs into their dotage. A report produced by the UK's Department for Trade and Industry in 2003 pointed out that many of those choosing to work beyond traditional retirement ages were either self-employed or working in small businesses.

Today about a quarter of the 1.325m people over state pension age who are still working in the UK are self-employed, many of them working as subcontractors and responsible for their own pensions provision. In spite of the Heyday ruling, there is no guarantee that a hard and fast retirement age, enshrined in law, can be preserved indefinitely in the UK. Gordon Brown's government promised a review in 2011, in other words nothing before a general election.

I don't play golf, but I do enjoy fishing and gardening and walking, all pastimes beloved of the retiree. But I can't imagine spending every waking hour on hobbies or going out to find some new diversion in order to fill this ever-lengthening stretch of time between traditional retirement age and death, although I appreciate that hobbies do provide enjoyment for hundreds of thousands of active pensioners.

The problem is that state pension ages and retirement ages (the two often become confused) were created in the nineteenth-century industrialized world when most men didn't live so long after retirement. Just as it did with the pit ponies that spent most of their lives underground, the promise of being "put out to grass" held a lot of appeal for those among the laboring classes who were physically spent by the time they reached their mid-sixties.

Some of these Victorian laborers would have remembered the days of the "work houses" created for the poor and the aged who often equated to one and the same. Anyone who could not work was viewed as a drain on society. Perhaps we should think again about the workhouse in a modern context—not as a place where aging people must work as an economic necessity, but where people of all ages across all strata of society might converge by choice to do a variety of work that meets their social requirements and matches their economic needs.

I hesitate to say this because it's a line that could be easily misconstrued. I am not advocating a return to the kind of Dickensian conditions described in *Oliver Twist*. Nor am I suggesting that the residents of old-folk's homes should be pressed into sewing mailbags. But community hubs where people of all ages could gather to undertake varying types of work and learning could help to revive the social significance of work.

We might call them workshops or work centers or we could dispense with the word "work" entirely to allow for their social function. Public libraries are beginning to perform such a function today. No longer are they the stuffy places of book lending where everyone is expected to keep silent (although there remains a need for quiet reading areas). Today they are becoming learning centers with computing courses and wi-fi networks. Why couldn't they become informal centers of work? Or perhaps they are already. The British Library has created the biggest public wi-fi area in the UK to encourage just such a working, reading and social environment.

But if there are to be such centers in every village and town they need to be recognized for what they can offer. Perhaps we need to revisit the concept of the library. Today the library is more of a knowledge center—a place where people go to extract knowledge. But the kind of working hub I have in mind is more of a knowledge exchange. It would need experts in information technology, librarianship, research and teaching who can help people to learn new skills. Ideally it would be a public service governed, as libraries are today, by a pass system. People should be able to enter these hubs and set up their office for the day if they so wish.

The public funding of such a system would be preferable to wasting money on a benefits system that can create an incentive for people to do nothing with their lives. A working hub system could also replace outmoded job centers that have become stigmatized in catering for the lowest common denominator both in job openings and job applicants. Potential job candidates and potential employers deserve better.

Today, of course, we must recognize that there is less of a need to concentrate people in one place so older workers—indeed workers of any age—can be networked in their own homes. But they will need to be supported, hence the concept of age management that has emerged in Finland.

AGE MANAGEMENT

Age management has become a significant political and corporate concern in Finland where the government has responded to demographic trends by introducing both pension reforms and a national program on aging workers. It is a simple concept that involves looking at older employees in the organization and arranging work in a way that best marries their needs to the needs of the employer.

The program requires employers to manage the way that older people work by focusing primarily on health. People's ability to do specific work is measured against a "work ability" index that gives an indication of people's abilities at different stages of life.

Declining capabilities, however, are not viewed negatively. Instead they indicate that certain jobs may need to be better managed during later career stages, sometimes through a combination of training, more flexible working, or different physical working arrangements. "Sometimes adjustments may need to be made to work duration. The new thinking involves fitting the work to suit a person's abilities that may have changed with age," says Chris Ball of TAEN.

TAEN believes the Finnish model has much to offer other European systems. But Ball warns that attitudes need to change on both sides of the employment contract, suggesting that final salary expectations may need to be muted in future if people wish to remain with an existing employer. "It's unrealistic to expect your salary to keep on going up. The idea of an age-related escalator is not sensible but it has a bearing on pensions for those in final salary schemes," he says. "This is not to say we should get rid of final salary and defined benefit schemes but a somewhat more pragmatic approach needs to be applied in dealing with this issue," he adds.

One answer could be to extend assistance to older people choosing to establish themselves in self-employment. PRIME, an organization dedicated to helping the over-fifties set up in business, estimated in one of its recent reports that something like 800,000 people between 50 and state pension age are currently inactive but want to work in the UK.

PRIME's chief executive Laurie South has called for the UK government to do more for this group which, he points out, will grow as the population ages in the next few years. "In the meantime," he says, "self-employment remains the best option for many of those individuals eager to work. It's something you can do for yourself. You don't have to wait for government."

Nor should people wait for the prompt from their employer. We all need to recognize that our attitudes change with time. Chris Ball argues that most people know themselves to the extent that they know when it is time to give up or move on. I agree. There needs to be some mature thinking and discussion about later working patterns at an individual level for everyone concerned. To be working full on one day and finding one's self in retirement the next is simply not natural.

Just as young people can benefit from transitions into the workplace through part-time work and internships, so older people need to transition from an industrious peak where they may be experiencing steep learning curves and relatively stressful workloads to other ways of using their knowledge when they possess the kind of "been there, seen it all" wisdom that only comes from time in the job.

In the UK, parliament has the House of Lords where government has acknowledged there is a serious reviewing role for "wise heads." The House of Lords is no longer a gentlemen's club for the aristocracy. It is a place of work where members are expected to use their experience judiciously, balancing the work of the elected House of Commons.

But it has no mirror in wider society except, perhaps, for various governance boards. The peerage ensures that politicians can maintain a voice and an active role in society well into old age. One of the UK's oldest institutions, the monarchy, has no retirement provision so why should the rest of us?

The late Bill Deedes was an exceptional example of what can be achieved by working into old age. As Lord Deedes he could have enjoyed the trappings of peerage and as a former cabinet minister and ex-Fleet Street editor he could have basked in past glories, but instead, when his editing days were over he took out his notebook and went back to writing and reporting, working right up to his death in 2007 at the age of 94. Even after suffering a stroke during a five-hour helicopter trip to an earthquake zone in Gujarat, India, he still managed to file his copy.

His obituary in the *Daily Telegraph* described his approach to work thus:

> Most men of such distinction and age (he was already well into his seventies [when he retired as editor]) would have opted for a distant and honourable retirement. Deedes, however, almost immediately returned to the Telegraph as a reporter and columnist.
>
> Those who sneered at his talent for survival entirely missed the point. It was not calculation but humility—together with his understanding that it is preferable not to rust unburnished but to shine in use—that gave him another lease on life.

The obituary went on to explain that perhaps because of his age and changing attitude to life, he attracted an appreciative audience in the newspaper readership:

> He shrugged off the tedium of the daily trek to the Telegraph's new offices in the Isle of Dogs, mastered the new computer technology, and settled down with unflagging energy to the final fulfilment of his gifts.
>
> Though he wrote both regularly and often, he could never write often enough for the readers, who relished the extraordinary length and breadth of his experience.[7]

It takes a combination of qualities and conditions to emulate such achievement. The first and most important is the acknowledgment among employers that older people have much to contribute in ways that might not be immediately obvious to a younger cadre of management. The second is the confidence, desire and opportunity to carve out a niche where experience is respected and sought after. To create this niche in our middle years requires a degree of self-knowledge and a willingness to let go of some working arrangements and positions that we may have worked hard to secure.

On a recent fishing trip to the River Dee I was sharing a hut with three businessmen, all entrepreneurs in their own way, all exposed to the uncertainties of the markets, all trying to second-guess the future. Each of us was unburdening problems and each listening to mutual advice. One telling observation made by a fishing friend was that the year he spent away from his business just over 10 years ago was one of the best things to happen, both to him and the company. "Up to that point I thought I had to be at the centre of every decision. Now I know that it's far more important to recruit good people and let them get on with it," he said. Today, he and his business partner rarely interfere with the day-to-day running of their companies, concentrating instead on deal making, developing business opportunities and taking life a bit easier.

This last part is not as simple as it seems for the restless entrepreneur. Retirement and everything that might go with it—serial cruising or visiting the ruins of yet another lost civilization—just doesn't seem to press the right buttons.

It was noticeable that everyone in our hut, most of whom are now in their mid-fifties, was thinking ahead, not to a life of retirement, but a life of work; only not the work of career-building. For want of a better word, it was the work of creating some kind of legacy, although no one said as much. This was the word used more than once by Tony Blair during his last year in office as the UK's prime minister.

I think it's a good way to look at the future when approaching the later stages of a career. The legacy I'm thinking about is not so much how we shall be remembered—memories fade quickly, so such vanity-inspired reflection is going to be misplaced—but how we can make a difference. We all want to make a difference in one way or another, and what better way than through our work.

Andrew Carnegie, the US steel magnate, wrote an article in the late nineteenth-century entitled *Wealth*, (later known as *A Gospel of Wealth*) in which he laid down what he believed was a duty among the rich to ensure that their accumulated wealth was put to good use.[8] His thinking is as influential today as it was in its time.

Serious, directed, philanthropy has become a full-time job for Bill Gates, the cofounder of Microsoft. Over two years from 2006 to the summer of 2008 he slipped from a full-time executive role at Microsoft to full-time working for the Bill & Melinda Gates Foundation, the charity he set up with his wife to invest his wealth in medical research, specifically to the goal of eradicating malaria worldwide. Warren Buffet, another of America's wealthy elite, was so impressed with the Gates' work that he announced he would be giving much of his own vast wealth to the foundation.

While Buffet and Gates are investing billions of dollars into charitable research, thousands of other people all over the world are devoting their later years to charitable causes, be it teaching in Africa through Voluntary Services Overseas, or in charity administration closer to home. The loss to business and other parts of the economy has been charity's gain.

One thing I have noticed about many later-life careers is that they become multifaceted, often reflecting a series of individual personal interests. In later life, at least, Charles Handy's portfolio work is becoming a reality. But it may not be sensible to view this work as a career since the portfolio may have a mixture of rewards and responsibilities. Often the reward will not be financial but the satisfaction of putting something back. In that sense it might be viewed as more of a vocation.

Philanthropic work is likely to be viewed as a luxury for most people although there are thousands more today among the middle classes than in my father's day who might question the need for their growing material portfolios that might include a cottage in the country or an apartment in the city in addition to their everyday address. Such portfolios can be viewed as a kind of insurance policy, ensuring potential rental income in old age, but often they are a drag on the economy assuming the status of "parked" wealth.

But increasing wealth provides us with choices and there is no reason to believe that, even with an option to work longer, there will be a stampede to join the daily commute when it is no longer a financial imperative. The evidence still suggests that most people still look forward to an active and comfortable retirement that is distinct from their working lives.

For this reason I believe that industry fears over mandatory retirement are misplaced. I doubt whether its abolition would lead to a mass clamor to stay on at work, certainly not if people have adequate pensions in place.

In time this debate may seem academic. While unemployment figures are rising dramatically across the world just now, looking ahead over a longer time horizon of 10 to 20 years, the demographic squeeze will mean that other administrations will need to respond as Finland has done by looking at age and the workforce more thoughtfully, and not before time.

Social and economic pressures are combining to force changes in both employee and management attitudes to retirement and pensions. The pressures have been building in the past few years as increasing numbers of companies replace final salary schemes with defined benefit schemes resulting in dwindling pension pots.

This means that more people who once might have looked at a comfortable retirement are seeking to supplement or defer their pension incomes by working longer in full- or part-time roles. Why should employers object? Some don't. In 2005 Nationwide building society announced that its employees could delay their retirement until they were 75 if they wished. Meanwhile at B&Q, the do-it-yourself store that introduced a popular policy of re-employing older workers in 1989, a quarter of its 39,000 workforce is aged over 50. Its oldest worker, customer advisor Sydney Prior, is 95 and didn't join the company until he was 77.

But these examples remain in the minority and do not reflect people working in the best-paid jobs. Let's be frank here about the reasons that employers would seek to retain the power to enforce retirement. Companies do not want to be saddled with aging and often better-paid employees working into their dotage with all the attendant consequences for lower productivity and deteriorating health. Rarely is this stated so starkly but I believe it to be a fair summary of employer concerns. The productivity argument simply doesn't stack up. According to a study published five years ago by the then Department of Trade and Industry, there is no evidence that older workers are less productive. Additionally, their absence records are better than those of younger workers. Moreover, both B&Q and Nationwide have found that older workers have a better rapport with their customers.

There is, however, a legitimate concern about more expensive older workers doing the same work as lower-paid younger workers who are just as capable. To manage age effectively in workplaces I believe that older workers will need to buy in to the idea that their best earnings days should not necessarily be at the end of their careers.

But there's a snag here for the decreasing number of employees who are working toward final salary pensions. It is one of the flaws of such pensions that often stands in the way of people working toward retirement in their sixties.

When early retirement is mooted it's tempting to take the pension shilling, negotiating a lesser pension with a lump sum to go before the appointed age. Financially both sides of this arrangement may appear to be winning. In reality, however, it is often the case that both are losing—the employee in pension benefit and the employer in retaining the skills of an experienced worker.

It really shouldn't be like this. There has to be a fundamental shift in attitudes toward retirement and the working contribution of people later in their careers. At the moment only people who can exercise a degree of control over their role, as a business owner, for example, or as a niche specialist or high-earning professional who cannot be replaced easily, can sit comfortably as they approach their sixties or even seventies.

As a society we need to be addressing the whole idea of retirement in a fundamental way, approaching later life in a way that allows the meaning of retirement to change so that it no longer represents the end of working life. That would allow the word to drop out of common usage. In the US pensions specialists are beginning to talk about "phased retirement" where older people might arrange part-time working or shorter hours.

Shakespeare may have been right in the sixteenth century to write of the "Seven Ages of Man," but today it is not so simple to pigeonhole everyone at work. Those who look after themselves in mind and body can look forward to many years of productive life. As it is employees in their fifties and sixties are looking after their health more than their younger counterparts. A study by Chicago-based ComPsych Corporation, the world's largest provider of employer assistance programs, found that older employees had healthier diets, exercised more and experienced less stress than their younger colleagues, many of whom were busy raising young families.[9] This is a generation that simply will not lie down.

We need, therefore, to establish new meanings, new words and new descriptions for the things we do in later life. We need to understand and we need to establish, possibly through legislation or taxation and pensions reform, if necessary, that we have choices—choices to work on our own terms in our later years, doing work that we enjoy, either for the fun of it or for a useful income that might supplement income we earn from pensions, savings or other investments.

The boomer generation, my generation, has a duty to work longer, if differently, to support itself into old age and to relive the burden of support that would otherwise fall on subsequent generations. The alternative is increasing resentment among those who are still in education or embarking on careers today. Besides, we owe it to ourselves to work longer where we can; as Eleanor Roosevelt once said: "When you cease to make a contribution, you begin to die."

Since pension arrangements are unlikely to be as generous tomorrow as they were in the immediate past, the next generations will need to think about their later career as they enter their middle years. Planning too soon is not a good idea in my opinion (which I appreciate will not be shared by all) as it stifles spontaneity and agility in career progression. Mid-career fixation on a pension is an energy-sapping and psychologically inhibiting mindset (a bit like taking out insurance—sometimes sensible, but oh so dull). Youth has no time for gray hair anyway and the best-laid plans can be overtaken by changing circumstances. But once in our late thirties and forties, we have to look to the long game and we must recognize that it's a game that will demand new skills, new relationships and new understandings. Of one thing I'm sure, age power is going to be a significant force in the future of work. As Abraham Lincoln once said, "In the end, it's not the years in your life that count. It's the life in your years."

CHAPTER 4

Whatever Happened to Lunch?

Health is the first of all liberties.

Henri Frederic Amiel (1821–81)

It's small, looks like a stopwatch, has a digital screen, fits on your belt, measures the number of steps you take each day, and it racks up "health points" in company incentive schemes. It's called Fitbug and it's helping to revolutionize the way employers respond to the health and fitness of their staff.

I first came across the Fitbug at a conference in Edinburgh when I noticed that one of the speakers was pacing the stage with more energy than most. It turned out he was wearing one of these gizmos. The more paces he could do in a day, the more he stood to earn in a year-end health bonus.

The device is more than a pedometer. It links to a designated page on the Internet that acts like a personal well-being coach, allowing users to monitor their eating, drinking and exercise regimes and awarding points for healthy behaviors.

In one incentive scheme that uses the device, accumulated "health points" at the end of the year are converted into a cash payout. Typically this might be around £150 for anyone maintaining a reasonably healthy lifestyle. This is not an exceptional amount relative to an annual salary, but a welcome addition to the wallet for many people wondering how they're going to find the money for Christmas presents.

Most of us need incentives, and a cash incentive to help individuals maintain a healthier lifestyle makes a lot of sense for employers who can reap the benefits in lower staff-insurance premiums and fewer days lost by staff to sickness.

The cost of poor workplace health in absenteeism alone is alarming. The Confederation of British Industry estimated that the annual cost of absences among UK employers was £13bn in 2006.

Many companies have introduced absence management regimes such as back-to-work interviews. Some have tried rewards for good attendance or penalties, such as withholding sick pay for those with poor attendance records. But few of these schemes address the symptoms of absence, be they health problems, personality clashes or dissatisfaction with the job.

When the Royal Mail decided to manage its absence rates it introduced scheduled weekly sessions between managers and staff called "Work Time Listening and Learning" (WTLL) sessions, allowing people to discuss a range of issues, including health, with their line managers.[1] The system recognizes that there is a big difference between an informal discussion and one where staff members are called in to the office like naughty schoolchildren to explain themselves in what amounts to an interrogation.

The listening approach is just one of a number of polices introduced to help cut down absenteeism at the Royal Mail. Others include the provision of a health screening service for employees, a telephone health advice contact center for employees and their families, and the provision of health clinics at 90 of its depots. People returning to work can use a national physiotherapy and occupational therapy service. Its larger sites around the UK have fitness centers and trained instructors on hand to give exercise and nutritional advice. More recently it has introduced an online health checking and assessment service.

This comprehensive response to health management has paid off. According to a London School of Economics' analysis of health and well-being policies across the group, such initiatives have saved the Royal Mail as much as £227 million over three years by reducing absence across its 180,000 strong workforce from 7 percent to just under 5 percent between 2004 and 2007.

That's a substantial drop, achieved by a combination of stick and carrot. The worst way to approach absence is to ignore it. If people are away from work, without any follow-up by management, it can send out a message that managers do not care and that perception may be part of the problem. Neither does it help those who are genuinely ill, since they will feel less likely to rush back to work if it appears that no one is too worried whether they turn up or not. People work best when they feel needed and inquiring about an absence is a natural thing to do in small teams.

The need for people to feel wanted in the workplace was acknowledged by Dame Carol Black in her 2007/8 review of long-term sickness and benefits which, among other things, discussed the idea of family doctors substituting sick notes that sign people off work, with electronic "fit notes". The fit notes would indicate to an employer what type of work someone might be capable of doing. The proposal turns the sick note philosophy on its head and, as working from home gains more acceptance among employers, it might be the right time to challenge the assumption that people are totally incapacitated when ill. Surely it depends on the nature of the illness. Why can't people do a bit of work while convalescing at home? It's amazing what you can do when your income depends on it. I know from personal experience.

The Black review estimated the annual cost to the economy of illness among the working-age population of the UK at more than £100 billion. Highlighting the significance of absence to the bottom lines of businesses, it called for companies to include absence and well-being reporting in their annual reports. More important still, however, was the general recognition that workplaces had a role to play in helping people maintain their health.

The antecedents of these policies can be traced back at least 200 years to the textile mill complex established by Robert Owen in New Lanark. Owen angered his business partners when he built schools for employees and their children on plots that had been earmarked for production. At the time he recognized his employees as "vital machines." While today's employers would no longer describe employees as machines, we still seem prepared to describe people as "human resources."

Quaker entrepreneurs in Britain and the US were in the vanguard of a social welfare movement that established sports and social clubs to promote health and well-being among employees. The movement flourished in the 1920s and 1930s when sports fields were laid down by many big companies, some of which (or their inheritors) began selling them off for development during the 1990s. It seems odd that they should do so when the most enlightened planners and designers are trying to create workplaces with in-built social structures and sports facilities. Why has this happened? One answer is that working patterns have changed so much that people have less time to take advantage of such facilities, even though more sedentary lifestyles mean that exercise is as important today as it ever was and probably more so in many sectors. Another, more cynical, view is that raising cash through land sales is too tempting a proposition for those who look after the accounts. Healthy balance sheets are more attractive than a healthy workforce for those who think of a number when asked to imagine a figure.

The health hazards associated with work are also changing. One of the fittest looking workers I ever saw was lying on his side in the depths of a coal mine, shoveling hunks of coal on to a conveyor belt behind his back. He was a Polish-born face-worker who had been hewing coal down that pit for 27 years. The hard physical labor ensured his muscles were toned to perfection.

But mining presented its own specific health dangers, such as the threat of pneumoconiosis. In the same way those working in shipbuilding and other building trades during the early and middle part of the twentieth century risked contracting mesothelioma, the asbestos-related cancer.

While the prevalence of such diseases has decreased with the decline of their associated industries, the rise of sedentary office work in the latter part of the century has been accompanied by its own associated health problems—obesity, heart disease and type 2 diabetes.

The World Health Organization estimates that more than 180m people worldwide have diabetes. This number is likely to be more than double by 2030. WHO projects that diabetes deaths will increase by more than 50 percent in the next 10 years if urgent action is not taken. While diabetes is a problem for all countries, its spread is particularly noticeable in the rich West. According to WHO, diabetes deaths are expected to increase by more than 80 percent in upper-middle income countries between 2006 and 2015.

Mirroring these increases, global obesity levels are also set to increase markedly in the same timeframe. According to a 2008 BBC report, drawn from WHO statistics, some 2.3bn adults will be classed as overweight by 2015 and more than 700m of them will be clinically obese. In 2005 the corresponding figures were 1.6bn and 400m.

The report described obesity as a "modern problem" exacerbated by the increase of convenience foods, labor-saving devices, motorized transport and more sedentary jobs. Each of these factors can be related in one way or another to the way we work.

We are reaping the unwelcome dividends of wealth. During the Second World War food was rationed, and people enjoyed healthier lifestyles as a result. Today we have more choice over what we eat than ever before, but often we choose poorly, sucked into corrosive eating habits by brand-hungry advertising and work-styles that encourage snacking and grazing as a substitute for the designated square meal.

The workplace lunch today is laden with choice. At one end of the spectrum is the sandwich box, at the other the expense-account working lunch, chatting with a business contact. So what has really changed, you may ask? The business lunch existed in Charles Dickens' day, as did the sandwich for the hungry laborer. The humble Cornish Pasty—as neatly packaged a meal as you will find anywhere—thrived for centuries as the staple of tin miners. Today you can buy pasties from fast-food outlets in any big city. In Patagonia or Spain the same arrangement is an empanada—a pastry-cased packet of food.

As in other aspects of our working lives, we need to peel away layers of familiarity to expose the changes to workplace eating. Some changes are for the good. Health and safety laws, for example, forbid the consumption of alcohol in many forms of regulated work. Elsewhere abstinence has been influenced by habit.

Most of us will have noticed the slow but perceptible shift away from lunchtime drinking. It still happens, but less than it once did. When I started working for the *Financial Times* in Bracken House, just across the road from St Paul's Cathedral during the late 1980s, there was a bar serving beer and spirits in the basement not far from the printing presses. Close by was a comfortable dining room that must have hosted some fascinating gatherings over the years. It was here that the editor and other department heads would host politicians, economists or visiting foreign dignitaries.

Every department head was designated the room two or three times a year to use as they wished. Sometimes the whole department would descend there to experience a four-course meal with fine clarets, cigars and after-dinner liqueurs. Lunch would run long in to the afternoon.

London's financial traditions revolved around the social lunch; not busy, clock-watching exchanges, but a more languid, eclectic discourse that had as much to do with pleasure as business. Yes, deals were sealed, often over coffee. But these were not strictly managed, agenda-led occasions. They were the best part of the working day.

But a combination of health concerns and more puritanical approaches to work put a stop to all that. When the *FT* moved to its new premises at Southwark Bridge on the south bank of the Thames, a few of the old lunchtime and office traditions disappeared. The new building was non-smoking throughout. A change of premises had lent an opportunity for a change of regimes. It was noticeable that it was years later that smoking restrictions were introduced for lobby journalists and other staff working from the Palace of Westminster.

So it was out with the lunchtime cigars. The port and brandy disappeared at the same time and so, regrettably, did the atmosphere. The high-rise plate-glass dining room could not recapture the sense of timelessness possessed by the former venue, hidden away in the bowels of a building that combined the dissemination of information and word craft with the grind and dirt of manufacturing.

Gradually the wine became rationed and so did the time. A 1 p.m. lunch would start promptly and end at 2.30 p.m. sharp. Adequate enough you may say, and that's exactly what people did say. The old regime became indefensible. Why should anyone need two hours or more for lunch? The old-style journalists' lunches, however, were not defined by need but by enjoyment. They were occasional, not daily get-togethers, and that made them special. In a high-pressure job they were a kind of reward like a release valve, an opportunity every now and then to relax and let your hair down.

But the health police would argue that alcohol is a poor way to deal with pressure. Far better, perhaps, to jog your way through a chunk of your lunch hour leaving time to eat a brief, balanced, light meal at the end. It's difficult to argue against these changes except to say that such healthy regimes are ignored by the majority either through procrastination, poor time management, existing work pressures or simply because it doesn't look much like fun, unless, of course, you happen to enjoy running for its endorphin-raising potential.

I visit my local authority gym once or twice a week to stay fit. It's more important now that I don't have my daily walk to work or, indeed the safety net of sick pay. I noticed one of the gym assistants grabbing a sandwich behind the counter. "Don't you have a lunch hour?" I asked. "Well we do technically," he said, "but in reality there is no time to take lunch. I don't have any cover."

For my generation, reared on collective agreements arising out of reasonable assumptions that people need time during the day to eat and digest their meals, this is a shocking development. Yet for hundreds of thousands of people working today it is simply the way things are. It is nothing less than the exploitation of people's goodwill. Workers have been let down by their employers in the socially damaging, stressful and blinkered pursuit of ever better productivity. Productivity for what? Better lives? I don't think so.

Among these corrosive developments, however, are beacons of enlightenment that recognize the advantages of healthy living and working. Exercise is being encouraged by the installation of gyms in some companies today. In the more progressive workplaces there is a menu of healthy options for break-time exercises and other social opportunities.

At Chiswick Park in London, a 33-acre business park developed by Stanhope and designed by the Richard Rogers Partnership, there is a large yellow toy box full of games and a sports arena with organized sports leagues plus a social events program on Friday lunchtimes.[2]

The park is focused sharply on the needs of employees among the companies based there. Are you happy enough with a cubicle and a chair or would you prefer an office with a view from the window or lawns with deckchairs? How about a lake? What about dropping your keys off at reception so you can have your car washed and polished or being able to order groceries to be delivered to your car boot, or booking a massage at your desk in the afternoon? Is this employee-cosseting on a grand scale, or the shape of things to come?

The office park is organized through a branded, employee-focused service aimed at creating contented, productive workers. The concept, called Enjoy-Work, is based on the theory that happy workers do better work. The friendly atmosphere starts at the entrance with yellow-shirted support staff. Most business parks would refer to these people as security guards and the on-site companies as tenants. Chiswick Park calls its tenants "guests" and its security team "guest support."

These hotel service undertones are no accident. Kay Chaston, chief executive of Chiswick Park Estate Management, whose job is to deliver and develop the Enjoy-Work concept, has a career background, not in human resources management, but in the hotel industry. This explains why each reception desk is equipped with the kinds of odds and ends you would expect the concierge to produce in a five-star hotel: sticking plasters, glue, needles and thread, shoe polish, and so on. They even have a fleet of free bicycles.

"We are trying to create something here that recognises that the war for talent is over. The employees have won the argument and those who can supply the best talent are adding true value to an organisation. But people need support and our job is to reduce the hassle for those who work here," says Chaston.

All the services are listed on the Enjoy-Work intranet which also includes contact numbers for hand-picked tradespeople such as electricians, plumbers and decorators. The estate managers have negotiated discount deals with some suppliers. Most of the 400 listings on the intranet are local services—in line with the park's policy of building strong links with the Chiswick community.

The sports program has been designed to promote contact between the different businesses on the site. "A sense of community doesn't exist in society any more. How many of us know our neighbors? Yet this is something intrinsic to the human spirit so we are developing a sense of community here very quickly," says Chaston. "Anyone who comes down to one of the events can join a team and there is no quicker way to establish relationships than by playing sports together."

Friday lunchtimes are designated for special events such as a remote-controlled speedboat competition on the lake, tai chi, fencing or golf. The complex also includes a gymnasium and employs a sports coach for consultations on personal training. While sports events and in-house services are not so rare these days in city firms, what sets Chiswick Park apart is the detail, the variety and the constant refinement of employee services.

Underneath the apparently soft center of these support systems are measurable advantages for businesses. When the Disney Corporation came to the Chiswick site, it expected to lose 5 percent of its staff in the move. In the event it lost hardly any.

Companies that have moved to the site believe the environment is an important factor in attracting and retaining good staff. "It means that people's expectations have grown. We have a young workforce and for some people this is their first job. When they move on they will have quite a shock when they see what it is like to work elsewhere," says Andy Porter, resources manager at France Telecom, one of the businesses on the site.

Mary Finucane, product development manager in the commercial development team at Teletext, another of the site's "guests," says: "I love it here. I absolutely love it. There are so many little services they provide to make life easier, such as umbrellas when it rains and the bikes."

There may be some who believe that the well-being and leisure of employees should not be the responsibility of the employer. But even the most puritanical of managers must accept that a stimulating workplace is far more likely to lead to good work than a job in a dreary office with colleagues who remain strangers.

This is why job design and environmental design in workplaces is important. But employers don't have to be large blue-chip companies to make a difference. VieLife, a health consultancy based in the UK and US, has been one of the pioneers of preventative health interventions in the workplace.[3]

Its first office in the UK was a modest space but there were many little touches that advertised its concern for employee health. There was a bowl of fruit on the meeting table, and in the gents' toilet, over the washbasin, there was a chart allowing users to compare the color of their urine with the shades on the scale (the lighter the better). VieLife stresses to its clients the potential of health monitoring for cutting private medical premiums that in the early 2000s were rising at the rate of between 10 and 20 percent a year.

In the US, access to private medical insurance is a significant source of staff retention. While the UK has the National Health Service, the lions' share—some two-thirds of the system—is funded from employers' national insurance contributions.

Those who characterize the British system as the "national ill service," have a valid point since four-fifths of the health service budget is concentrated on remedying the illnesses of 20 percent of the population.

Across society, institutions are slowly waking up to the valuable roles they can play in improving the nation's health. Jamie Oliver, the celebrity chef, secured government support in the UK for his nationwide campaign to improve the healthy eating options in school dinner services.

The workplace, arguably, has been even slower to respond, preferring until recently to treat health as a matter of regulatory compliance. This is the occupational health legacy of labor market regulation that focused traditionally on the safety aspects of "health and safety" law.

More holistic corporate initiatives have been sporadic and piecemeal. When BT, the telecommunications company, decided in 2005 to launch a company-wide health and fitness drive it was staggered by the response as nearly 13,000 employees signed up to the 16-week program designed to help them get fitter, trimmer and healthier. Behind the program was a discovery by Dr Paul Litchfield, BT's chief medical officer, that in the previous financial year 26 of the company's employees had died prematurely of heart-related illness. The average age of BT employees at that time was around 47 with a significant bulge of people in their mid-forties and early-fifties.[4]

Dr Litchfield looked in to the mortality rates of employees and found that one was dying every two weeks from heart-related illness on average. The statistic matched that of the general population but to see it among company employees was a shock, nevertheless, he said. The findings led BT to launch what it has called its Work-Fit program. Initially the medical team issued pedometers, diet and exercise regimes linked to the company intranet, encouraging an element of friendly competition among teams of employees.

"We started the Work-Fit programme really because we had been thrashing around for a little while trying to think what we should be doing in the health promotion space," says Dr Litchfield. "But we didn't go down the traditional route of 'well person health screening.' Those were programmes we had run in the 80s and

90s—they are resource intensive, they are a nightmare logistically if you are a company like our's with people spread all over the place, and their effectiveness is so so."

"The programme was created jointly with the trade unions and we deliberately branded it as a joint brand. The philosophy has been to encourage people to make small but sustained life-style changes that will have longer term benefits for their health." During the program BT has run various campaigns focusing on a range of topics or themes such as heart disease, diabetes and smoking. The first was looking at nutrition, fitness and the causes of cardiovascular problems. A second, about six months, later looked into smoking abstention.

"We deliberately didn't do the smoking campaign at the same time as we ran the nutrition and exercise programme because, although those are the triumverate of big risk factors, smoking tends to have negative connotations as well as positive connotations. If we ran the programmes together non-smokers might say 'this is all about smokers so nothing to do with me.'"

Of about 1000 employees who registered for the Quit Smoking campaign, roughly a third had stayed off cigarettes when the health team looked at the results six months later. The campaign involved a "carrot and stick" approach. Material was available online to help with abstention but at the same time, in advance of national legislation to ban smoking everywhere in the work-place, the company closed down its designated smoking rooms and banned smoking in its vehicles.

Another theme that led to a campaign was mental health, one of the last big health taboos of the workplace. "I think we have done a lot at BT to break down the stigma around mental health," says Dr Litchfield. "These days someone would quite happily tell their line manager that they have been off sick as a result of depression. Ten years ago a proportion would have substituted another problem. It still seems to be less acceptable to talk about mental health, the more senior people get, but generally there is a much more accepting attitude."

The approach at BT, he says, has been to drip-feed a healthy lifestyle message in all of its campaigns. "Whether it's heart disease or diabetes or cancer or mental health, the fundamental message is if you lead a healthier lifestyle, you take some regular exercise, you are sensible about what you eat and you don't abuse on substances, this applies to all of these health issues in terms of prevention or reduction of risk. It really doesn't mater what the disease is, if you do those simple things you reduce the risk."

Since the program began, sickness absence rates have been reduced by more than a third, saving some £30m a year on the sick pay bill. Looking at wider benefits, in terms of recruitment, retention and better productivity, for example, the company may have saved up to £100m since the beginning of the program for an outlay of not much more than £1m. "It's been a very good investment," says Dr Litchfield.

"A lot of people were telling us that they had not succeeded in losing weight when they had tried before, but with the encouragement of the programme that provides a series of small achievable targets, they were telling us they were sticking to this one," he says.

A web-based approach has been adopted by Standard Life Healthcare, a private medical insurer and subsidiary of Standard Life Assurance. Its online health management system includes a confidential questionnaire looking at various health issues and provides a health rating with suggestions on how to improve the score. The system is voluntary but has been adopted by 85 percent of staff, saving the company £1m. Staff turnover has been reduced by 13 percent and productivity has risen by 25 percent since the system was introduced.

AstraZenica, the pharmaceuticals and health care services business, has also used staff surveys to identify the factors that can cause health problems. Access to gyms and sports grounds, healthy eating options in its canteens, screening medicals and employee counseling are all available within the company. Such visible commitments to take health seriously encourage employees to help one another lead healthier lives. Companies can no longer afford to ignore the health of their employees no more than they can afford to ignore the health of the business. One very much depends on the other.

These individual organizational responses in the workplace are ahead of government policy in the UK which, to a large extent, continues to focus on occupational health. Even now, in spite of measurable economic benefits, most corporate health initiatives are classed in tax law as employee benefits. In the UK, subsidized gym membership is still regarded by the Customs and Revenue Service as a taxable perk. So you pay out of your taxed earnings in order to get fit and stay fit for work, thus contributing to the income of the nation and avoiding any cost burden to the health service. For this commitment you receive no tax incentive whatsoever.

If insurers can see the benefits of preventive health care why can't the government and local authorities respond by providing fitness-building facilities in the same way that they provide doctors' appointments and subsidized medicines on prescription? The national insurance covers the pill taken as a remedy but not the work that might be undertaken to avoid any curative medicine.

There is growing evidence to suggest that a preventive approach to health care in the workplace can produce measurable improvements in productivity. We know this because companies that have adopted the WHO's health and work performance questionnaire are beginning to track their employees' health.[5]

The questionnaire, devised by Harvard Medical School, asks employees to rate their physical and mental health. It then asks questions about specific medical conditions and symptoms, including notes on the numbers of visits to hospitals and surgeries in the previous year. The responses allow employers to build up a picture of the health problems affecting their workforces, enabling them to direct interventions to the issues that matter most. Subsequent staff surveys allow year-on-year comparisons to measure improvements.

Employee health improvements can make a big difference to workforce productivity, according to the initial findings of research among a number of leading UK employers undertaken by Vielife. Early results showed that the most healthy quartile of a workforce is more productive by seven hours a week than the least healthy quartile. Health-related metrics beyond those related simply to absence would appear, therefore, to offer significant benefits to employers.

It would be wrong to say that the office vending machine with its fizzy drinks, potato crisps and chocolate bars has become a thing of the past, but the new-age thinking has switched to salad bars and fruit juices. I'm sure that office cleaners just love this change as they endeavor to separate the paper waste from the apple cores and orange peel. But they must get used to it because health evangelism has now entered the boardroom in a campaign to include employee well-being in annual company reports.

A group called Business Action on Health set up by Business In The Community and some of its member companies, has committed itself to raising the level of FTSE 100 companies measuring and reporting on employee health from a rate of seven percent at the beginning of 2008 to 75 percent by 2011.[6]

The group, chaired by Alex Gourlay, chief executive of Boots UK, the retail arm of Alliance Boots, is seeking to extend measuring and reporting within four areas:

- The promotion of employee health and absence measurement.

- Filtering health programs into the brand image for potential recruits and customers.

- Improving levels of employee engagement by encouraging healthier lifestyles.

- Reflecting a healthy working environment through reduced employee turnover

"We want to make the business case that investing in those elements that drive your people engagement and well being is also going to help drive your business and the bottom line. If you don't do this you're missing a business opportunity," says Gourlay.

Standard Life, another member of the group, he says, believes it has improved productivity by 25 percent in the past four years by promoting healthy working practices.

So what kind of things does Business Action on Health believe is going to make a difference? Gourlay points to what he calls "simple pragmatic things" such as installing showers, clothing lockers, more spaces for bicycles, fruit in the office and cutting out stodgy food in staff canteens.

The UK campaign is import for two reasons: first, if successful it will introduce some much needed standardization around employee measures used for reporting purposes; second, it is capable of mustering substantial peer pressure to fall into line among the biggest UK companies.

While I admire the aims of the campaign which appears to have secured the support of the Department of Health, I don't think that companies should lean too heavily on government support. Instead they should be listening more to their employees because some of the best health initiatives are at the grassroots.

A 2007 study carried out by Adecco Institute, the research arm of the staffing company, looking at the potential for employers across Europe to confront demographic change, found that health management was "an area ripe for improvement." While three quarters of European companies, it said, were offering medical check-ups, only one in 10 companies were giving dietary advice or providing relaxation programs.[7] "Long term health options such as sports facilities, back strain reduction and healthy catering remain the exception," said the report.

The corporate neglect of employee health that seemed to characterize the late twentieth-century flowering of capitalism, as it struggled to break from union agreements on demarcations and working hours, has meant that too often health symptoms such as workplace stress and muscular skeletal disorders have been ignored. Companies have been content to regard other health issues, such as the endemic growth of diabetes and rising obesity levels as a problem for society as a whole, rather than something that should be addressed as a corporate responsibility.

This attitude is no longer sustainable as employees not only hold their employers to account for their health, but begin, increasingly, to factor in health care and fitness facilities when choosing an employer at the start of a career. Fitness to work and healthy workplaces, therefore, are going to be an increasing feature in the new work. While once recruiters may have been asked about rewards and holiday entitlements today they are just as likely to be asked: "How good is your gym?"

CHAPTER 5

Women or Children First?

Life is too short to stuff a mushroom.

Shirley Conran (1932–)

Anna Sam worked on a supermarket checkout in France for eight years up to the beginning of 2008. While formally her role was described as a *hotesse de caisse* (till hostess), more colloquially she was known as a *beepeuse*—a woman who beeps.

Her book, *The Tribulations of a Check-out Girl*, a catalog of social behavior, reflecting Sam's gift for minute and detailed observations, could also be read as a treatise on the dehumanization of work. As such it should be required reading for anyone in human resources management.

Sam often heard mothers admonish their children as they approached her till: "If you don't work hard at school you'll end up like that lady behind the counter," they would say. Every one of her colleagues heard similar comments.

The book charts the degradation of human relations in one of the few situations where strangers meet, the so-called point of sale. Supermarket transactions have been sapped of their humanity through processes that even govern the way assistants say "hello" and "goodbye."

Anna Sam would say "goodbye and have a good day" around 250 times in every shift. Sam, who took her checkout job initially to fund her French literature studies, went back to the supermarket when she graduated and stayed in the job for eight years. She started a blog about her day-to-day experiences that attracted a big following and became a basis for her book.[1] Today she is consulted by politicians and supermarket chains for advice on shop work and customer service. But it took a book for businesses to wake up and recognize that here was not a human machine, but a living, breathing and thinking human being.

You don't see many men working on supermarket checkouts apart from students working in part-time jobs. Polly Toynbee, the

Guardian columnist and commentator on social affairs made this point in her book, *Hard Work*, where she explored the disadvantages for those in low-paid work by undertaking a series of poorly paid and poorly regarded jobs.

Toynbee was 55 when she undertook the exercise, attempting to live off the meager wages from a succession of jobs, often working as a casual agency employee for earnings at or near the minimum wage. Not only was her experience an indictment of polices that have broadened the gap between rich and poor in the UK, it also highlighted the working realities for thousands of women. As Toynbee pointed out, some 80 percent of the ten lowest-paid occupations are undertaken by women.

This, I fear, is another future of work. If successive Conservative and Labour administrations have been unable to make any fundamental changes to the social disparity in British society, why should we believe that the future will deliver a better deal for those in low-paid jobs?

One way to do so would be to declare war on drudge work through a thorough dismantling of attitudes and conditions surrounding low-paid work. What is the work of a cleaner? Could such work be undertaken by people doing other jobs? Could people doing apparently one-dimensional tasks be give greater responsibility for other work? Or could some work simply be channeled into obsolescence through automation or reallocation?

When I started working at the *Financial Times*, there was a contract for telephone cleaning undertaken by women who came around the office once a week. I would sit back while the cleaning woman applied a cloth, impregnated with sterilizing fluid and a cleaning agent, to the mouthpiece and key board of my desk telephones. It was a non-job. Had management provided a box of cleaning tissues in every department, the journalists could and would have cleaned their own phones. The contract was later canceled. If the job disappeared, did it deprive some women of work? Obviously it did, but is this the kind of work we need to preserve for the future?

Another feature of *FT* office life, consigned to history, was that of the morning and afternoon refreshment trolley dispensing tea and cakes. I know journalists who regret its passing. But today they make their own tea and this self-service has attained a social significance in that it gets people away from their desks for a while, allowing them to encounter their colleagues.

The tea and cakes trolley was handled by a woman. Why was it that some types of work, particularly in the service sector, came to be regarded as women's work? During the early 1990s I visited Teeside and interviewed shipyard workers who had lost their jobs. They were all men, used to tough physical labor, often working outside. They had a pride in their skills but did not expect to work again.

Part of their problem, as some readily admitted, was their attitude. They were unionized workers who did not take kindly to detailed supervision and would have been highly suspicious of anything described as "change management." While the relatively new Nissan car factory in Sunderland was recruiting at the time, it was choosing mostly younger men with limited work experience. "They don't want us. They think we're difficult," said one of the shipyard men. "There's nothing left for us around here now apart from women's work in shops and supermarkets."

In less than a quarter of a century since I heard those remarks attitudes have shifted dramatically, yet there are many jobs, often those which can be filled part-time, that are predominantly undertaken by women. Toynbee notes that unionization was strongest and made the greatest difference around the kind of work, such as that in production, manufacturing and transport, that would suffer immediate tangible losses were the work to be withdrawn. Much of this work was historically undertaken by men.

Some work has jumped between the sexes (see Figure 5.1 outlining the feminization of the workforce over the past 40 years). Few roles can better demonstrate the way that attitudes toward women and the status of women in work can change than that of the secretary. Historically the secretary was an important job in government, recognized in UK cabinet and senior civil service positions today. In business the role maintained some importance in the job of the company secretary but it became downgraded through commoditization within the typing pool during the 1920s and 1930s. The acquisition of shorthand and typing skills during this period were seen as a woman's passport to office work. Such skills could benefit anyone using keyboards today yet, for some

FIGURE 5.1 A more feminized workforce

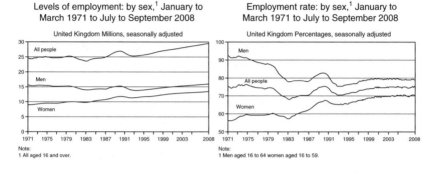

Levels of employment: by sex,[1] January to March 1971 to July to September 2008

United Kingdom Millions, seasonally adjusted

Note:
1 All aged 16 and over.

Employment rate: by sex,[1] January to March 1971 to July to September 2008

United Kingdom Percentages, seasonally adjusted

Note:
1 Men aged 16 to 64 women aged 16 to 59.

The US – workforce participation by gender and age

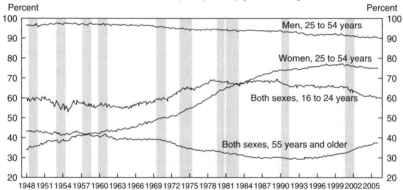

Note: Shaded areas represent recessions. Beginning in 1994, data reflect the introduction of a major redesign of the current Population survey. Additional adjustments to population controls were incorporated into the data in January of various years. These changes can affect comparability with data previous periods.

Source: Labour Force Survey.

unfathomable reason, they are largely ignored in the education sector.

The personal assistant to a senior figure—most often a woman—retained a degree of status which has grown somewhat in recent years after the removal or automation of some of the job's more mundane tasks. The ubiquitous BlackBerry has become the PA in your pocket.

An Institute for Employment Studies report in 1996 noted how changes in organizational structure and working practices had allowed for some management functions to be transferred to more senior secretaries. At the same time the role of the personal secretary working for one boss had declined in favor of team secretaries.[2]

Indeed many former secretarial functions have become so intrinsic to the role of management that it is difficult to understand why a divide between the manager and the secretary should persist. Today much work that would have been described in the past as secretarial is undertaken by trainee managers on graduate programs. The value of such work distribution is that future managers will have a much better idea of the necessity and usefulness of certain jobs, simply because it is work that they will have undertaken themselves.

But while there is a need for better career structures and promotional ladders available for those undertaking secretarial work, there is a need also to recognize that not everyone in these roles will have aspirations to move into senior management, particularly if the work is going to mean long hours and periods away from home.

While such issues do not concern all women they cannot and should not be dismissed when evaluating the future role of women in work. A better understanding of women's relationship with the workplace is important because women have been securing an ever-larger share of it over the past 50 years so that in the UK and the US they are close to filling the same proportion of jobs as men in the overall workforce (see Figure 5.1). Indeed the 2009 recession, where most job losses in the UK involved men, may have accelerated the rate at which women are moving to an equal share of the labor market in terms of numbers.

As we move into the second decade of the twenty-first century, therefore, it is tempting to view the future for women in work optimistically. Demographic shifts in Western society suggest that as more women attain better education they will be a significant source of future skills for employers.

Women have been forging ahead of men educationally on both sides of the Atlantic. Higher Education Policy Institute research published in June 2009 revealed that in the UK 49 percent of university-age women were attending university compared to 37.8 percent of men in the same cohort, reflecting an underperformance of men compared with women in education.[3] The study showed that women achieved better degrees than men, with 63.9 percent achieving first- or upper-second-class degrees against 59.9 percent of men. In the US educational differences are even more marked with women gaining 60 percent of all college degrees.[4]

The progress of women in the US workplace was emphasized by the disproportionate number of men who were losing their jobs during the 2008/9 recession. US jobless figures in May 2009 showed unemployment rates at 9.4 percent, a 25-year high. While rates for men and women, however, were almost equal in 2007, two years later 10.5 percent of men were unemployed compared with 8 percent of women. Part of the reason for this imbalance was structural. Male-dominated blue-collar occupations were bearing the brunt of job cuts while white-collar work, most attractive to women, particularly in the public sector, was less affected.

The path to a more equitable working life for women seems clearer than ever before, partly as a result of significant social changes that occurred within a generation during the late twentieth-century. Catherine Hakim, a sociologist at the London School of Economics, has identified five separate changes in late twentieth-century society that, she argues, have transformed options and opportunities for women in their choice of lifestyle and work:

1. The contraceptive revolution that from around 1965 onwards gave women reliable independent control of their fertility for the first time.

2. Equal opportunities and sex discrimination legislation.

3. The expansion of white-collar jobs that are more attractive to women.

4. Expansion of work for secondary earners who may want to retain other interests beyond paid work.

5. Increase in significance of attitudes, values, personal preferences and lifestyle choices in modern, liberal societies.[5]

Contemporary attitudes are changing in ways that would have been unthinkable a quarter of a century earlier. In January 2009, for example, when Johanna Sigurdardottir was named as Iceland's prime minister she became the first openly lesbian head of government in Europe, with barely more than an acknowledgment in the press, indicative of an overwhelming "so what?" across society.

So many obstacles to workplace progression have been lifted that women are finding themselves in the vanguard of an economic revolution, argue Avivah Wittenberg-Cox and Alison Maitland in their book, *Why Women Mean Business*. If women can achieve greater representation in careers and positions that have been hitherto dominated by men, the prize for business and the economy will be substantial, say Wittenberg-Cox and Maitland, quoting from a body of research outlining the advantages of employing more women in senior posts.

Goldman Sachs, for example, has suggested that gender equality in the labor force could boost gross domestic product by as much as 9 percent in the US, 13 percent in the Eurozone and 16 percent in Japan.[6] Research published in 2004 by Catalyst, a US thinktank, found that the Fortune 500 companies with the highest representation of women in their top management teams significantly outperformed those with the lowest averages. Return on equity was 35 percent higher while the total return to shareholders was 34 percent.[7]

Catalyst found the out-performance was even more impressive when three years later it compared the financial results of companies with the highest and lowest representation of women on their boards. The authors quote many such studies telling a similar story. There is no shortage of evidence supporting the contention that the promotion of women to senior roles is good for business. Yet Wittenberg-Cox and Maitland write with a sense of frustration since they also recognize that, in spite of such positive evidence, women remain underrepresented in senior roles and in significant sectors of the economy such as science and engineering.

While women such as Angela Merkel, the German chancellor, Benazir Bhutto, the late prime minister of Pakistan, and Hillary Clinton, secretary of state in the US administration, have demonstrated that political power is no longer beyond reach, women remain in a minority among those who choose to view themselves as the power elite, gathering annually at the World Economic Forum in Davos, Switzerland.

Ahead of the 2009 meeting the 22-member foundation board included just four women while no women sat on the managing board responsible for running the forum. Lower down the management chain the gender balance was restored where slightly more than half of the functional directors were women.[8] The influx of women into middle management has been noted by Wittenberg-Cox and Maitland who suggest that women are prized in such roles for their organizational skills and work ethic.

But there are other types of work where stereotypical attitudes and old fashioned management practices still lead to sexual discrimination in ways that do nothing to help the employers involved. This discrimination works both ways—through women being overlooked and through women overlooking certain jobs that, by their nature or in the way they are organized on highly competitive lines, can prove more attractive to men.

Take the motor industry. While female car sales assistants do exist, they are not widespread. Typically the customer sales experience involves chatting with a certain type of sales-driven male who is working on commission. In these discussions I never feel that the salesman is concerned for my interests but I do have the strong impression that he cares about the sale, rather like some Lothario intent only in adding another notch to the bedpost.

Carlos Ghosn, chief executive of Renault and Nissan, speaking at the Women's Forum in Deauville, France, in 2006, said that women directly made or influenced two-thirds of car purchases in Japan. Nissan had carried out surveys, showing that 80 percent of women buyers and half of men wanted to see women sales executives in car showrooms. Yet only one in 10 of the salespeople in the Japanese car industry are women.[9]

Clearly attitudes to women in the workplace have not yet changed enough. Fiona Bruce, the BBC television newsreader has complained that, unlike their male counterparts, female newsreaders are judged by their looks. "Of course we are," she told the *Daily Telegraph*, "And I can't see myself changing it, though no-one has ever said or intimated to me that I am a bit of window dressing. It would take a pretty bold and, I would suggest, foolhardy person to say that to my face."[10]

Other female newsreaders have experienced discrimination associated with age. In November 2008, Selina Scott won compensation and an apology from Channel Five when it reneged on an agreement to employ her as maternity cover for another newsreader, Natasha Kaplinsky on Five News. Scott was initially told that her pay would match that of the woman she was due to replace—about £500,000 for six months' work—and gave up her other professional opportunities to take the job. But the news station employed two younger newsreaders instead.

Scott then launched an action to take the broadcaster to an employment tribunal, claiming it had turned her down for the job because she was too old. As well as age discrimination, she also claimed she was the victim of sexism and breach of contract. "How many women are there on mainstream current affairs programmes over fifty?" she asked.[11] Such experiences continue to be endured by women in the workplace long after a revolution in circumstances, attitudes and legislation created an environment where women can exercise some measure of control over their career choices.

But as women stand on the threshold of power in business and politics, as the door to the corner office has been thrust ajar and some of the biggest jobs are there for the taking, should women be made to feel that they are betraying their sex if they hesitate and ask themselves: is this for me?

Compelling arguments surrounding what Catherine Hakim calls Preference Theory, suggest that women can and will continue to exercise choice over their career and lifestyle, and this includes the choice to reject the traditional male-defined and male-dominated career path.

The way this choice manifests itself among women and men is significantly influenced by different attitudes to careers, work and home-building among the sexes. It is not so much priorities toward child-rearing that differ between men and women; both sexes would take a "family comes first" approach in most cases. But while women often interpret this priority by seeking to increase direct involvement with their family, men tend to pursue external avenues—such as wage-earning—in order to ensure the welfare of their families. Breaking down these diverging responses, if indeed they may be broken down, will underpin continuing tensions surrounding the future of family life.

What is Preference Theory and why does it need to be understood in creating effective workplace policies that will enable women to define for themselves both fulfilling roles in their careers and in rearing families?

Hakim laid down four main tenets of her theory. Tenet one embraces the five changes listed earlier. Tenet two notes that women are heterogeneous or diverse in the way they handle the conflicts between family life and employment. In the same way they adopt diverse approaches given the broader choices arising from Tenet one.

Tenet three notes that this very diversity of choice creates conflicting interests between groups of women. Women who opt to build a family with several children, for example, are likely to have different career experiences and priorities than those who opt to remain childless. These conflicting interests, says Hakim have handed career advantages to men who, for various social, historical and biological reasons, are relatively more focused on their careers.

Her fourth tenet again centers on the diversity of choices, options, desires and perceived duties of women that, she argues, has hampered attempts to establish unified social polices governing women's relationship with work and family. Each of these tenets and changes that constitute Preference Theory, she maintains, should be considered when contextualizing the future direction of women in work.

So while Wittenberg-Cox and Maitland present powerful evidence to show how women could be contributing so much more within business, with potentially dramatic results, Hakim's research suggests that it would not be helpful for policymakers to work from the premise that most women are seeking career paths that will propel them to the most responsible leadership roles in organizations.

CONFLICT BETWEEN PRODUCTION AND REPRODUCTION

What Hakim calls the "conflict between production and reproduction," is always going to queer the pitch of career-centric women, even to the extent that it distorts the intentions of the most family-friendly of workplace policies.

A case in point is that of Sweden, where long established family-friendly employment policies have allowed women to combine child-rearing with part-time employment. But these policies mean that careers assume less importance for women who take advantage of their options than they do for men pursuing full-time careers. The result is that men climb higher than women in careers and occupy most positions of responsibility and leadership in companies.

Hakim points out that there are proportionately fewer women in senior management in Sweden (1.5 percent) than in the US where about 11 percent of senior managers are women.[12] She estimates that women in Sweden are paid about 20 percent less than men on average, similar to gender pay differences in the UK. In Italy the gap is 15 percent, Spain 12 percent and both Belgium and Portugal, 8 percent. Hakim also notes that in Nordic countries there is a pay threshold below which 80 percent of earners are women and above which 80 percent are men.

One of the problems with generous maternity leave provisions, she says, is that these do not work in favor of women who may want to move up the ladder in a corporate career. Family-friendly policies, she says, have led private companies to reduce the number of women they employ in order to avoid the costs of maternity packages. The upshot today is that 75 percent of Swedish women are working in the public sector, while 75 percent of men are working in the better-paid, more performance-driven private sector.

This is food for thought for those policymakers who believe the answer to equal opportunities in the workplace is to provide ever-more generous maternity packages for women. In Sweden it hasn't helped, either, to provide equally generous paternity arrangements for men since very few men take them.

While Hakim has the statistics to support these findings, I'm sure that most of us have anecdotal experiences of the way what, at face value, appear to be enlightened-workplace policies for the benefit of women have worked against them. I discovered during my own career that while job-sharing between women might be accepted in some workplace roles, the more these roles involved senior management positions, the more difficult it was to sustain them, particularly in the face of intransigence among a male-dominated hierarchy. So the most enlightened family-friendly policies can and do backfire.

Sometimes they backfire during a job application. No employer would ever admit openly to sexual prejudice in turning down a woman. In the UK and many other countries it is against the law. But some employers, particularly small employers, do weigh such possibilities when choosing a younger woman over an older woman, for example. I know this because they have told me. I do not envisage that such covert calculations will be abandoned in future. On the contrary, I believe they are an unwelcome but understandable by-product of family-friendly legislation.

I agree with Catherine Hakim's argument that policymakers need to be more imaginative in the way they frame their workplace interventions in support of women who seek to balance their career and child-rearing priorities. She has suggested that men might be more attracted toward having career breaks to spend more time with their children at later stages in their upbringing. Hakim has also written of the polarization of behaviors and attitudes between women who focus their efforts on child rearing and the family and those who enter the man's world of competitive career making, while trying to rear a family at the same time.

Looking at various research evidence drawn from what she calls "advanced modern societies," she groups women into three categories: about a fifth, she says, are "home centred," preferring not to undertake paid work, some 60 percent (but as much as 80 percent) she describes as "adaptive," a group that includes women who want to combine career and family. Another fifth she categorizes as "work centred," often childless women whose prime focus is either their career or an equal commitment to a particular pursuit such as a sport or role in the arts.

These differences present some of the biggest difficulties for policymakers since, as Hakim points out, it is wrong to suppose that all women harbor maternal instincts. A significant minority do not. Equally, a significant minority do not seek to combine a family with a career and would like to enjoy child rearing and homemaking while maintaining the respect of those among their peers who are more career-orientated. Why should those who choose to focus on the next generation—a vital undertaking in any society—feel that they are second-class citizens?

The differences identified by Hakim present difficulties for women as a group in seeking to find consensus in career-focused strategies. What may be desirable for some is irrelevant for others.

It is tempting to suggest that men have taken advantage of these diverse characteristics and, as a man, I know that men together will often throw up their hands and make the point that "we're not the ones who have the babies," an argument that tends to be dismissed witheringly and justifiably by women as unacceptable when it is used as an excuse for dodging domestic chores around the home.

Today there are so-called new men who are doing far more than their fathers ever did to share child-rearing responsibilities. This is particularly true where both partners are pursuing successful careers. But these accommodations can put strains on all relationships—those between parents and those between parents and their children.

The rights of children are becoming a significant influence in the division of career aspirations and choices within the nuclear family. A two-year investigation into what constitutes a good childhood, commissioned by the Children's Society, a UK charity and published in February 2009, reached some disturbing conclusions for working mothers, suggesting that children had suffered as a result of the trend toward dual-income families.

The report, *A Good Childhood*, based on interviews with 35,000 children, found that in spite of better health, education and more possessions, children's lives today were tougher than those of their parents, leading to widespread parental guilt.[13]

The report noted that some 70 percent of mothers with babies of between nine and 12 months old were doing some kind of paid work, compared with about a quarter just 25 years earlier. Additionally more children were experiencing the break-up of their parents' relationships, with one in three 16 year-olds living apart from their father.

The report's authors, Richard Layard and Judith Dunn, said the findings represented a massive change in people's way of life. They blamed an individualist culture that encouraged people to pursue their own success in ways that did not always take into account the consequences for their children.

Looking specifically at the impact of working parents, the Children's Society survey asked adults whether "nowadays parents aren't able to spend enough time with their children." Some 60 percent of those questioned agreed. When asked whether "these days more and more parents have to put their career first, even if this affects their family life," almost half agreed. The report exposed the encroachment of careers into family life and the extent to which dual-earning arrangements were compromising relationships between parents and their children. One of the strongest symptoms of this encroachment is parental guilt.

"Life remains a succession of uneasy compromises, but this report on childhood has changed the way I think," wrote *FT* columnist, Lucy Kellaway, describing how such parental guilt was manifesting itself among the professional classes when she was called to her son's school to discuss his course work:

> Cursing at having to leave work early, I showed up at the school to find that all the other mothers looked uncannily like me. They were almost all white, professional, middle-class women with that hunted look that comes from having cut short work in order to receive a bollocking on behalf of one's child.

She went so far as to suggest that the affluent white sons of two working parents were becoming "the new underclass."[14]

While the report was criticized by some columnists, Kellaway admitted that "Though I don't like the conclusion any more than they do, I can't dismiss it quite so conveniently. Usually I try to ignore things that damn working mothers, on the grounds that guilt is uncomfortable and unhelpful, but this time there was a word in the report that has lodged itself in my mind and won't go away. That word was *selfish*."

The report, as Kellaway acknowledged, was unlikely to persuade professional women to change their lifestyles markedly, but it did promise to pile on the guilt that many experienced already. And in not a few cases it stimulated angry responses, questioning why mothers and not fathers were expected to share the greatest burden of guilt? But if the report exposed degrees of selfishness and guilt it also exposed some ignorance of the extent to which parental relationships influenced the emotional well-being of their children.

"It is crucial how the parents get on with each other. It is remarkable how many parents do not realise how important this is for their children," wrote Layard and Dunn.[15] This gap in understanding was revealed in the survey that asked teenagers and parents whether they agreed with the statement: "Parents getting on well is one of the most important factors in raising happy children." Seven in ten of the teenagers agreed, but only a third of the parents did so. In other words, teenagers understood the potentially harmful effects of parental strife far better than their parents. Layard and Dunn quoted studies showing that, on average, some 50 percent more children with separated parents, than those without, experienced a range of problems, including lower academic achievement, lower self-esteem, behavioral difficulties and depression.

Among its recommendations the report said that working parents should be entitled to leave of up to three years between them, with no loss of job security—an entitlement that is provided for parents in France and Germany.

The report made for uncomfortable reading among hardworking parents. Asked to look into this mirror of modern society, many did not like the reflection. Little wonder, then, that more and more women today are choosing a career over raising a family. In June 2009 an Office of National Statistics survey of 12,700 women born between 1956 and 1960 found that one in five of them had chosen to remain childless.[16] The proportion of those without children had almost doubled since the 1990s. The study found that pursuing a professional career was one of the prime factors, a finding supported by the discovery that there were more women without children in managerial roles than mothers.

Women who are better educated or who have better qualifications than their partners are more likely to remain childless, said the study. "These women are marrying their careers," Anastasia de Waal, director of family and education for the thinktank Civitas told the *Daily Telegraph*. "It used to be that one of the most important boxes to tick was getting married and having kids but that is changing. The question it raises is: are we going to see a polarisation between the poor having children and the rich not?

We have not got the balance right between wanting children in our society and wanting work."

It is a supreme irony for women that at the very time that their career prospects appear healthier than they have been at any stage in history, with better education, greater opportunities and various anti-discriminatory safeguards, they are being urged to reflect on their family responsibilities and social roles. The saving grace in this debate is the acknowledgment that they must not do so alone, but with the compliance and involvement of men.

The work of men and their future domestic engagement is inextricably linked with the future relationship between women and paid work. This relationship can only develop productively and fairly if men are prepared to examine their own approaches to work and the home. As Avivah Wittenberg-Cox and Alison Maitland have suggested, this must include a much deeper understanding of what it is that alienates women in the workplace and whether mechanisms can be installed to prevent unfair exploitation and exclusion of women.

But are male-dominated boardrooms ready to undertake such fundamental appraisals and accept the consequences? Are they prepared to discount pushy male behavior that ensures better pay deals or the failure among women to advance themselves through a lack of confidence? Are they prepared to encourage flexible working and career breaks for men as much as women in ways that will not derail careers?

The prize of greater productivity, better competitiveness and simply a better way of doing business than deal making on the golf course is too important to ignore. Neither can companies divorce themselves from the social imperative of stimulating healthy, happy upbringings for the next generation. Employees, both men and women, need the breathing space to develop sustainable domestic arrangements.

As the husband of a professional woman, I understand the domestic juggling that characterizes child-rearing among dual-income couples. I also understand the compromises we make. I do believe that children are remarkably resilient where they can rely on parental support. I also believe that the involvement of third-party child-carers can add another dimension to a child's upbringing. It is not as if parents have all the solutions since parenting is something for which we receive little training beyond the memories we retain from our own upbringings.

The need for employers, therefore, is to be focused not only on the bottom line, the end product and the customer, but also on the social bottom line that dominates the concerns of every individual in work. This is not about some artificial arrangement called "work-life balance" but about genuinely balanced lives for all. It is why the future of women in work should not be treated as part of a separate agenda, shunted into the company diversity policy, but as integral to the way people are managed, recruited, promoted and rewarded.

For women the message must be that in future they do have choices over their work even if the choice ultimately is to vote with their feet, gravitating to the workplaces and management cultures that value, recognize and reward their skills and distinctive qualities. Women's networks and employer comparison websites such as Wheretowork.com are monitoring employers constantly so that poor practices and attitudes are noticed and highlighted. It is Preference Theory in practice.

Sadly that prize in the short term is there, mainly for middle-class educated women. Improving work and pay in low-paid jobs such as cleaning and shop work will not happen overnight, ensuring that some types of less desirable work will continue well into the future. Eliminating poor work will take generations, but it is a goal worth pursuing nevertheless if governments are genuine about building a fairer society.

Overall, however, the future for women in work must be perceived as encouraging if employers are willing to embrace more enlightened management rather than persisting with the power plays that have dominated corporate hierarchies in the past. Mary Parker Follett, the US management theorist, set a management agenda for all, not just women, during the 1920s when she argued that those in authority should develop the idea of *power with* rather than *power over* those who they managed.[17] The distinction was so subtle for male-dominated management that her ideas have been largely ignored for the best part of 80 years. But Parker Follett demonstrated that there were alternative forms of management. Perhaps their time has come.

As Catherine Hakim notes, the needs, perspectives and ambitions of women are diverse and cannot be pigeonholed by employers or policymakers. But that very diversity is a strength, not a problem. Women have needed to demonstrate remarkable adaptability to survive in a man's world. In future business will rely on that ability to adapt and women must show the way.

CHAPTER 6

Technology—Scourge or Savior of Work?

We are becoming the servants in thought, as in action, of the machine we have created to serve us.

John Kenneth Galbraith (1908–2006)

Joe Macri sits in Microsoft's Dublin-based headquarters for Western Europe, talking with the members of his team. There's Erik in Munich, Lukas in Vienna, Marco in Zurich, Ian at home in Reading and Pedro in his Algarve Villa.

"No we don't have an office in the Algarve. I'm not sure why Pedro's here if he's on holiday. I'll need to speak to him," jokes Macri, Microsoft's general manager for business marketing in Western Europe. A few months ago such meetings would have been held in Amsterdam at least once every three months.

Today the team meets face-to-face no more than once or twice a year. The rest of the time they meet using Microsoft's "unified communications" technology—a system that allows team conferencing using multi-angled cameras enabling everyone in the meeting to see everyone else at the same time.

The technology allows instant messaging too, so while one member of the team is speaking, two or three others could be exchanging messages about the content of the meeting.

"Now, if anyone falls asleep—and it has been known in past phone conferences," says Macri, "we can all see who it is." He admits that conferencing technology cannot replicate the eye contact and subtleties of human interactions that feed and nourish relationships. That's why some meetings are still held face-to-face. "But once you know people it makes it easier to meet this way and there is no doubt it is saving us money," he says.

Macri believes he will be at least halving his team travel budget currently running at more than a million euros a year. "It saves money, increases productivity and reduces our carbon footprint as a company," he says. "Also, from a personal point of view I no longer have to get up at some God awful hour to catch my flight to the Netherlands."

Microsoft, of course, has a vested interest in developing communications software for the workplace. But this also means it has needed to acquire a deep understanding of working patterns, not least to ensure that its own workforce is maintaining healthy working and living habits.

It hasn't always been the case. In the early days of the company, when developers were working on the first Windows program, some resorted to sleeping under their desks, such was the obsession to get the new operating system completed.

Those days are in the past although the company still runs offices that are open all the time for staff to work whenever they want. Home working is not discouraged either but Theo Rinsema, general manager of Microsoft Netherlands, says the company has become much more aware about the risks associated with overwork.

"We know that people don't stop working when we don't see them and we know from the feedback in employee satisfaction questionnaires that this can be a problem. So now we try to help people make the right decisions about work," he says. "When work shifts from a place where you do things to an activity that you control, you need to develop the competence of when to stop working."

It's worth dwelling on this point. Who would have thought that "downing tools" as it was called in the heyday of the trade unions would one day be described as a "competence"? Yet there are thousands of us working today who find it difficult to stop working. Like drinkers at the all-night bar we don't know how to say "enough." New technologies are emerging constantly but most take time to embed themselves in our lives and some have unforeseen social consequences, sometimes beneficial, sometimes detrimental, occasionally both.

Technologies have always excited people, often in ways that magnify and overstate the social benefit of innovation. Walking up 22,841 ft (6962 m) Acongagua in January 2003, I had regular updates on our altitude from climbing partner Charles Godden reading from his Garmin GPS (Global Positioning System) device. Godden likes gadgets and has a gadget fund to satiate his appetite.

A lot of men like gadgets. It's why they are married to the TV remote control. The Garmin didn't get us to the top or aid us in any way but I suppose it helped to pass the time as we acclimatized on the way up. I'm sure that the Garmin is a very fine and useful instrument in all kinds of circumstances. I can imagine it could be handy if you were lost and needed rescuing and you happened to have your mobile telephone with you and a reasonable signal. But wouldn't it be better to concentrate on not getting lost in the first place?

I want to spend the rest of this chapter exploring the way technology changes lives, how it changes the way we relate to the world and each other, and, most of all, how it changes the way we understand and undertake work. But I think it is also important to recognize how much it does not change lives, how deep down, the way we feel about each other as people has little to do with the latest gizmo. That understanding should never desert us as we move through life. That said, technology has shaped the way we have evolved over the millennia. Its history is our history.

Some might argue that developing the power of speech was the most revolutionary human advance in the whole of human history. Written text and artwork must be up there for consideration and so must the creation of that first tool millions of years ago that almost certainly predated language itself. Ever since that time work and technology have been bound together, a combination of aim and execution, invariably growing in complexity and input with not a hint of irony that technology emerged to make life easier and work to make life better.

As brains developed, this simple cause and effect relationship of labor-saving aim, innovation, and related work accompanied every step of human progress down the centuries. The means to sustain fire demanded the gathering of wood. Fire, water, shelter and the access to food formed a platform, not just for survival but for every subsequent social and technological advance. Most technologies are logical developments designed to solve a problem or fulfill a need. Today technology continues to shape and influence the way we work although not always in the way envisaged by its originators.

The desktop computer, some said, would create the paperless office. It didn't happen. In the modern office, digital technologies share an uncomfortable interface with more traditional practices. Paper files exist alongside electronic data banks. Photocopiers work overtime printing out electronic reports that could be accessed on screen. Notepads sit alongside palmtop devices and diaries, card indexes and contacts books compete with digital databases on mainframes and on line.

The more venerable the office, the more resistance there seems to be to new technology. When Barack Obama moved in to the Oval Office in the White House, he became the first US president to sit with a laptop computer at his desk.

Some reports prior to his inauguration said he would be forced to abandon his BlackBerry hand-held device that he had used so adroitly in the presidential election campaign. The security services feared that any messages conveyed through such devices could be intercepted. White House spokesman Robert Gibbs later confirmed, however, that Obama would be keeping his BlackBerry device through a compromise that would allow him to stay in touch with senior staff and a small group of personal friends.[1]

Obama discovered that there are times in any job when technologies are eschewed entirely since nothing yet has been invented to replace basic human values such as integrity, honesty and trust. A promise is a promise and while few of the millions around the world who watched Barack Obama recite his oath of office during his inauguration as the 44th president of the United States had any doubt about the validity of his swearing in, there remained enough of a niggle among constitutionalists for the process to be repeated the next day, simply because one word had been repeated out of order.

One of the most frustrating and yet the most endearing qualities of people is that their behavior continues to defy the best efforts of technology. When Neil Armstrong stepped on the moon for the first time he could be heard on the recording saying: "That's one small step for man, one giant leap for mankind." To make grammatical sense forever more the written quote must appear like this: "That's one small step for [a] man, one giant leap for mankind," thus recording what Armstrong meant to say.[2]

Only a short time earlier Armstrong himself had exposed the limits of existing technology by landing the lunar module manually as it was running low on fuel. While works of science fiction, such as Arthur C. Clarke's *2001*, might contemplate the dominance of artificial intelligence, the unpredictable nature of human thinking always intervenes. We love technology, but not as much as we revel in the sheer unpredictability of human nature.

It's clear therefore that while technological change may experience what Malcolm Gladwell calls "tipping points" it also has sticking points and some of these are generational. Someone who has relied for most of their career on a Filofax organizer for maintaining their lists of contacts, say, may be less willing to change to an electronic hand-held device. But this should not always be regarded as a failure to move with the times. The benefits of some technologies are overblown but fashion consciousness and a desire to imitate means that very often people fail to make a sensible evaluation. Once they have stepped over a technological threshold it is difficult to step back.

In some cases it may simply be that the technology does not suit a particular way of working. Julian Richer, founder of the Richer Sounds hi-fi chain of shops prefers to work off a piece of white card rather than use a computer or notebook. He lists his "to dos" in tiny writing, crossing off the list as he works through it.[3] Richer takes a practical approach to technology that says from the outset: what does it do for me? But the marketing of communications technology today has as much to do with desirability as it has with function. When mobile phones began to appear in numbers during the early 1990s they were still relatively large—although not so large as the brick-like devices of the 1970s and 1980s—with low battery life. One of their features was the ability to send SMS (Short Message Service) text messages, dispensing with the need to make a call in some circumstances.

At this time many mobile workers could be contacted through pagers which required a message recipient to call in to an office manager. The pager was a tool of management control, keeping employees on a kind of leash where they could be reached, sometimes during inconvenient parts of the day or evening. But it was also useful for those, such as doctors "on call," who needed to be contactable in an emergency. The BlackBerry has taken this "always reachable" concept to new and often intrusive levels. Nevertheless in spite of initial fears among those who noted the addictive nature of BlackBerry use (hence the nickname

"Crackberry"), there seems to be a consensus that the advantages of such hand-held devices outweigh the disadvantages in day-to-day management roles.

Management, after all, has long been recognized as something of a plate-spinning exercise, as Henry Mintzberg, the management writer, noted in his 1973 book, *The Nature of Managerial Work*. Mintzberg spent much of his early career observing what it was that managers actually did with their time. "Jumping from topic to topic, he (the manager) thrives on interruptions," he wrote, "and, more often than not, disposes of items in 10 minutes or less. Though he may have fifty projects going, all are delegated. He juggles them, checking each one periodically before sending it back in to orbit."[4]

He argued that Henri Fayol's four definitions of management, laid down as early as 1916—those of planning, organization, coordination and control—were barely recognizable in the daily routine.

Mintzberg found in a study of British managers that they spent very little time each day on concentrated work and worked for half an hour or more without interruption only once every two days. E-mail interruptions from the always-on BlackBerry must have reduced that time to a fraction of what it was in the 1970s. It only confirms Mintzberg's conclusion that "The job of managing does not breed reflective planners; the manager responds to stimuli as an individual who is conditioned by his job to prefer live to delayed action."

But while Mintzberg's manager preferred to pick up information verbally at meetings and on the telephone, today's manager is absorbing and responding to a series of e-mails as *Financial Times* writer Lucy Kellaway so sharply observed in her satirical series of columns on e-mail management, featuring the fictional Martin Lukes. Lukes was a parody but it was a parody that worked because people could recognize flashes of their own experience within the fictional exchanges. But even Lukes would have struggled to keep up with the social networking innovations that began to invade managerial and employee e-mails during 2007. The Internet social network began somewhat earlier but 2007 was the year that it moved into the mainstream of common usage.

THE RISE OF FACEBOOK

Facebook first came to my attention through my eldest son who told me of "a great system" for keeping in touch with university friends. "But you're not allowed to belong to it," he said, with a degree of satisfaction. It was true too, for a while. University exclusivity did not last long, however, and the system was soon made available to the general population. By this time, however, it had built a critical mass within the universities and a cache, therefore, associated with the college experience.

Online social networking systems are equipped to scan our e-mail messages if we are looking for potential "friends." New sites are emerging almost daily that can read our various online data. Routinely many of us add contact details with our e-mails in the common sense recognition that information networks need information if they are to function.

Journalists used to be known for the depth of their contacts books yet rarely these days do I consult my lists of contact numbers. Firstly, it's easier to search within my stored e-mails or find a number online. Secondly, people are moving jobs so frequently the updates would take too much time.

But paper isn't dead. If paper had been invented yesterday we would treat the invention quite differently. It would be celebrated for its ubiquity, cheapness, ease of use and disposability. Here is a technology that can be used once, then thrown away. It's the perfect green product, easily recyclable and manufactured from managed, sustainable woodlands. Paper script is comfortable to read and it's easy to annotate. The book in your pocket is your master document, not something that has been copied or updated several times on the computer. A small book can fit into a coat pocket. It also has another advantage, something that would have not been recognized less than a decade ago. It is unconnected.

It explains why I am writing these words just now within the sanctuary of a notebook, detached from communications technologies that have become so successful in the storage and exchange of information that we feel to be drowning in knowledge, our senses overpowered by unadulterated intellectual stimulation. We live in a Midas world of knowledge where every click of the BlackBerry—that symbol of professional connectedness—every stroke of a keyboard, every glide of a computer mouse brings exciting new discoveries with all the shiny luster of gold. And, just like Crete's mythical king, we're finding that gold and only gold is meaningless in life. Knowledge and only knowledge, bouncing randomly and unconnectedly in perpetual Brownian motion, is blurring the lens through which we make sense of our working lives.

The first time I wrote a book I adopted a well-worn pattern of research, using books, interviews and geographical site visits. I referenced various websites, accessed through a modem. The visits were brief, focused and research-specific. Today I sit in front of my desktop computer like a child let loose in a toy shop the size of Hamley's with permission to play with whatever I choose within the bounds of legality. At one level there are games— thousands of them in every shape and size, at another naked people performing any number of sexual contortions. Elsewhere there is news, instantaneous with analysis and reactions rolled into one.

There are archives, photographs, artworks, stories, statistics and new, new, new sparking, sparkly, exciting things all of the time and everywhere. When Microsoft launched its Windows operating system it asked us: "Where do you want to go today?" Now we're asked not only where we want to go, but what do we want to do and, if we are fans of virtual world Second Life, who do we want to be?

For the unrestricted office worker every visit to the Internet is like passing by the island of the Sirens. Not even Odysseus could resist their seductive calls. In the office the web has become an alarming source of distraction.

BlackBerries too demand attention, signaling every new e-mail in a way that proves difficult for even the most disciplined of individuals to ignore. Yet the BlackBerry, the iPhone, the mobile telephone and broadband wireless connections have been hailed as liberating technologies emancipating employees from fixed, static workstations.

Today we're told that much of the work we do can be accomplished anywhere. Home-working is spreading, encouraged by companies such as British Telecommunications which has made significant savings in office space by giving some employees the option to work from home.

BT began what it called its "freedom to work" initiative in 1998 when it launched an experiment, allowing about 600 employees to design their own working patterns. Within five years some 6000 employees were working from home, producing a one-off saving of £36m in office costs and countless savings in fuel costs.

The need for home-office space is influencing house designs and home interiors. My own home-office is a tiny room bounded on one side by a bookcase. The key to its success is that most of the things I need for work are directly to hand. Like many home workers I have a separate telephone line for business calls manned not by a secretary but by a built-in recorded answering system, allowing voicemail.

In the past computers have been swapped frequently—every two or three years but there are signs that memory and processing speeds have grown sufficiently for a modern computer to deal efficiently with most multimedia demands—whether accessing a podcast, a YouTube video or taking international calls on the Skype system.

The growth and popularity of broadband has challenged traditional pricing mechanisms imposed by hotels. During my early career I became accustomed to rip-off rates charged for hotel room-based telephone calls, sometimes four times the fee charged by the line supplier.

Today some hotels—usually those who rely on company-employed business clients—are applying similar pricing models to bandwidth rentals. But not all do this. Some hotels—particularly at the budget end of the market—will include broadband access as part of the service you buy with your roomrate. Many of these hotels are competing for traveling business clients. As company expenses budgets tighten increasingly, traveling employees are encouraged to make savings where they can. For the self-employed such savings are taken for granted.

The mobile worker is not a new phenomenon as thousands of traveling Willie Lomans—the subject of Arthur Miller's 1949 play, *Death of a Salesman*—could attest. But increasingly sophisticated mobile technologies are extending choices to ever-growing areas of employment.

But are they limiting choices too? I discussed earlier the way that the pager and now the BlackBerry have enabled people to stay in constant touch with their offices, clients and customers. The BlackBerry and other hand-held devices like it are information in a pocket. But do they withdraw just a little bit of freedom for those who use them? And have they become too much of a crutch in corporate life?

I recall the distaste of some journalists I knew when they were first handed pagers. While some—the anxious ones—drew comfort from being constantly in touch, others hated the Big Brother feeling that they were always working on a leash, just a bleep away from the news desk, the nerve center of daily print journalism.

The BlackBerry can do so much more but does every office-worker need one? The point was made by a friend who works for one of the big accountancy firms. "We've removed BlackBerries from junior staff because we didn't think their use justified the costs," he said.

"But won't that turn BlackBerries into a status symbol, desirable because they are only handed out to partners?" I asked.

"You could say that. But you can look at it another way," he said. "If you have one of these devices it means you are always contactable. You are never away from work. Do you think every big shot carries one of these around? I doubt it very much. In fact I would argue that not possessing a BlackBerry is a kind of status symbol."

Mobile phone use, too, is restricted now when driving in the UK after a series of high-profile legal actions resulting from accidents caused by telephone distractions. Offenses of using a hand-held mobile phone while driving and failing to have proper control of a vehicle attract an endorsement and a fine with discretion for disqualification and hefty fines for those cases that reach court.

While the use of hands-free telephones or Bluetooth systems have not been banned, the courts can now take their use into consideration in any prosecution alleging poor or dangerous driving. If a vehicle has been in an accident the driver's phone records can be checked to determine whether a phone was being used at the time. Evidence of phone use could be assessed as a contributory factor. This means that people making work-related phone calls from their cars are putting themselves at risk of prosecution, losing their licenses and possibly their jobs, as a result of technology allowing them to "work anywhere."

In these cases enabling technologies are disabled by legal interventions. In some train carriages restrictions on mobile phone use have been imposed as a result of social consequences—complaints from passengers about the insensitivity of fellow commuters disturbing the rest of the carriage with loud and irritating conservations.

In aircraft curbs on mobile telephone use are imposed for safety reasons, for fear that telephone signals could disrupt aircraft controls. Is this fear reasonable? Surely if there was a real danger from mobile telephone signals, flight authorities would ban phones altogether. People are not infallible and "live" phones travel every day in the pockets of passengers who have forgotten to switch them off. Several attempts have been made to shed light on the ban with unsatisfactory answers. Suffice to say that the use of mobile phones remains restricted.

Curbs on usage in cars and aeroplanes have given a new lease of life to the bus and the train as mobile workspaces. Traveling on the M40 from Oxford to London in 2008, I noticed advertising on a coach exterior extolling the virtues of bus commuting, adding useful office time through on-board wi-fi broadband networks. Train services are now offering power points and some, such as GNER, that initially reserved wi-fi access to first class passengers, have now rolled out wi-fi for all their passengers.

This broader availability of Internet communications means that people are making trade-offs constantly in the use of this technology. Aircrafts may have faster journey times, but how much of this time is useful? Airports trying to cash in by charging for broadband risk losing custom to hubs that provide such access as a customer service.

Air travel as a technology has lost its luster anyway. Action film-makers in the 1960s, aware of the status-value and romance attached to air travel, would often include aircraft take-off and landing shots to emphasize the exotic quality of international travel. Today they no longer bother. In *Mission Impossible III*, the action cuts instantly from Washington to Shanghai, emphasizing the seamlessness of the urban landscape in our twenty-first century global village. Shangri La for busy executives nowadays, is their own back garden. Besides, there is money to be saved in working from home.

Some companies are cutting their travel budget by millions of dollars by holding international team meetings, using audio and video links. Cisco's TelePresence conferencing system has set the standard for such meetings, having overcome many of the issues that have dogged video conferencing systems in the past. Lack of eye contact, voice delays and detached voices have all been put right in this system. While the system is expensive at more than $300,000 for the top end of the range, competition will bring the price down over time. Others competing in this market include Hewlett Packard with its Halo system, the Tandberg Telepresence T3 and Teliris.

The Cisco system would seem ideal for the rental market and pay-per-use conferencing facilities. Using this system within the company requires some time discipline because of its popularity. Demand is so high that meetings are booked by the hour. This means that there is an incentive to get on with the business in hand.

Cisco's chief executive John Chambers has said that where he previously spent 60 percent of his time on the road seeing customers, he can now do most of this from his office in San Jose, holding the meetings via TelePresence instead. With more than 200 fitted teleconferencing rooms around the globe, Cisco was able to cut its travel budget by $150m in its first year of running the system, all but covering the project and installation costs.

Technology works best when you hardly notice it and during a demonstration at the company's UK headquarters in Surrey I soon forgot that I was not sharing the same room with everyone else in the meeting. Indeed the sound quality is so good you can engage with people in just the same way as you would face-to-face. This system and other systems like it have enormous potential for remote working. And this is just the beginning. While faster and cheaper air travel helped bring the world together, there was a price to pay in fuel and fatigue. Today we're coming together without leaving our offices. Tomorrow we'll do so without leaving our homes.

One of the great things about many modern Internet technologies is that they are freely available to people who need not pay corporate rates. The Internet telephone system, Skype, for example, has transformed the way I keep in touch with home when working overseas. Back in the 1970s, the idea of a videophone was seen as futuristic and, even though the technology was possible, it was expensive and difficult to envisage in that it would only work if both the caller and the recipient were equipped. The same problem was a feature of early fax use. When my father-in-law installed a fax machine for his business for the first time during the 1970s he had to call around his suppliers in order to persuade them to buy their own fax machines.

But Skype simply took advantage of growing computer ownership coupled with the widespread availability of broadband that resulted from the first dotcom boom and the laying down of far more capacity in fiber-optic cabling than the world could use for years ahead. While large corporations such as Cisco and Microsoft are plowing ahead with conferencing technologies, a traveling student living off a subsistence budget can talk to friends all over the world, face-to-face, via laptop screens for free, using hotel lobbies or any other source of publicly accessible broadband.

When fishing in Mongolia in 2007 I found that the Skype connection to home from my hotel bedroom in Ulan Bator worked perfectly, and the connection cost nothing. While 30 years ago futurists were certainly envisaging such connections, they did not dream that the communications platform would be anything but a telephone, nor would they have believed that it could be delivered free of charge.

Skype is able to provide this service by charging for telephone services elsewhere. In so much of today's Internet technology, free services are piggy-backing on fee-charging systems, either that or they are earning their income through advertising revenues.

It means that fabulous numbers—in terms of users—do not necessarily translate to fabulous wealth. But many of the networking pioneers searching out the big numbers seem to be concerned first with conquering the world in clicks, initially, only turning to more robust revenue models as their creations are valued by potential stakeholders.

While communications technologies have demonstrated that they can bring the workplace into the home, even allowing potential for monitoring of some work such as the kind that might otherwise be undertaken in call centers, they struggle to replace the kind of relationship-building that has characterized working arrangements for hundreds of years.

Many managers still place a premium on up-front relationships defined by eye contact and handshakes. But is the value of such relationships over-rated? We still live in a world where business is decided by the meeting. The meeting is not the engine room of work. It is the power source. Almost every decision or idea in democratic society is subjected to discussion at some stage. Yes, some businesses are still run by autocrats but even Sir Alan Sugar in his television boss persona, consults his assistants before firing contestants on *The Apprentice* TV show.

So the power of argument and the art of persuasion continue to be robust components of working life. The problem with these behaviors is that they can very easily tip over into intimidation and aggression, which can open the door for less desirable traits such as vanity, avarice or a desire for revenge.

For years before the banking crisis of 2008, the business world had lived with the cult of the omnipotent chief executive. In public companies a self-serving industry has emerged around succession planning and so-called talent management that has promoted the power of the leader. Indeed the worldwide head-hunting business has been built around the myth of transformational leaders.

But the events of the past two years have proved that corporate leaders are no better than anyone else at reading the economic runes. Even worse, some seemed to be lured into a destructive path of gambling the future of their institutions on an unsustainable property boom.

The voices of restraint, sometimes among non-executive directors in board meetings, were stifled. Suppose people could express themselves in meetings without fear that their views would be condemned or ridiculed?

Voting technology is available today that allows people to register their opinions anonymously. The technology is becoming popular in conferences for registering votes among delegates, using hand-held calculator-like gadgets that are distributed as people enter the room. Imagine using such devices in the boardroom when faced with the kind of headstrong boss whose idea of consensus is to bulldoze policies through meetings, using a combination of fear and intimidation. The boss probably wouldn't allow it. But when management consultants introduce such methods it is regarded as a legitimate deployment of technology from their box of tricks. Mary Meaney, a partner specializing in performance transformation at the London offices of McKinsey & Co opted to use audience response technology among senior executives at a company she was advising during a change program.[5]

Asked whether the company had a clear and consistent strategy for the business, the answer was a unanimous "yes." However, when asked, using the confidential voting technology to agree or disagree with various different descriptions of the strategy, the executives were divided with an even distribution over six different responses. "The CEO exploded," says Meaney, "but it brought out in to the open what had previously been hidden under the surface: no one had any clear idea of what the strategy was. The next step was to sit down with the senior team and create a new strategy."

This confidential voting has exposed the weaknesses of committee debates in the presence of a headstrong leader. But it shows how a comparatively simple technology, when exercised with care and discretion, can ensure that contentious issues are more thoroughly debated than would otherwise be the case.

But such technologies must be given an opportunity to demonstrate their strengths. Too often the committee and the board are viewed as political arenas that are exploited by those who know how to manipulate and intimidate.

In the collaborative world of the Internet, where much of tomorrow's work will be undertaken, the face-to-face encounter will become less significant and its power will be diluted, possibly for the better. The winners in this new world will be those who understand the strength of their ideas but who might not be able to express themselves so well in the debating chamber atmosphere of a business meeting. The meek really are about to inherit the earth.

CHAPTER 7

Making Sense of Social Networking

The most powerful force in the universe is gossip.

Dave Barry (1947–)

Some years before the advent of social networks I was asked to join an online network called Sense Worldwide.[1] Sense drew its members mainly from the arts and creative industries. It saw itself as a platform for collaboration, but, unlike the later social networks that would draw most of their revenue from advertising, its commercial model was linked to market research.

Market research departments pay Sense to produce reports based on research, surveys and focus groups among its membership. I went along to one of these focus groups. It was a pleasant evening, spent enjoying drinks and nibbles among interesting people meeting in some vacant shop premises in London.

Without being given any knowledge or background of the product interest, we were guided through various projects exploring issues such as brand imagery and personal tastes. It was clear by the end of the evening that the exercise was looking at a new brand of beer. As we left the shop each of us was given a brown envelope in which was a crisp red £50 note. That was when I realized that for the past two hours I had not just been enjoying myself doing interesting stuff with interesting people, but that the things we had been doing were perceived as having some value for someone. The payment only confirmed a nagging suspicion that what we had been doing could be described as work.

Another Sense project involved members in China, or with friends or contacts there, photographing the interiors of Chinese homes. A television manufacturer wanted to build its knowledge not only of TV watching habits but also the specific locations of TVs in Chinese households. Today Facebook would allow such research through user groups but the Sense network emerged in the late 1990s before developments that would come to be known as Web 2.0.

It was around that time—just after the euphoria surrounding the first dotcom boom had deflated—that I began to research network theory and the history of networks in some detail. The concept of networking in companies was already well established although I found some networking practices distasteful. In business the idea was that you went into a room at any function with your pocket charged with calling cards and began to "press the flesh," shaking hands and speaking briefly with anyone and everyone. As you held a conversation with one person you were already supposed to be looking over their shoulder for the next, trying to work out the "must meets"—those you considered the most important people in the room.

I hated this kind of networking, partly because I'm not very good at it, and partly because I think it takes time to strike up a relationship. I understand that all human relationships are transactional. There is something mutually exploitative about the networking process. It says: I am meeting you because you might be useful to me while I acknowledge that I might be useful to you. What's so wrong with that? Nothing at all, according to many of those in executive management I know who regard such networking as the most natural thing in the world. But when I meet someone, I want to engage with them, get to know them a little and to chat on a level somewhere beyond the superficial. I don't want to be looking over their shoulder for the next introduction, or to witness them looking over my shoulder. It's rude.

One of the aims of this kind of networking is to get to the gatekeepers—the influencers, the power brokers and the budget holders. Politicians are the gatekeepers of legislation so companies pay lobbyists large sums to ensure that their corporate interests are represented in the legislature. There is one big sell going on out there, almost all of the time. Companies have become so accomplished in the methods of selling—marketing, advertising, branding and public relations—that it's difficult to recognize real quality and authenticity any more.

In future individuals will need to become just as talented in such practices, be they working for an organization or working for themselves. Branding has become an important part of how

I work. Arguably it always has been for those in the media, trading on their recognition either through broadcasting or in print. Today, however, the Internet and social networking media enable anyone to brand themselves or to brand their area of expertise. Some who have dedicated websites present themselves as a company talking in a collective sense about "us" and "our" products. It's like an Internet version of that scene toward the end of the Wizard of Oz when Dorothy and her friends discover that the terrible wizard is a mild old chap on his own, sitting behind a big screen that magnifies his size. But nobody in Oz can see that. It means today that each of us in self-employment can think of ourselves as an organization of one.

My own branding is hardly sophisticated and breaks most of the rules in that it does not focus on the one speciality responsible for most of my earnings—writing about work and management. Instead I have chosen the Cromwellian approach of "warts and all." This means that my website is sectionalized into three different areas of interest—work, sailing and fishing, plus a personal blog. As a business proposition this is not very clever since those who are interested in fishing columns are unlikely to be interested in sailing or work. The website, however, is not designed as a business tool but as a repository of thoughts and ideas, creating a web identity that I hope is a rough approximation to my genuine identity, including anxieties, foibles, prejudices and grievances. I suppose human resources professionals would call it a 360-degree portrait except that it's a self-portrait and does not represent the views of others.

It seemed to me, when I created the site, that everyone, sooner or later would have personal web pages, possibly allocated with a birth certificate. Work experience, educational qualifications, photographs, holiday diaries, could all be recorded there. That was before Internet social networking began to deliver just this facility with a few other additions to boot, such as the ability to interact with friends on each other's pages.

The astonishing growth of social networking was highlighted in a Nielsen Online report in March 2009 that found that social networking and blogging was now accounting for almost 10 percent of all Internet time and had become the fourth most popular Internet activity ahead of e-mailing, behind search, portals and personal computer software, while growing twice as fast as any other of these activities.[2]

"Social networking has become a fundamental part of the global online experience," said John Burbank, chief executive officer of Nielsen Online, a company that provides analysis of Internet use. "While two-thirds of the global online population already accesses member community sites, their vigorous adoption and the migration of time show no signs of slowing. Social networking will continue to alter not just the global online landscape, but the consumer experience at large," he said.

The report confirmed that people using social networking sites were growing in age diversity and that usage was becoming more integrated with mobile telephone and palm device access. In the UK some 2m people were using a handset to visit social networks, compared with 10m in the US.

The Internet has not quite satiated the kind of yearning expressed by Andy Warhol for "fifteen minutes of fame." You don't get that on Facebook. But it has given people the opportunity to establish their identity in a web-based format. We can list the books we like, the places we have visited, the films we have enjoyed and our favorite music. At one time you would need to be invited on to the BBC's Desert Island Discs to choose your 10 favorite musical pieces. Now you can list them on Facebook. My generation, accustomed to a centralized delivery of services and so-called government initiatives, might have expected such developments to emanate from the state. We find it difficult to assimilate the idea that a college student could build an international infrastructure that has caught the attention of millions of people worldwide. But the state couldn't have created Facebook without creating widespread suspicion among those worrying about threats to their civil liberties.

But what do these sites have to offer in our working lives and do they have a future? As a source of information they are already attracting the attention of recruiters. Research by the talent management consultancy DDI in 2009 suggested that a quarter of job interviewers worldwide were checking social networking sites such as Facebook and MySpace for information about job candidates.[3]

Among those who had carried out online searches, just over half said they had used the information to make recruitment decisions. People using such sites, however, are less aware of this use. Less than a third of job candidates surveyed by DDI believed that the information they disclosed on social networking sites could affect their chances of securing a job.

Is this kind of vetting worthwhile, beyond exposing the naivety of some job seekers? Steve Newhall, vice president for Europe at DDI, says: "While job candidates should consider the sort of information they post online, interviewers should also realise that much of what is put there is for fun, and is unlikely to reflect a candidate's on-the-job demeanour or performance." Such character trawling should be discouraged by employers who need to understand that potential employees have a right to a social life beyond, or even within, their jobs.

Too many employers reject this right today. Nearly one in four companies were blocking access to such sites, according to a US survey published in 2008.[4] One in three of the survey respondents considered the sites a "major drain on worker output." Others worried about the drain on bandwidth. There are other fears too. When social comment crosses the boundary into public comment on work issues, employers are proving sensitive.

In October 2008, Virgin Atlantic dismissed 13 of its cabin staff for criticizing the airline's flight safety standards and describing its passengers as "chavs" during a group discussion on the Facebook site. The company said the staff had insulted passengers and had brought the company into disrepute.[5] The chav comment was somewhat reminiscent of the costly joke made by Gerald Ratner, when chief executive of the Ratners' Group chain of jewellery shops. Speaking at the Institute of Directors' annual meeting in 1991 he denigrated the company's products saying that some of its earrings were cheaper than a Marks & Spencer's prawn sandwich "but wouldn't last as long." After his speech the company's value dropped some £500m and Ratner lost his job. Little wonder then, that companies are sensitive to criticism from within.

When companies first became aware of staff visiting social networking sites, some banned office-hours usage while others drew up policies to deal with what they regarded as an invasive technology. Social networking not only had the potential for distracting staff, but could also become a focus for dissent either against an organization or of individuals within the organization. Teachers and lecturers in schools and universities were among the first to find themselves targets for abuse or mockery. Some companies installed blocking filters but this kind of technological response can invite counter technology. A number of bypass filters are available on the web.

If Internet-based social networking has revealed anything about companies, it is the extent of paranoia that exists in some managements. But any company confident about its working conditions should have nothing to fear. When I tried a few work-related words in the search filter of Facebook I came up with one or two revealing entries. A group focussing on Foxtons, the estate agents—"Foxtons is a great place to work"—was largely complementary, including a few reassuring comments for some who were facing their first day at work. The group, however, was formed in response to an earlier and slightly larger one called "Former Foxtons employees who are scarred by the experience."

Some groups such as "30 things to do at Walmart" seem little more than sources of juvenile amusement, in this case at the expense of the world's largest superstore chain. Equally there are several "I love Walmart" groups, the biggest of which has more than 2000 members and numerous "Boycott Walmart" groups, one of which also has just over 2000 members. Reputationally, it seems that within the social networking arena, companies must learn to take the rough with the smooth.

McDonalds, as might be expected, has moved in to Facebook with a commercial presence, sponsoring the "McCareers" group advertising job openings at the company. But anyone who runs the word "McCareers" in the Facebook group search engine will find that this too has its detractors.

The problem with special interest groups on Facebook—and the reason that company heads should not get too worried about them—is that there are so many of these groups and those that do exist are rarely a source for intelligent debate. The biggest workplace issue raised by these sites is not about employer reputations or security fears that are usually overblown, but about time frittered away online in offices when people should be working for their employer.

The office was barely prepared for Facebook. Managers were already concerned about time lost to other forms of web surfing before they discovered that many of their staff were happily spending parts of their working days posting and messaging on social networking sites.

In his 2005 book, *The Living Dead*, David Bolchover documented the amount of office time that was being wasted. He quoted research revealing that some 14.6 percent of US workers admitted to surfing the web constantly. Another survey found that workers were spending more than one working day each week visiting websites that had nothing to do with their job.[6]

Three years later, management concerns were growing for good reason. Office workers in one UK survey admitted to spending at least 30 minutes a day visiting social networking websites and corporate information security officers were pointing out that these activities were using large chunks of company bandwidth. One FTSE 100 security officer said the company had been forced to block access to Facebook from the office because it was consuming 30 percent of the company's bandwidth.[7]

There have been mixed reactions to tighter Internet controls. Some employees, worried about the addictive nature of web surfing, have welcomed the removal of what they considered a temptation they would rather do without. Others regard such moves as management shooting itself in the foot by removing an important tool of information gathering. Yet others value the ability to search the Internet to such an extent that they raise the question of web access at their job interviews, the implication being that they will not accept a job with such restrictions. "I'm finding that our policy on such sites is raised at every interview these days when I am recruiting new staff. These sites are not important to me but they are to young people," said one recruitment company boss.[8]

The management dilemma raised by these responses has led some companies to change their approach to the undertaking of work in fundamental ways. At present many companies focus management attention on hours worked or hours spent in the office. The realization that a bottom on a seat does not always equate to good work has led to the emergence of an ugly phrase—presenteeism—acknowledging that people in work can be just as unproductive as those who are absent through sickness.

The observation is not new, but it was novel enough for Cali Ressler and Jodi Thompson to write a book about it: *Why Work Sucks and How to Fix It.* In the book they stake a claim to something they call the Results Only Work Environment or ROWE. Have they not heard of Peter Drucker's management by results? While the claim might have been somewhat audacious, valid for little more than the phrase they have adopted and trademarked to describe it, their book was a timely injection of common sense into discussions on workplace organization.

Ressler and Thompson make the following assumptions in their book:

> "We go to work and give everything we have and are treated like children who, if left unattended, will steal candy."
>
> "We go to work and watch someone who isn't very good at their job get promoted because they got in earlier and stayed later than anyone else.
>
> "We go to work and sit through overlong, overstaffed meetings to talk about the next overlong, overstaffed meeting.
>
> "We see talented, competent, productive people get penalised for having kids, for not being good at office politics, for being a little different. ... We play the game even though we know in our hearts the game doesn't make any sense."

Such comments are symptomatic of the frustrations that many people are feeling in the workplace today. Ressler and Thompson's solution has been to create a laissez-faire workplace where people can do whatever they want, whenever they want, as long as the work gets done. "You get paid for a chunk of work, not a chunk of time," they write. Anyone who undertakes project work will be familiar with this proposition. Even among permanent workforces the concept of piecework—where employers pay for the completion of a specific job in a set time—has been tried with mixed results.

There are fears that unsupervised work could lead to some employees shirking in their jobs or to employees cherry-picking convenient jobs and working times. But Ressler and Thompson say such fears are misplaced. People behave responsibly about their work, they argue, when they are trusted to achieve results without too many concerns about when or where they get the work done. The ROWE system they instigated at Best Buy, the US consumer electronics retailer, they say, led to productivity gains of 41 percent and reduced staff turnover by 90 percent in some divisions.

Perhaps the biggest challenge in the creation of a results-based workforce is the determination of expectations. This requires a deep understanding of the job by managers who should understand the quality of work when they see it. But how many of them do? The question may be academic because employers that fail to respond to employee needs for greater flexibility are going to find themselves losing out when labor markets tighten as they surely will in future.

Besides, is it feasible for employers to maintain a highly controled atmosphere in the workplace? As home-working spreads, managers are being forced to trust employees to deliver work. At Microsoft, employees are judged during their appraisals on the work they have achieved and the extent to which it has met various designated targets.

This seems a reasonable management approach. The role of performance appraisal is growing in the workplace. But individual contributions are not always easy to measure when work is undertaken by teams. In these cases it can be useful to encourage team-based appraisal when every member of the team, including the leaders, appraises each other.

People get to know each other well in good work teams and this self-knowledge promotes efficient working practices. In his 1947 book *No Gold on My Shovel*, Ifan Edwards exulted in the rhythmical movements necessary for shoveling when loading skips with a partner. In this sense workplaces are social networks in their own right. Long before Internet social networks became popular, the *Financial Times* had an internal messaging system that allowed the creation of user groups. One of the best patronized of these was the Pub message group, not only used for pub gatherings but also to share comments on people outside the group.

When considering the influence of social networking, therefore, we need to acknowledge that workplaces have always been arenas for social interaction. In the past the noise of machinery, demands of the job or management sanctions precluded much socializing. This remains true in call center and production-line work, not to mention the ubiquitous office cubicle, but modern offices allow more freedom for conversation among staff, particularly around the water cooler.

Companies have been slow to embrace Internet social networking technologies but this is beginning to change. Zappos.com, an online shoe retailer, has pioneered the use of Twitter.com as a means of promoting dialogue between staff and customers.

Twitter.com, sometimes described as a micro blogging service, burst on the social networking scene in 2006, when its Silicon Valley–based founders, Jack Dorsey, Evan Williams, and Biz Stone launched the service that allows users to post brief messages of not more than 140 characters each.

Users attract followers on the strength of their messages and/or become followers of others. In its early days Twitter was a classic communications technology seeking a use. Because its potential wasn't spelled out, and possibly because it was free to users, there was no rush among businesses to adopt the system. But those who were prepared to experiment found that it was one more way to broadcast ideas, links and messages.

A fellow tweeter, David Creelman, a Toronto-based human resources specialist who runs Creelman Research, suggests how it might be used in project work. Imagine, for example, you are working on a project with five other people in the team. You all sign up to Twitter and have your own twitter group. At a glance you can see how each other is progressing.

He puts it like this: "It could be almost like overhearing the buzz of background conversation:

A—can't get the new motor working, called in for service.
C—arrived in Frankfurt, will see Tony later.
E—finished the code for sorting.
F—J is sick so I'm at home.

The messages here would be distinguished from email because there would be nothing that is 'need to know.' At the same time if you glanced at this from time to time you might pick up useful information. Not only that, simply the buzz would make you feel you were part of a team (if you were in a remote location) not a guy alone in his home office wondering why he wasn't rich like his friends."

Unlike Facebook that continues to reflect the demographic of the younger users who first populated the site, growth of site traffic on Twitter has been strongest among 25–54 year olds. More specifically, 45–54 year olds are 36 percent more likely than average to visit Twitter, making them the highest indexing age group, according to comScore.com, a website that tracks consumer behavior on the Internet. ComScore's research shows that social networking can no longer be viewed as a youth movement. Nor are there signs of the upward trends in use abating just yet. Worldwide unique users of Twitter climbed from less than 2m unique users a month in February 2008 to some 10m in February 2009.[9]

It is vital for the future of knowledge work that we continue to experiment with Internet social networking, even if the initial rush to these sites begins to wane among the *fashionistas* who will always graze and move on to the next new thing. In the same way businesses should be monitoring various forums in order to measure the pulse of society. The nature of forums, where members are able to cloak themselves in anonymity, adopting user names and nicknames, allows a candid exchange of views and opinions unrestrained by the need to be guarded about what is said, as we often are in an office.

Forums, more than social networking sites, can prove to be exceptional clusters of expertise, often regulating themselves on the power of knowledge, common sense and courtesy expected of members. Those who transgress open themselves to ridicule among fellow posters or sanction by moderators who have learned that forum threads can be undermined by poor and sometimes boorish behavior among obsessive posters.

Many of these Internet behaviors are replicating social norms that have existed for centuries since historically networks have undertaken an influential role in spreading new ideas (see Box 7.1 on page 136). The difference today is that the web has made them more open, accessible, broad, swift in their scalability and difficult to control. Perhaps we can learn from looking in to the past.

Box 7.1   Networks in history

Centralized control has often sought to undermine networks in the past. The perceived potential of new ideas for influencing sedition forced some of the earliest networks to operate clandestinely. The early Christians, for example, used networking principles to spread their religious doctrines. Later, during the Reformation, networks maintained contact between dissenters and, after Protestantism gained the upper hand in Northern Europe, between the Roman Catholic minorities.

Sometimes their function was practical in development, for example early postal and communications systems. A thousand years before Christ, the Egyptians and the Chinese had courier relays using messengers on horseback, similar to the nineteenth century Pony Express. The Romans had a sophisticated postal system, vital to the maintenance of their empire. The Roman Imperial postal system had 10,000 miles of roads in Britain alone with horses stationed every 20 miles.

During the Renaissance, the exchange of ideas stimulated by the rise of the Italian academies would challenge the position of the established church and promote scientific experiment beyond its teaching. A new knowledge network based on scientific inquiry, not religious doctrine, would shift our worldview to such a degree that in some countries the old order would be swept away in revolution.

Knowledge networks began to spread in the seventeenth century after the establishment of the Academie Francais in 1634, the first of a new network of academies that would emerge across Europe. Correspondence and cooperation between these societies was able to mobilize some 500 observers taking readings of the transits of Venus between 1761 and 1769. In an effort to organize the profusion of scientific correspondence, The Patriotic Society of Hesse-Hamburg administered a network of correspondence bureaus connected to a central coordinating committee.

These new scientific societies espoused an egalitarian knowledge-sharing culture elevated to a level above politics and national interest. When the American, Arthur Lee, resigned from the Royal Society during the War of Independence, he was the only one of his countrymen to do so. In fact he was admonished by the society for forgetting that he belonged to a universal fraternity of knowledge.[10] Benjamin Franklin, one of Lee's fellow American members of the society, had no such scruples and maintained his membership throughout the war.[11]

It is worth recalling older networks when looking at the development of modern Internet-based networks. The nature of the social network means that it is in a constant state of fluidity and adaptation. For this reason we should be wary about viewing networking sites as permanent institutions. Indeed they must maintain a permanent state of flux to ensure their continued usefulness.

The relatively brief flourishing of Friends Reunited, a website that allowed old school friends to renew their acquaintances, has shown how quickly use of these sites can be overtaken by fashion or innovation. While Friends Reunited survives, it has lost the buzz it once enjoyed among Internet users.

As social networking sites continue to struggle in establishing themselves as profitable businesses, potential investors might learn lessons from historical examples. Even the bonds linking the academies fractured over time. "The solidarity uniting the Academicians of the world was based on a fiction, namely that of a society of equals pursuing a common goal," writes Francoise Waquet in the Encyclopedia of The Enlightenment.[12] Jean-Paul Marat, the French revolutionary politician, went further declaring that they were not "the refuge of new truths but the asylum of old prejudices."[13]

If the future development of Internet networks remains unclear, we must continue, nevertheless, to assume that they will endure since networks, in one form or another, are a feature of most living systems, down to the smallest microbe. This means that we need to develop a deeper understanding of their dynamics and the context within which effective network operates. The danger in approaching networks is to assume that simply because a network exists it can deliver some benefit to us as individuals. But it cannot do so without our inputs. Some people are more adept at using networks than others and these are the ones who are likely to derive most benefit from them in their careers.

SMALL WORLDS

When Stanley Milgram, the US sociologist, carried out his "small world experiment" in 1967 he measured the number of links it took for people chosen at random in Kansas and Nebraska to send parcels to a named recipient in Boston. The senders were simply asked to send the parcel to someone who they thought was likely to be more closely connected with the recipient than they were. Although the average number of links was close to six, in some cases the parcel made it with just two links; in others it needed as many as 11. It was clear that some people were better connected than others. As Malcolm Gladwell noted in his book *The Tipping Point*, "Sprinkled in every walk of life are a handful of people with a truly extraordinary knack of making friends and acquaintances. They are the connecters."

If connections are confined to specific industries, the degrees of separation tend to be even smaller. A few years ago, a group of students from Albright College in Reading, Pennsylvania, entertained viewers of a celebrity talk show by demonstrating the close connections of Kevin Bacon, their favorite Hollywood actor. In fact Mr Bacon proved to be far less well connected than many of his fellow actors. At the time Rod Steiger was the best-connected Hollywood actor, ahead of Donald Pleasence; Kevin Bacon came 876th.

These rankings were established by another group of students, at the University of Virginia, when they set up The Oracle of Bacon website (www.oracleofbacon.org) using statistics from an Internet database of films, www.imdb.com. It takes just two films, for example, to connect Richard Branson, chairman of Virgin, and Shirley Temple. Shirley Temple appeared in *Miss Annie Rooney* in 1942 with Noel Neill who appeared with Richard Branson in *Superman Returns* in 2006.

Unfortunately there is no website out there that makes similar connections for executives, but studies have been carried out into the connectedness of board directors among the Fortune 1000. A team of academics from the University of Michigan Business School looked at the web of connections between 7682 directors who between them held 10,100 directorships. While most of them served on no more than one board, a privileged 7 percent held three or more directorships.

The Michigan team calculated that the members of this smallest cluster of directors were, on average, just 4.6 handshakes away from any other director of these top companies. One director, the Washington lawyer Vernon Jordan, had collected 10 directorships that put him, on average, just three handshakes away from the rest.

But it is one thing to have connections and quite another to use them as Jordan clearly did. LinkedIn, an online business network launched in 2003, before people were using the term "social network" in a web context, has begun adopting the characteristics of some of the later social networks in order to avoid the sterility of representing nothing more than lists of names and contact numbers. More than 38m people have signed up to it but usage varies widely.

One of its advantages is that it allows people to go beyond their personal network and tap into the separate networks of those they know. These wider networks can be important in job hunting as Mark Granovetter, a Stanford-based professor, discovered during the 1960s when he published a paper called *The Strength of Weak Ties* that investigated the way people used social connections to secure jobs. After interviewing dozens of managerial and professional workers, asking who had helped them find their job, he kept getting the same reply. The job contact did not come through a friend but through someone who was no more than an acquaintance. His subsequent paper proposed that when it came to finding a job our relatively weak social connections were more important than close friendships.

The reason is that our strongest friendships usually involve tight-knit clusters of friends in which everyone tends to know everyone else. Acquaintances, on the other hand, have their own friendship clusters, so the acquaintance, rather than the friend, is likely to have the more useful connection. The same applies with close colleagues and the more distant contacts we have through our work.

The ideas surrounding the strength of weak ties suggest that sector-based connections, while useful, are far less impressive than those maintained by true connecters such as Vernon Jordan, who are comfortable crossing boundaries between different walks of life. These individuals act as hubs in successful networks that do not consist of randomly distributed individuals. This is fundamental to understanding how networks can be exploited in the distribution of work, because it reveals that positioning is vital if people are to take advantage of potential opportunities. If we assume that there is plenty of work out there for all of us, it follows that the better connected we are, the more choices we are likely to have over the tasks we may wish to undertake.

If the influence of networks is growing in business through the popularity of alliances and partnerships, their cooperative nature is likely to change the way we compete, possibly leading to different patterns of employment. Conventional hierarchies may begin to change, emphasizing qualities such as connectedness. One day, perhaps, it may be commonplace to see enterprises guided by freelance influencers or connecters, charging market rates, rather than relying on the increasingly costly presiding presence of an incumbent chief executive. But we should not assume that this is already happening. Michael Moynagh and Richard Worsley warn in their book, *Working in the Twenty-First Century* that it is still "too early to predict the death of hierarchical organisations."[14]

Networks rely heavily on trust and mutuality for their cohesion. The Chinese have a word for the connections at the heart of their many family business networks—guanxi. Think of the old school tie, the favor system and mutual back scratching, seasoned with family ties and clan loyalties and you begin to get a flavor of guanxi. Indeed we've witnessed features of guanxi in the 2009 scandal over UK MPs self-regulated expenses.

Guanxi is the lubricant in a network of long-standing fealties. It is not so very different from the family ties and solemn understandings that bind together criminal organizations such as the Mafia. Even these organizations are united as much by trust— honor among thieves—as they are by fear. The best networks are suffused with trust which, once established, begins to feed off itself like a perpetually nourishing fruit, powerful yet fragile and easily bruised. When trust fails, the ubiquity of the network begins to fade, leaving the kind of rooted, structured and rigid institution that can survive perfectly well in a stable system, but which can become paralysed and unresponsive when the climate in which it operates begins to fluctuate. This is happening today as business struggles to adapt to the chillier climate of recession.

The meeting of the G20 group of nations in London during April 2009 was in itself the convening of a network of power brokers in order to find common ground and strategies for battling the recession. The role of networks in the future of work is likely to grow in importance rather than shrink as fast communications bring the global village ever closer. The late Marshall McLuhan, a prophet of the Internet social network and the man who coined the term global village, once wrote: "Gutenberg made everybody a reader. Xerox makes everybody a publisher." Had he been alive today he may have been tempted to add: "And the social network makes everybody a player." Today we can all join the game.

CHAPTER 8

The Inheritors

> *We live in an age when to be young and to be indifferent can be no longer synonymous. We must prepare for the coming hour. The claims of the future are represented by suffering millions; and the youth of a nation are the trustees of posterity.*
>
> Benjamin Disraeli (1804–81)

In the summer of 2008 as the campaigns of Barack Obama and John McCain went in to overdrive before the US presidential election in the autumn, a website was created called www. Iftheworldcouldvote.com.

The site allowed anyone in the world with access to the Internet to register their preferences for the presidential candidates in the form of a web based "vote." Some 868,844 individuals took the trouble to record their votes, a third of the total on the day of the actual election.

Its creator, Bragi Thor, a 23-year-old psychology student, lives in Iceland. "The idea came to me one night when I was lying in bed," he says. "I was thinking about how incredibly powerful the American president is. What he does has an influence on the whole world, and as a result of that the whole world has an opinion on who should become the next president. I wanted to give those millions of people from around the world one united place to voice their opinion, and, while doing that, show the American public that they live in a world where nations need to work together."

With two friends, Htjor Smarason and Steinar Hugi, he put together the site that could register votes from anywhere in the world. They launched the site on June 10 and advertised its existence on the Facebook social networking site. Within a few days they had registered a few thousand votes and the numbers ticked over through most of the summer at about 50 votes a day.

"It wasn't until early September that the site started picking up," says Thor. "From then on each day we had we had fifty percent more hits than the day before. And, as expected, the site peaked on November 4th with about three times as many hits as the day before." Interest began to build when the site came to the attention of the mainstream media and various blogs. "I did between thirty and forty interviews with radio and television stations and newspapers from all over the world," he says.

The site developers were surprised at the number of direct hits they registered as a result of people typing in the web address. Nearly 55 percent of all votes arrived in this way. "We think that because of all the media coverage we received, a lot of people saw the URL in newspapers," says Thor. Initially, however, word had spread from a group established on Facebook. Gradually people who heard about the site sent the address to their e-mail contacts. I found the site when a link was posted on a forum I had visited.

Malcolm Gladwell wrote in his book, *Tipping Point*, about the bandwagon effect that can gather around a successful idea or product. The Internet has created the means, through social networking sites, forums and video sites such as YouTube for anyone to achieve almost instant global coverage in a matter of days, even hours, as long as their message, picture or story is strong enough to create that essential buzz, beloved of the media.

In the past this process was in the hands of professional groups—journalists, public relations agents and marketing professionals. These groups remain important in the sphere of communications as Thor and his colleagues recognize, but they no longer control everything that we see and hear.

If the world could vote was brilliant in its simplicity and breathtaking in its global reach. Analysis of the voting highlighted some important messages. Almost every country voted in large proportions for Obama, usually far higher than the actual popular vote. In the US the website voting split was 80 percent for Obama, 20 percent for McCain, a marked difference from their respective shares of the popular vote in the election (53 percent for Obama, 46 percent for McCain).

The difference, I am sure, had everything to do with the Internet demographic although we have no definitive proof since the site did not collect data on voters, other than the national origin of the vote. It would be safe to say that many of the voters would have been young people and a proportion would have been below voting age, venting their opinion simply because they could.

But there were other details that would have interested Barack Obama's foreign policy advisors. In what the United Nations diplomatically calls the Former Yugoslav Republic of Macedonia the Republicans enjoyed an 84 percent share of the vote with just 16 percent going to the Democrats. The vote reflected unhappiness among Macedonians with Obama's support in the Senate for Greece in a bitter dispute between the two countries.

Thor is so excited by the result he plans to follow up the experiment with a global vote on the death penalty. "I would expect most people all over the world to be against it with possible exceptions of the Middle East and the United States. That would be interesting."

On rare occasions when every section of the media ignites at once, the tipping point phenomenon can be startling. The moment that Susan Boyle, an obscure Scottish singer, sang the first line of "I Dreamed a Dream" from *Les Miserables*, the musical, in the first round of the TV show, Britain's Got Talent, in 2009, television audience reaction, the Internet and mainstream media went in to overdrive, startled by the unexpected power of her voice. Within a little over a week of that single performance combined viewings of that and other appearances on video websites had topped 100m worldwide, more than the combined viewing figures for Barack Obama's presidential inauguration.

The reason that Susan Boyle's story attracted so much attention is that it forced people to examine preconceptions based only on appearance. Boyle, a somewhat dumpy middle-aged spinster, did not look the part of a glamorous stage singer. It was a salutary lesson, indeed, for the recruitment industry. The adage that you should never judge a book by its cover was never so powerfully proven.

Even on a much smaller scale the speed of take up on the Internet can be staggering. In the introduction I wrote of the snowman video made in a morning by two of my sons, George and Robert. Encouraged by this brief venture onto the Internet, Rob, a 23-year-old Mathematics student began to experiment with Adobe flash games software during his summer break from university. He made a game called *Salmon Survival* for my website representing salmon migrating back to their spawning grounds.

He acquired his game-making skills from web-based tutorials and by conferring with others on games forums. While studying in Lille after the summer, he began to research flash gaming in a little more depth. The flash gaming world is indeed a phenomenon. The games are free to play in this advertising-driven medium. The best can rack up millions of plays and some can earn their originators tens of thousands of dollars. Worldwide these games are attracting a following to match that of international TV audiences

Rob discovered that one of the most popular genres among the biggest user group—teenage adolescent boys—is the so-called sniper game. These games are tests of speed and accuracy as the player lines up various shots on a screen-based cross-haired sight. Rob prefers problem-solving games so he took the puzzle concept and united it with a sniper game. He didn't want representations of bloodshed either, so he built the game around furry animals.

The result was a game he called Panda: Tactical Striker. He e-mailed his finished game to a website owner he contacted over the Internet. The site owner liked his work and offered him $2000 for the game plus up to $3000 in bonuses if the game proved a success. Additionally Rob could earn extra cash through flash game advertising run on a pay-per-click basis by a company called Mochiads.

The game was launched on a single site on a Monday when it was still in Beta development in case of glitches that would be spotted by early players. By Thursday it was ready for a full launch. In its first full day on the web it notched up 190,000 plays in 156 countries and was adopted on to 146 websites.

These figures are by no means exceptional. In the space of two weeks the game had been played 800,000 times and Rob was confident of reaching his target of 1m plays. In fact within three months he had notched up 2m plays and a few months after that, 3m. But by this time he had already completed Panda II and has since launched the third game in the series. I stood behind him as he watched an online clicker notching up playing figures after publication. They were rising in fives and tens every second.

The life of many of these games is almost as short as the attention span of those who play them. They flower and fade. But a few have attracted a strong following. Take Bloons. Bloons is an online game launched in 2007. It's a simple game where players use their computer mouse to launch a dart at a bunch of colorful balloons on the screen, trying to burst as many as possible. At the time of writing, less than two years since its launch, the game had been played more than 340m times around the world. Since the game and various derivatives have been notching up more than 500,000 plays every day, by the time you read this that total will be far higher.

The game was created by New Zealand-based brothers Stephen and Chris Harris. The Harris brothers, one a scientist, the other a financial planner, both gave up their jobs to work full time on their game websites, earning enough to support two families, with the promise of much more to come.

Initially their games were made to be adopted by other sites in the gaming community, earning fees through accumulations of advertising revenues. The brothers then created their own website to host their games. Soon after that they created another site, Bloonsworld.com that enabled their growing army of fans to create and contribute their own levels of the game.

Thus the Harris brothers have created a collaborative Nirvana from which they can draw advertising profits. They have the ideas and make the initial games, but once the games have attracted a following, they can attract intellectual input from all over the world—hours and hours of work from enthusiasts who are simply happy to have the honor of seeing their own input featured on the web, like bricks in a growing online edifice. Internet experts refer to this as user-generated content and it is probably the biggest driving force in Internet growth today. Teachers are helping to spread good practices by posting their classes and methods on sites such as YouTube. One of the most popular in 2007 was the last lecture of Randy Pausch that has been viewed some 10m times on YouTube.[1] Pausch, a computer science professor at Carnegie Mellon University in Pittsburgh, died in 2008 from pancreatic cancer. He knew he had little time left when he gave his lecture that was packed with good advice for young people seeking to develop a career. He spoke of the "brick walls" standing in the way of ambition. They are there for a reason, he argued, testing the depth of desire among those who will need to overcome them. "The brick walls are there to stop the people who don't want it badly enough. They are there to stop other people," he said. Many companies erect their own brick walls to deter prospective recruits, so some students are exploring different avenues on the Internet that may turn out to be career openings.

Rob has tapped in to the appetite for user involvement, creating a game called Popopop where followers can make their own levels of the game with varying degrees of difficulty. He features the game on his games website BadViking.com that he created, adopting free-to-use open-sourced website building software. A site such as this can be built and maintained with pocket money.

Unlike the readerships of popular authors, the enthusiasts who follow some gamemakers are being invited to contribute creatively. Imagine an author asking readers to shape the sequel to a best-selling novel. In some ways the flash games industry is not so very different from book publishing. But while book publishing is a retailing model, flash games are free to users and website hosts, relying mostly on advertising for income. Those websites that do pay to publish a game are embedding a link to their own site, and sometimes buying first use of a new game can adorn their site like the star attraction in a shop window display. Just as books have a shelf life, flash games are discarded and forgotten like yesterday's newspaper, relying on new editions for their continued success. The market cycle is somewhat like a Mexican wave in a sports stadium.

If students can achieve this kind of entrepreneurial success while still at university, how can established employers win their talents? In some cases, they can't. Instead of applying for a corporate internship, Rob spent his spare time building up his games portfolio that is already earning him a reasonable income. Rob is still thinking that he may enter a career in advertising or another of the creative industries, but his dream is to build an Internet business. The model that has interested him most is Club Penguin, known in the gaming business as a massively multiplayer online role-playing game (MMORPG) that took advantage of the online social networking phenomenon of the early to mid 2000s.

The difference between Club Penguin, however, and social networking sites such as MySpace and Facebook is that it offers a virtual world where its young members adopt penguin characters. Basic membership, enjoyed by 90 percent of its members is free, but 10 percent of those who have joined have opted for enhanced membership for which they (or their parents) must pay a fee.

The Walt Disney Company acquired New Horizon, Club Penguin's owner, for $350m in 2007 with a clause allowing for payment of a further $350m if various targets were met in 2009. On the back of this deal Disney has now introduced more traditional revenue streams such as merchandising, including books, figures, puzzles, Nintendo games and trading cards.

Some of the best new web-based businesses are creating strong levels of community involvement. Take Omlet.com, the creation of four former Royal College of Art industrial design students, James Tuthill, Johannes Paul, Simon Nicholls and William Windham. The business began as a college project to create a design-based product. When looking around for a final-year project, Tuthill's mother suggested they tried to design a better chicken hut.

The group had been looking for something that would be straightforward to market and could be sold directly to customers. The resulting design, a colorful plastic hutch called the Eglu has achieved what all great products do, stimulating a market that hardly existed, feeding a yearning among suburban families to rear some livestock and feed themselves with something sustainable.

Another success was the website. Web-based forums and contributions from users have created a community of interest and a tutorial network for educating prospective chicken-owners in the mysteries of chicken rearing. Its online niche is so vibrant that if you look up the word "chicken" in the Google search engine you will find Omlet among the top ten entries.

None of this was created by expensive in-house IT departments or by outsourced specialists. The Omlet team did the work themselves, sourcing useful software on the web. The business was turning over £4.3m a year when I met them in the spring of 2009 and the business was still small enough that the partners could arrange their employment pragmatically, handling the work that they needed to do without recourse to traditional corporate structures or even to executive titles. They did not have a designated managing director.

Much of tomorrow's work will depend on this kind of collaboration among people building alternative careers, avoiding, where they can, the paraphernalia, rituals, titles and hierarchies of corporatism as it has become manifest in the big company. Many young people are becoming increasingly disillusioned with a world that even their parents have grown to distrust. The result is a growing non-conformism.

RISE OF THE CHECK-OUT CULTURE

Christopher McCandless graduated from Emory University in Atlanta, Georgia in 1990 with the world at his feet. He came from an upper-middle class business background and his parents had ensured that he would start his career with their financial support. He left university with nearly $25,000 in his bank account and a car provided by his parents.

He gave away the car and donated his money to charity, turning his back on the middle-class lifestyle of his parents. A corporate career, he said, was nothing more than a "20th century invention."

McCandless pursued an itinerant existence, dreaming of what he called an "Alaskan Odyssey." In 1992, with little preparation, he journeyed into the Alaskan wilderness with the intention of living off the land. Starved of supplies, he died there. Since then his life story has attracted a cult following among young people and subsequent book and film coverage.[2]

It could be argued that adventurers and "drop-outs" have been a feature of almost every generation. In the 1960s cinema audiences were entertained by the story of young Ben Braddock's seduction by Mrs Robinson, a friend of his parents in the film, *The Graduate.*

Braddock, the graduate, had been advised by another parental friend to follow a career in "plastics." Instead he prefers to float on an airbed in the family pool as he is accused by his father of throwing away four years at college. "What was the point of all that hard work?" asks his father. "You got me," says Braddock.

So there is nothing new about disaffected youth. The difference between today's younger generation and that of the 1960s is that there are more opportunities than ever before for young people to make their way in life. Today's Dick Wittingtons leave not with some bread and cheese wrapped in a spotted handkerchief, but with a backpack, laptop and a link to the travellers' network, WAYN.com. Or they do not leave, remaining often in their parents' homes to avoid the expense of buying or renting accommodation.

The 1960s generation also had opportunities. "Doors are opening to you, doors of opportunities that were not open to your mothers and fathers," Dr Martin Luther King told students of Barratt Junior High School in Philadelphia in 1967. King was attempting to imbue in the students a sense of self-worth. "Don't allow anybody to make you feel that you're nobody. Always feel that you count. Always feel that you have worth, and always feel that your life has ultimate significance," he said.

> If it falls your lot to be a street sweeper, sweep streets like Michelangelo painted pictures, sweep streets like Beethoven composed music, sweep streets like Leontyne Price sings before the Metropolitan Opera. Sweep streets like Shakespeare wrote poetry. Sweep streets so well that all the hosts of heaven and earth will have to pause and say: Here lived a great street sweeper who swept his job well. If you can't be a pine at the top of the hill, be a shrub in the valley. Be the best little shrub on the side of the hill.
>
> Be a bush if you can't be a tree. If you can't be a highway, just be a trail. If you can't be a sun, be a star. For it isn't by size that you win or fail. Be the best of whatever you are.[3]

Barack Obama invoked similar sentiments in his presidential inauguration speech in January 2009. His appeal was entirely to the work ethic, evoking "the risk-takers, the doers, the makers of things—some celebrated but more often men and women obscure in their labor.

He said:

> Time and again these men and women struggled and sacrificed and worked till their hands were raw so that we might live a better life. They saw America as bigger than the sum of our individual ambitions; greater than all the differences of birth or wealth or faction. ...

> Starting today, we must pick ourselves up, dust ourselves off, and begin again the work of remaking America. For everywhere we look, there is work to be done.

Obama was appealing for the kind of collective spirit in which nations pull together during wartime. But this has not been the spirit that has characterized graduate recruitment in the past 10 years.

Increasingly companies have been fostering elites and focusing their selection on rigorous academic sifting, often concentrating on specific universities such as the Ivy league in the US, The Russell Group in the UK and the grandes écoles of France. The problem with this concentration on academic excellence is that the employers that do so are perpetuating a tradition based on systems of working and employee and managerial development that belongs to the world of Ben Braddock's parents.

This is the twentieth century industrial model of structured working focused on the big employer. Business, education, legislation, pension systems and economic assumptions continue to rely on this model, but it is a model that is poorly equipped to deal with the fluidity and dynamism of ideas and learning distributed through the Internet.

Looking at the broader working landscape, where formal graduate recruitment represents only one avenue for shifting people out of the education system and into work, perceptions of change are beginning to emerge.

One phenomenon that is beginning to trouble recruiters is what Tom Mason, managing director of Hudson Solutions, part of the Hudson human resources group calls "the check-out culture."[4] This refers to graduates who look for alternatives to the typical graduate job, either by traveling the world or in setting up their own businesses.

This culture of exploring alternative lifestyles—if only temporarily, before undertaking the responsibilities of formal career-based employment—began to emerge during the 1990s with the advent of the "gap year" in the UK. Gap years were not a product of government legislation or the education system. They were the product of an informal movement that stared sporadically then took root. Initially such breaks were most popular between graduation and starting formal work. Then in the 2000s increasing numbers of young people began taking gap years between school and university.

The practice became so popular that employers often welcomed gap year experience provided that graduates could show some evidence of having done something wholesome during time spent traveling. Hanging around doing very little at home was unlikely to increase one's chances of finding a graduate career opening.

I raised this notion of the check-out culture over lunch with Robert Walters, founder of the recruitment business that shares his name. In a discussion that bordered on one between grumpy old men stereotypes, we both agreed that today's youth wanted it all, straightaway and preferably with the work taken out. But underpinning the grumbles that "it's not the same as it was in our day" was a general observation that some graduates, sometimes highly qualified individuals, are less than enamored with big company graduate programs.

The way that attitudes among young people are changing was given some definition in research undertaken in 2006 by Henley Centre HeadlightVision, trend-spotting and research consultants. The study, based on 1500 interviews with a representative sample of people aged between 14 and 30, grouped young people into six significant categories: young self-starters, hesitant creatives, corporate strivers, drifting opportunists, traditionalists and avoiders.[5]

While companies could rely on traditionalists who represented about 20 percent of the sample, the only other category that appeared to tick most of the boxes for big company graduate-recruitment schemes was that of the so-called corporate strivers. These were defined as ambitious, career-focused team players who fear failure and who are motivated by status and material wealth but who are also keen to give something back to society. They like to have the stability of an organization around them and they are risk averse.

How many graduate management programs would turn away this kind of candidate with the right academic qualifications? These are people who know what they want and who, with the right pay, conditions and training, just might stay with an employer. They are the kind of people who fit the model of the corporate steward. But recruiters should not expect them to innovate or to take risks.

Leaving aside the traditionalists and the avoiders, for each of the other three featured categories of young people, it was clear from the research that there were going to be issues in graduate programs. The self-starters were described as "naturally enterprising forward-thinking optimists, able to see commercial opportunities."

While recruiters may be willing to accommodate the risk-taking behavior of this group, they might struggle with their reluctance to plan, their lack of sustained focus and their impatience. This is a group, said Henley, that wants it all, and now.

What about the hesitant creatives? These are said to be "practical, pragmatic individuals, natural planners who like to feel in control." The trouble is that their creativity does not sit comfortably within boundaries or the kind of conventions—such as dress codes—imposed by many employers. Another issue for business is that these people also tend to be risk averse and can lack confidence and self-belief.

Then there's the fourth group—the drifting opportunists: the "live for today fun-seekers who are not natural planners." For these people friendships matter more than being part of an organization. Their social life matters as much as their work. They can be enterprising and they will take risks if there is a clear short-term benefit, but they can lack self-belief and drive.

Attitudes not only vary among different generations, they also vary among different nationalities. A 2008 report, Young People Facing The Future, based on a survey of close to 23,000 people in 17 countries, discovered broad differences in young people's attitudes to work, depending on their nationality.[6] Most of those surveyed were in the 16–29 age range, but with a proportion in the 30–50 range, allowing comparisons of responses between age groups.

The study found evidence, for example, of much more conformist attitudes among young people in France and Italy, than those in Nordic countries. Some 54 percent of young French adults agreed with the statement that "to have a successful career you must conform to the expectations and wishes of others." Only 26 percent of young Britons endorsed that.

Not only were young Britons less conformist, they were far less enamored with the idea of conventional work than the French. While 70 percent of the French sample said they believed a fulfiling job could deliver a happy life, no more than 43 percent of young British adults said the same. But French conformity should not be interpreted as optimism; far from it. Only a quarter of young French adults in the study thought their personal future looked bright. In the UK, the proportion was just over a third while in Denmark nearly two-thirds of those surveyed were optimistic.

Anna Stellinger, director of economic and social research at the Fondation Pour L'innovation Politique, who headed the research, believes these results reflect the variety of employment systems in different countries. Jobs in Scandinavia and the UK, where protection is weaker than in France, are much more accessible to young people as a result, she says. Young people in France, she says, believe there is less they can do as individuals to alter the course of their lives. They feel they have less freedom and control over their careers.

A general observation in the research that counters some beliefs about the latest generation of young adults was that collective structures were still important to young people. Individual expression goes only so far since belonging to a group remains a significant concern.

Why should these findings matter to recruiters? Because they tell us two things: the first is that the attitudes of young people are shaped by the society in which they are raised and educated; the second is that for all their national differences, young people share much the same priorities about careers.

Interesting, meaningful work was the highest priority of all, cited as the top concern for 70 percent. Second on the list was personal health, third was security, fourth, pride in the job, fifth was good colleagues, sixth a good boss, and seventh, good career opportunities. A high salary was at eighth in the wish list. Travel opportunities, fixed working hours and jobs with lots of responsibility were less highly rated.

You would think that with such a variance in attitudes, both generationally and nationally, recruiters would encourage such diversity. Yet in attitudes and personality types they often recruit too narrowly, focusing selection decisions on desired competency sets. While competency-based recruitment makes some sense—an extrovert, for example, is unlikely to be satisfied doing a job best suited to an introvert—sets of competencies, laid like templates over human characteristics and skills, have come to be too rigidly defined within the human resources community.

There needs to be room for a mixture of approaches in the workplace that does not exclude the range of different attitudes outlined by the foundation's study and by the Henley Centre. Too many companies, however, are sifting out the very people who would add diversity to their employment profile. Moreover, the way that many companies are refining their competency models and raising their academic hurdles in candidate sifting has created an impression of exclusion among graduates, particularly those who are made to feel they belong to second-string universities. Many online recruitment offerings are designed not only to encourage what companies regard as the right type of people but also to discourage others who might be persuaded the job is not for them.

Self-exclusion appears to be happening, but not necessarily to the advantage of traditional employers. Statistics gathered by the Department for Business, Enterprise and Regulatory Reform's Small Business Service for the second quarter of 2006 revealed that something like 3.7 million people in the UK were self-employed, some eight percent of the population over the age of 16. Five years earlier the figure was 3.3 million and 10 years earlier it was 2.8m. In 2007 there were 4.7 million small- and medium-sized enterprises in the UK, the largest volume since estimates began in 1980. Enterprise was growing in spite of the existing education and employment system that leaves little room for an enterprising spirit within an exam-obsessed curriculum.

How many of these businesses, I wonder, were started by older workers, discarded by or disillusioned with former employers? How many were launched by young people disenchanted by what one of my friends, a partner in a large accountancy firm, describes as "the hamster wheel" of modern corporate life?

Rajeeb Dey, president of the Oxford Entrepreneurs Society, a group he established at Oxford University, says that too little support is extended to those graduates who want to establish their own businesses. "You may want to set up a business but because you have no immediate support you get tempted in to going down the big recruiter route for a little while, maybe two years, then you find you can't get out."

Support is arriving for young entrepreneurs in a new UK National Enterprise Academy, backed by £30m from the tax-payer, matched by employers. The initiative has been headed by self-made millionaire Peter Jones, one of the entrepreneurs who make up BBC TV's Dragons' Den panel.[7] The academy will offer vocational qualifications in enterprise and entrepreneurship for more than 11,000 young people, mainly in the age group of 16 to 19 in its first three years.

While formal assistance is to be welcomed, some will continue to carve out their own individual niches. One who did succeed in following his own distinctive star was Matt Harding, a former games software producer. Harding decided, like many young people, that he wanted to travel the world. On one of his trips he took a video camera and did a little jig for the camera. Soon he was ensuring that he had shots of himself doing dances before some of the world's great landmarks.

Later he edited some of these dance scenes and set them to music, a haunting song called Sweet Lullaby that used lyrics from the Solomon Islands. He also attracted sponsorship for his video from a chewing gum manufacturer called Stride Gum. The popularity of the video spread first by word of mouth and then through media interest, so much so that today it has been viewed on YouTube more than 12m times.

On the back of this initial success, Harding has furthered his travels, logging his progress on a website called *WherethehellisMatt. com*. There is not a careers service of any shape or form that could prepare a young person for such an individual approach to living. Is this work? Whatever it is, Harding seems to be happy with his chosen path, for now.

These alternative career or lifestyle options are sometimes forced on individuals either through poor work experiences or through rejection that is no fault of their own. As the recession began to bite in the City of London, hundreds of graduates who had joined banks and other financial institutions just three years earlier, were finding themselves redundant. Many did not look for other work, but used their redundancy cheques to finance traveling projects.

Thousands more new graduates were finding it increasingly difficult to find traineeships as companies squeezed their recruiting programs. One of the biggest mistakes that large companies can do in a downturn is to freeze the recruitment of entry-level employees—young people who are starting work for the first time as trainees and who just might be prepared to forge a long-term career with the company.

Companies must recruit at all levels, but it is often the long-term career prospects, prepared to invest their ambitions in the business, who become the leaders of the future, not necessarily in the top job but in positions where they can maintain and influence the culture of the enterprise.

A graduate recruitment freeze, even for one year, deprives a company of an age cohort that will not only help to maintain age diversity as the company grows in future, but will also ensure the distinctive culture of the business is retained. Employers need a healthy distribution of age groups progressing through the ranks.

Age diversity is just as important as other forms of diversity as a company moves to maturity. It is natural that some people will move jobs and there will always be a need to recruit from outside the business. Not even the civil service can fill its needs entirely from within as it once did. But the key to effective workforce management is to maintain flows of able people through the system, while maintaining sustainable levels of staff turnover and recruitment.

Yet what happened in the recession of 2008? According to a survey of UK employers published in May 2009, less than half of the companies questioned said that they planned to recruit from that year's crop of new graduates. No more than one in six companies would be offering jobs to 16-year-olds and one in three would have openings for 18-year-olds, according to the research carried out jointly by the Chartered Institute of Personnel and Development and the accountants, KPMG.[8] The advice to graduates from both organizations was depressingly familiar: start looking for work earlier and try harder to market yourself.

Just for once I would like to see one of these professional bodies advising students to tell prospective employers to stuff their jobs. "Don't become wage slaves. Turn your backs on the labor market and do your own thing," they could say. Now that would be refreshing.

Turning recruitment on and off like a tap betrays potentially damaging short-termist behavior. It is difficult to assess the fall-out from such knee-jerk management, however, as companies seek more transparent explanations when their business is not doing as well as they hoped. You can't measure something that doesn't exist—such as the benefits that might have been gained from the employee-who-never-was.

To ignore the younger workforce today could have repercussions for years to come, for the simple fact that youth is a dwindling resource across the Western industrialized world. The point is made emphatically in Don Tapscott's book, *Grown Up Digital*, where he points out that young people are not only a limited resource but are the vital resource in shaping a future of networked, online digital business.

The real danger for employers today is the reverse of this proposition: that young people will ignore their offerings—the attractive starting salary, the training, the travel options, the benefits packages and prospects of promotion. Will these be enough in a contract that demands loyalty to a single employer, lines of reporting, dress codes and fixed hours of working? For now, for the majority of young people, the answer is probably yes. But will this hold true in future as a growing minority question the desirability of this contract?

More than half of the North American Internet savvy young people surveyed by Tapscott, in an extensive research study, said that they wanted to be able to work in places beyond offices. A similar number said they wanted flexible hours for undertaking work.[9]

What people want and what they get, however, is a different story. Why should employers respond to such expectations when they are sifting through thousands of applications for a handful of entry-level jobs? The question that employers need to ask is whether some potential candidates are making their choices before they embark on applying for work. What level of discrimination is applied by the sort of individuals who can transform a business as marketplaces change? Are highly structured working practices going to attract those people who will make a difference in business in future?

Microsoft believes it is creating the kind of atmosphere that will appeal to the Internet generation, focusing on measuring achievement by results rather than conformity to rigid patterns of working. When the company carried out research in 2007 looking at the attributes needed for success in the contemporary workplace, the most important capabilities, it concluded, were those involving critical thinking, problem-solving, communications, a capacity for team working, enthusiasm for work and self-esteem.

Most of these qualities fit with the eight most significant attributes of the net generation studied by Tapscott and his team. The features that typify behaviors among this group, writes Tapscott are: freedom, customization, scrutiny, integrity, collaboration, entertainment, speed and innovation.[10]

Stephen Uden, head of skills and economic affairs at Microsoft in the UK, believes such qualities can be found in the way young people use information technology. "Using systems such as instant messaging, young people today are helping each other with their homework in the same way that we expect employees to collaborate on projects," says Uden.

"The education system is biased towards knowledge and the ability of people to recall, and regurgitate remembered information, whereas technology is promoting the ability to source relevant information quickly. This is what is becoming important among employers such as ourselves.

"Problem-solving, good communications and collaborating in teams are happening all the time over the internet, but these skills are not valued in the way that young people are assessed in examinations. Collaborating in exams is called cheating. Yet the first thing we want to know when people come on board here is that they will collaborate."

Uden's remarks expose the inadequacies of an education system that stresses individual exam-primed competition that expects children to excel over each other. The same competition is required in employment selection but once in work, young people are expected to adapt quickly to team working where the priorities have shifted to the sharing of expertise in systems of working that emphasize the complementary nature of skills.

London's Cass Business School appreciates the contradictions in qualifications that measure individual knowledge and workplace requirements centered on team-working skills. Cass organizes its management coursework on team-based principles, while course tutors must monitor individual contributions in order to differentiate individuals in their final grades. The school has acknowledged that the artificial world of academic examinations and the real world of collaborative enterprise are poles apart.

Sports team managers understand these tensions and take pains to stress work-rate and team performances, often above individual flair which may count for relatively little when contrasted against the performance of the entire team. Indeed the attitude of some players with high levels of individual skills can be undermining to overall team performances. In an ideal world sports managers want players who can combine flair, work-rate, team spirit and a level-headed approach to their work, but the whole package is a rare commodity.

Highly talented people can be temperamental and difficult to manage. For every footballing midfield anchor holding a team together there is the goal poacher bent on personal glory. Teams may have to accommodate these distinctive personality types, but the contributions of the unsung players should not be overlooked. Sadly, the star system, where media commentators reduce every situation to the contributions of individuals, does little to foster team spirit. There is an apocryphal story of a cleaner at NASA during the space program in the 1960s who, when asked to describe his job, said: "We're putting a man on the moon." This helps to explain why Formula One motor racing drivers are conditioned to use the term "we" when explaining their actions in order to remind themselves and everyone else that they are involved in a team sport.

Don Tapscott has felt it necessary in his book to defend the net generation from critics such as Mark Bauerlein, an academic who described them in his book as *The Dumbest Generation*.[11] Some of Bauerlein's criticisms are understandable from the perspective of a generation encouraged to read, digest and store knowledge.

But even that generation, as most lawyers would attest, cannot store everything.

And what about this piece of advice for new graduates: "Turn off your computer. You're actually going to have to turn off your phone and discover all that is human around us." Who could be urging young people to disengage from the Internet? The Duke of Edinburgh perhaps? In fact the advice was dispensed by none other than Eric Schmidt, chairman and CEO of Google, speaking at the University of Pennsylvania in May 2009.[12] "Nothing beats holding the hand of your grandchild as he walks his first steps," said Schmidt. But did his advice fall on stony ground? The Internet generation, comprising what Tapscott calls "digital natives," engages constantly with the net, retrieving and transferring information. There is good reason for this since the Internet has placed so much information at our fingertips that to attempt to store it in our brains would overload our intellectual capacity. The new approach to information is to scan, select, analyze, disseminate and discard.

Others have sided with Bauerlein. Andrew Keen pursues a similar argument in *The Cult of the Amateur*. Tapscott points to one US employers' report that described high school students as "woefully ill-prepared for work." The criticism seems unfair. Much of today's workplace, buttressed by outdated support systems, is woefully underprepared for the kind of work that will be defining tomorrow's growing knowledge-based economies. The mismatch between young people's approaches and attitudes to work and the expectations of traditional employers could be good news for the older generation (some of whom will be welcomed back into traditional jobs as a result). But even among my own "boomer" generation attitudes are changing, particularly among those who have stepped away from permanent employment. It is as if the good life of the barely sustainable permanent job is sandwiched between polar attitudes at either end of the work spectrum.

These misguided attacks on the younger generation are an insult to the very people who will be inheriting a world despoiled by previous generations and brought to the brink of environmental catastrophe through terrible wastage and irresponsible use of the world's most precious resources—including people. If this—the Millenials—is the dumbest generation what does that say about the rest of us? Instead of heaping generational opprobrium upon young shoulders the boomers should be proffering what little wisdom they have accumulated in their lifetime in common cause to preserve what remains of the earth's resources for future generations. We owe this to our children and to those not yet born.

CHAPTER 9

Leadership, Teamwork and Collaboration

*In times of change, learners inherit the Earth, while the
learned find themselves beautifully equipped to deal with a
world that no longer exists.*

Eric Hoffer (1902–83)

Standing among the afterguard of a Volvo Ocean Racing boat
in the heat of competition is to witness an exercise in collective
leadership. Here on ABN AMRO One, nicknamed Black Betty
during the Portsmouth in-port race, June 2006, we're cutting
through the waves at 26 knots before making the slickest of
gybes in a 35-knot gust of wind. The gust is enough to shred the
spinnaker of the leading boat, Pirates of the Caribbean, just a few
seconds ahead.

Black Betty's skipper, Mike Sanderson, is helming while the
navigator and tactician are deep in conversation. Every other
member of the crew knows his individual job intimately. But they
also know other jobs and can break off or interchange roles the
instant they encounter a problem. This is teamwork performed
at the highest level involving something more than mechanistic
drills. Crewing a performance yacht requires highly adaptive
roles, engaging thought and judgment within an atmosphere of
mutual respect.

But sporting organization can't translate to business, can it?
We can't expect office workers to replicate the conditions of competitive sport can we? Not yet, perhaps, in most workplaces, but
the kind of collaboration achieved in sport can be replicated in
some organizational teams. Collaborative leadership, exchanging
the leadership role and leadership by consent are going to be far
more prevalent in organizations as we become more familiar with
new forms of working.

Not once during that Volvo race did I hear a raised voice or a barked command. What I did hear was calm discussion, inputs, thinking, consideration, quick decisions and reassessments if they didn't work out. Even the labored winching needed to trim the sails was achieved with quiet efficiency.

A month later, taking part in the two-week Sevenstar Round Britain and Ireland offshore sailing race, I was part of a crew of mixed ages and abilities experiencing ocean racing in the raw. Unlike the crew of ABN Amro, the relationship between this work team and its skipper was closer to that of an experienced corporate manager who understands the demands of individual jobs better than the members of his or her team. When boat speed is everything, when you're giving of your best and when you're still found wanting by the boss, relationships are going to suffer.

There were some harsh exchanges, yet at the end of it all we had a second place in class and the crew and their skipper remained friends. Why can't this happen in a conventional work-place? At sea you can't be dismissed, you can't invoke the griev-ance procedure, you can't even leave the office. All you can do, funnily enough, is get on with your work. In contrast, too often in offices, frustrations are allowed to fester, too many things are left unsaid, poor performance and poor management are overlooked. People leave, harboring resentment that is rarely subjected to any analysis. In the worst examples, disenchantment spreads like a malaise and no one can remember how it all started.

Fast forward three years to June 2009. I'm on the water again, this time with Dame Ellen MacArthur, the woman who shot to fame in her early twenties for her round-the-world sail-ing exploits, including breaking the record for a solo circum-navigation. MacArthur earned her reputation as a solo sailor yet constantly, throughout her career, she has stressed the value of teamwork. I have joined her on the BT Open 60, the yacht that was skippered by Sebastien Josse on the 2008–9 Vendee Globe round the world race. Today, however, we're sailing in the annual Isle of Wight round the island race.

Who is in charge? The badge on our foul-weather clothing says Team Ellen. But Josse is at the helm, making all the calls with a navigator. MacArthur, meanwhile is amidships with a BBC TV crew plus BT's head of communications and myself. "I'm here for you," she says. What's happening here? Who is making a living and how in this sailing race? No more than two or three of us on the boat are formally employed. The rest are freelances with a range of contractual obligations. The event itself, the boat and the water on which it is sailing create a kind of catalyst for various projects.

The BBC presenter and cameraman are filming an item on weather forecasting for a TV series on popular science called *Bang Goes The Theory*. The BT executive is representing the sponsor and I am writing a column for the *Financial Times*. Josse is keeping in shape for future events and MacArthur is representing at least three causes or organizations. In no particular order there is The Ellen MacArthur Trust, a charity that takes children aged between eight and 18 who have either cancer or leukemia sailing. Additionally there is Offshore Challenges, the business she runs with her long-term business partner, Mark Turner. Finally there is her passion to further understanding in sustainable living.

Various different agendas were coming together, therefore, for the length of a day on the deck of a 60 ft racing yacht. Where was the transaction? What was the product? Who was the customer? An exchange was happening and one that would involve money for some, but the real currency exchanging hands on this day was information. I was learning more about all of these ventures and about MacArthur herself. The BBC was using a well-known figure to inform and entertain its viewers. BT was getting some welcome television exposure—what sponsorship deals are partly about. The *Financial Times* meanwhile was getting a feature for its readers. JP Morgan Asset Management, sponsor of the race, was also benefiting in wider media exposure. Something else is worth noting: we all had a lot of fun. Was this work? Not as I knew it in my younger days.

But the information cycle didn't end there. I passed on my new knowledge—not all of which could be included in an *FT* article—in various blogs and among a number of influential organizations. Now I'm transferring some here in this book. Not only are the organizational and individual connections and agendas complex, but so are the leadership dynamics. MacArthur may have been the boss, but operational responsibilities, including all tactical and racing decisions were assumed by Josse and the crew. She broke off constantly, however, to undertake crewing duties and so did the rest of us where we could. Pulling in a spinnaker, bagging a sale, freeing a sheet—no crewing task was too minor for MacArthur.

But apart from ensuring a few basic safety drills, such as ducking under the boom on a tack, she left the rest of us to look after our own safety. The TV cameraman, wielding a bulky camera, wore a life jacket because it made sense. Some did not by choice. We must all take responsibilities for ourselves in the new work and that sometimes involves taking leadership roles. If you see a hazard on a boat you deal with it. If something needs to happen, you must make it so. The same must apply in all working life.

The people in charge with titles that cement their authority cannot possibly oversee a complex modern operation, be it a hospital, car manufacturer or fast consumer goods supplier. It was probably always the case. Even in military campaigns, leaders are only as good as their planning and strategies. Once in battle, the execution of maneuvers must be left to others.

The point was made by Leo Tolstoy in *War and Peace*, his epic novel about the events leading up to Napoleon's retreat from Moscow in 1912. Tolstoy argued strongly that the disastrous French campaign was almost doomed from the start. Napoleon had not initially sought the campaign. Once launched, however, events developed a momentum of their own and Kutuzov, the opposing Russian commander, simply allowed them to take their course, avoiding battle whenever he could.

When Tsar Alexander failed to capitulate after the French entered Moscow, Napoleon was left with the option of maintaining an increasingly undisciplined army in the capital during a Russian winter or of retreating West. Worried about the safety of his supply lines, Napoleon chose the second option and thereafter witnessed the steady destruction of one of the greatest armies in history.

Similarly anyone who has ever tried to unravel the causes of the First World War will recall how events conspired to defeat the best intentions of the leaders of the European powers to avoid conflict. Countries that had armed themselves for war and laid plans for war found themselves pulled inexorably into conflict once their armies were mobilized. Europe was dragged into war in spite of, not because of, the actions of its political leaders and monarchs.

Less obvious but equally powerful undercurrents are changing businesses today. Executives are being led into business strategies at times, not through any hard-nosed experience, but on a whim. I recall the comment of one senior executive I know in the earliest days of the Internet. "I don't really understand what it is or whether it will work for us," he said at the time, "But I think we have to go ahead and get on the web, then see what happens." There followed a multimillion pound investment and development program, accompanied by a spectacular rise in the company share price and an equally spectacular fall after the first dotcom boom.

Too often the decisions of company bosses are interpreted either as acts of genius or of folly when neither explanation is appropriate. "A king is the slave of history," wrote Tolstoy, arguing that the actions of leaders were the consequences of "thousands of minute causes fitted together." We might live consciously for ourselves, he decided, but unconsciously we are no more than instruments for the accomplishment of historical and social ends. In the same way a corporate boss is an instrument for the accomplishment of profit.

Harold Macmillan understood the biggest problem facing any leader. When asked to spell it out, he said: "Events, dear boy. Events." Tolstoy elaborated thus: "In historical events great men—so-called—are but labels serving to give the name to the event," he wrote, "and like labels they have the least possible connection with the event itself." Abraham Lincoln was aware of this phenomenon when he wrote to a friend: "I claim not to have controlled events, but confess plainly that events have controlled me."

Nothing illustrates these observations more emphatically than the events of May 2009 when over three weeks the Palace of Westminster, the mother of all parliaments, was shaken to its foundations by a series of front-page news stories in the UK's

Daily Telegraph newspaper, outlining abuses among members of parliament in the way they had exploited their expenses system. The detailed daily revelations led to the resignation of the speaker of the House of Commons, Michael Martin, the first time that a speaker had been forced from office in more than 300 years.

The expenses scandal exposed a failure of collective self-governance among the very people entrusted by the electorate to govern on their behalf. One of the most worrying features of the episode was the number of MPs who did not appear to appreciate that they had done anything wrong in spite of public outrage at the way MPs' allowances had been manipulated.

The allowance system had emerged to assist MPs in running two homes so that they could move easily between parliament and their constituencies. But the system was exploited by some who switched their choice of first and second homes to their advantage in a process known as "flipping." Others lodged expense claims for items or services that had little or nothing to do with the subsistence needs of a legislator. The MP for Gosport, Sir Peter Viggers, claimed £30,000 for gardening, including a £1645 submission for an elaborate duck house on his pond. The uck house claim was rejected by the Parliamentary fees office, but there was no denying the intent to heap the burden of these expenses on the taxpayer.

Apologizing afterwards for what he described as a "ridiculous and grave error of judgement," Viggers said he felt "ashamed and humiliated." He was not alone. Margaret Moran, Labour MP for Luton South claimed £22,500 for treating dry rot at her partner's house 100 miles from her constituency. Another MP, Julie Kirkbride claimed that she had needed a £50,000 extension—used by her brother—in a house that was already subsidized by taxpayers.

As the revelations continued, a mounting number of MPs announced they would not be standing for parliament again. What had they been thinking? Why did so many people entrusted with the laws of the land indulge in what can only be described as featherbedding on a grand scale and in some cases, plain fraud. In the aftermath some simply claimed they had "made a mistake," while others defended what they had done as "within the rules." It was all too clear that the test question asked by some as they made their claims was not so much: "Is this right?" but "Can I get away with it?"

The institutional apparatus that lent a veneer of normality to practices that shocked right thinking people in the rest of society only demonstrated the creeping nature of corruption, where questionable practices, little by little, assert themselves in the psyche. This builds to such an extent that some of those working in this atmosphere can be deluded into thinking that what they are doing is acceptable. Then there is the fallback of justification; in the case of MPs, some might have believed the allowance system was compensation for salaries which, while generous, paled in comparison to those in senior corporate management and the leading professions.

The danger is that some will always find justification for their individual "worth" whatever their level, if they seek to do so. Real Madrid's World and European Player of the Year, Cristiano Ronaldo, had no hesitation in agreeing that some football players were worth a £100m transfer fee. Asked to comment on the possibility when he was still playing for Manchester United, he said: "Special players are maybe worth that. I agree with that. When you are good, when you are a special player, you are more expensive than the other ones. That's normal. It's like cars. Some cars are better than others, that's why they're more expensive. It's the same with players."[1] Weeks later, he was transferred to Real Madrid for £80m in a deal that at the age of 24 would earn him £183,000 a week in the first year, rising to £556,000 a week in year six.[2]

Footballers and other sports stars inhabit the world of entertainment where rewards are measured by box-office appeal. This does not always equate to the out-and-out skills of an individual but may have more to do with their immeasurable "star quality." Is Samuel L. Jackson, one of the highest grossing actors of all time, a better actor than Sir Ian McKellen whose box-office earnings are somewhat lower? Some might argue that he is. On the other hand, others would point to Sir Ian's stage training and Shakespearean experience. That said, few would deny that Jackson has that certain indefinable presence that marks him out as a star.

What kind of factors are applied in such talent comparisons? Critical acclaim is one factor, but a much more important one in the film industry is box-office takings and the track record of actors in previous films. Most leading actors want rewards to match the expected success of the film. But some will take smaller fees to work with a favorite director or on the kind of project that they believe may deliver some artistic recognition, such as an Oscar.

Chief executives make much the same decisions. Some may be excited by the challenge of turning a business round or by taking a venture in a new direction. Just as professional footballers are approached by clubs, top executives are sounded out by headhunters. Indeed it is not uncommon for senior executives to maintain a close relationship with specific headhunters for most of their career at the top level. Once they signal a willingness to move, their packages generally will be negotiated by lawyers. The more risk attached to a potential move, the more they will be seeking in any future severance deal. It explains why executives often walk away from a corporate debacle with generous payments that are perceived by many outsiders as "rewards for failure" when in fact the potential for such an event had been envisaged in the initial recruitment package.

So how do big companies determine the pay of their top people? Is it the work that they do? Looking at international comparisons, the prime factor would appear to be geographical location. US-based executives earn far more than those with similar responsibilities in Japan and Germany, for example.

It's difficult in these circumstances to conclude anything other than that there is no fair system of reward for some of the stewards of the world's biggest companies. They get where they are and earn what they earn through a combination of talent, hard work, determination, playing the system, luck and geographical location. Yet many of these individuals, and the system they inhabit, believe that what they are bringing to the table are exceptional leadership qualities. It is one of the myths of modern corporate life.

This is not to deny that many corporate bosses have some impressive business skills, often coupled with inspirational qualities, not to mention hides as tough as rhinos'. But it is rare that we see the full package. Often we find that they have skills to match the aspirations of shareholders. Sir Fred Goodwin, former chief executive at Royal Bank of Scotland, demanded and achieved organizational excellence. His board was fixed on maintaining exceptional growth and they harbored strong ambitions to be the biggest bank in the world. In the acquisition of National Westminster bank, they demonstrated that they could swallow another giant institution whole, and accommodate the many difficult cultural and staffing issues involved in big mergers.

But, like many of his peers in other banks, Goodwin had steered his organization into the path of a financial tsunami building from the collapse of subprime mortgage lending. Crucially the bank had weakened its cash reserves at what would prove to be exactly the wrong time, in buying the Dutch bank ABN Amro—the same organization excited by an association with the extremes of ocean racing.

Without doubt, the failure of the financial system in 2008 was a failure of leadership. The very people who had been entrusted with the security of the capitalist system brought that system to the brink of catastrophe and only bold political intervention, indebting nations and their citizens for years to come, succeeded in restoring stability to sagging markets that came precipitously close to collapse. It wasn't the money markets that saved the system; it was governments, pawning yesterday's excesses against tomorrow's earnings. Politicians who the media love to hate were the ones who stepped up to the plate and intervened. There were howls of anguish from those who witnessed the virtual nationalization of some of the UK's most prominent banks. But the alternative of failure was unthinkable.

In the inquest that followed, the banking bosses who allowed their institutions to founder were demonized and none more so than Goodwin who was allowed to leave RBS on a £703,000-a-year pension for life, later reduced to £342,500 a year when he took a lump sum and allowed the remainder to drop by £200,000 a year. Not for the first time an individual and an institution would be brought down by the scale of their ambition. Before the collapse of RBS, Goodwin was feted as one of the leading chief executives of his time. In 2006 his name would have been topping almost any target list among headhunters. Corporately, Goodwin was what Hollywood calls "box office." He would have been welcomed almost anywhere with open arms, and had he moved then his reputation would almost certainly be quite different today. In leadership, just as in life for almost any of us, there are the "if onlys" that we recall with the education of hindsight.

Landing the ABN AMRO deal became a head-to-head for retail banking dominance between arch rivals RBS and Barclays Bank that was backing a rival consortium. Had Barclays and not RBS succeeded in the ABN AMRO acquisition it is very likely that the financial consequences of the credit crunch would have rebounded to a greater degree on Barclays instead. Goodwin's aggressiveness, seen as a virtue in a string of previous acquisitions, became the source of his downfall in the perfect financial storm of 2008. Did this make him a bad banker or was he simply a victim of circumstance? It seems unlikely that history will be kind enough to revise a popular image of Goodwin as synonymous with all that went wrong in the bank lending crisis.

Few would argue today that the ABN AMRO acquisition was anything other than highly imprudent. But at the time the most senior figures in the bank regarded the purchase as an acceptable risk, opening up possibilities for RBS to extend its banking empire in to many more countries. Dissenting voices—and there were some within the bank—were steamrollered by an individual who knew he enjoyed the confidence of investors.

This is how power manifests itself. There is no reason to believe it will not do so again, whatever checks and balances are imposed in future. There is something in the nature of leadership that confirms with a growing certainty for those in power the merits of their own judgments. This certainty is reinforced by previous successes. Unfortunately little is acquired from past successes other than a strengthening of hubris. The best lessons for future success are rooted in past failures.

Surely, then, great leaders should possess a sense of foresight. Isn't that a desirable quality in any organization? Warren Bennis, probably the world's most prolific writer on leadership, wrote in his seminal work, *On Becoming a Leader*, that vision was a crucial ingredient of leadership. This is the ability to map out a scenario, planning many moves ahead like a chess grand master. In an uncertain world, however, it is difficult to plan future strategies, envisioning future conditions.

The world changed for almost everyone after Adolf Hitler's Germany invaded Poland in 1939, but few in Britain at the time could have foreseen that within 10 months the country would be standing alone, its army decimated by victorious German forces poised to invade at the other side of the channel. When Winston Churchill became prime minister, Britain's position was desperate and some advised to sue for peace. But Churchill, as we all know now, was a man right for his time—belligerent, maverick, eloquent, lyrical and highly experienced in politics—whose speech-making rallied a nation at what none who lived through it would deny was its "darkest hour."

Most people have their own ideas of leadership and their understanding often overlaps with what they envisage as greatness. When the British public was asked by the BBC in 2002 to vote for who they regarded as the Greatest Briton, leadership was only one of the qualities in the mix. Winston Churchill came first in the poll, followed by Isambard Kingdom Brunel and Princess Diana. Each of the top nominations, however, was championed by a particular individual and the persuasiveness of these people, and how they assembled their arguments was a factor in the final poll.

Apart from those darkest days of the war, Churchill had a chequered performance in wartime leadership, often frustrating his generals and allies in equal measure. But, like most good leaders, he leaned heavily on the advice of others, including his military experts and the knowledge of his new allies, the Americans, when they entered the war. Churchill, for all his foibles, and there were many, had a very clear understanding of what Europe and the world might look like after the war. His reading of Joseph Stalin and the Russian leader's ambitions was far sharper than that of Franklin D. Roosevelt, president of the US for most of the Second World War.

It's not surprising, therefore, given Thomas Carlyle's "great man theory" of historical progress, that Churchill would have ticked all the boxes of what many people understand as great leadership. For most of history, military leadership has dominated the concerns of societies and their administrations, for good reason. Your system of administration or the strength of your economy would not matter a jot if your walled medieval city was standing in the way of Genghis Khan's hordes.

But the maintenance of power, as Julius Caesar discovered, was more than a matter of single-minded military leadership. It also involved political skills, one reason why Machiavelli's *The Prince* is still read by corporate bosses today. Knowing when to fight your battles, both in the boardroom, among investors and in approaches to takeover targets is a great skill, as corporate leaders can learn from the writings of Sun Tzu. To what extent, however, is this kind of knowledge going to be useful to those who seek to lead or who are chosen to lead in future? Is the definition of leadership undergoing change today in the same way that we can perceive that work is changing?

I examined the dynamics of competitive sailing at the beginning of this chapter to demonstrate how fluid leadership can be in the transfer and distribution of information. The scandal of MPs expenses was a timely reminder that those entrusted with leadership—in this case central to the UK's legislative process, passing laws that influence the way that all of us live and work—can sometimes fail to reflect the responsibilities of office. If legislators cannot lead by example, where should we look to draw inspiration for the future? Indeed, is inspiration the prime quality that we should look for in future leadership amid so much business failure today? And what price leadership today amid so much business failure? Are clues to be found in the vast literature on leadership?

Most books on leadership seem to place their faith in emulation, either choosing role models from history or from business or politics. The market for leadership books is a confusing place and the thirst for this genre among publishers seemingly unquenchable. Prospective corporate bosses can choose from an extensive menu of historical role models such as Sun Tzu, Nelson, Alexander the Great and Gandhi. There is even a title called *Jesus CEO*.[3] If all of these individuals have one thing in common, however, it is that none of them learned anything from each other. Does this suggest then that some are born to lead?

The question is debated as strongly today as it ever was, although the notion is largely dismissed in *Talent is Overrated*, Geoff Colvin's 2008 study of great performance, that outlines a compelling argument for acquired skills, needing thousands of hours of what he calls "deliberate practice" to achieve outstanding levels of performance. In leadership, the debate is complicated further. No one yet has managed to isolate all the traits required for sound leadership, not least since no one yet has managed to define what leadership actually *is*, although many have tried.

The best we can do is to focus on various lists outlined by those who have thought deeply about leadership or who have held positions of leadership. Warren Bennis was probably the first of the leadership gurus to suggest that leaders need a sense of vision. If only bank bosses and economists had possessed some vision before the financial crisis of 2008. If it was lacking then, can it be acquired now? The experience of the past two years suggests that society will need to lean on a body of fresh thinking if it is to sweep away the mistakes of today's generation.

In a 2003 revised edition of *On Becoming a Leader*, Bennis had shifted his thinking toward collaborations in leadership instead of the "solitary geniuses" described in school books. "The Lone Ranger is dead," wrote Bennis and Patricia Ward Biederman in their coauthored work, *Organizing Genius: The Secrets of Creative Collaboration*. Yet people still seek out leaders for information, advice and direction while others aspire to roles in which they can demonstrate responsibility, either through influence, organization or control; so we should not imagine that leadership itself is dead. But it is changing and must change further to accommodate the same forces that are changing the way we work.

The cult of leadership has been one of the most lasting facets of work over the millennia, as pervasive now as it was in the time of the ancients. Throughout history leadership has passed through several manifestations, including the power of the military, the influence of intellectual thought in the classical period, the inherited rights of monarchy and aristocracy, electoral mandates of modern democracies and meritocratic elevation in corporations. Examples of military leadership have become relatively unfashionable in contemporary companies but, on occasions, they still demand attention.

On the eve of the invasion of Iraq in what became the Second Gulf War, Lt. Col. Tim Collins, commanding officer, 1st Battalion, Royal Irish Regiment, assembled his troops together and gave them an extraordinary speech that was quoted verbatim in the next day's *Daily Telegraph*. His eve of battle speech, reminiscent of Shakespeare's St Crispin's Day speech in *Henry V* made Collins an overnight media celebrity. His regiment played an important peacekeeping role that he related later in his autobiography. Hearing him speak some time ago at an engagement in London, I was struck by several aspects of his delivery. One was his disclosure that everywhere he went he carried a copy of Machiavelli's *The Prince* in his battle dress.

The second was more of an observation. Women in the audience seemed captivated by his language. Was it sex appeal, something in the accent, or was it old-fashioned charisma, the quality that Jim Collins, the management writer, told us in his book *Good to Great*, no longer had much relevance in the running of companies?

Looking back at that speech by Col Collins, I think that its power was all about the language he used and the way it set forth a sense of purpose to the mission, dictating not only the intentions of the war but also the conduct in which it would be carried out. The Biblical lyricism of the speech only added to its strength.

Here is an excerpt:

We go to liberate not to conquer. We will not fly our flags in their country. We are entering Iraq to free a people and the only flag which will be flown in that ancient land is their own. Show respect for them.

There are some who are alive at this moment who will not be alive shortly. Those who do not wish to go on that journey, we will not send. As for the others I expect you to rock their world. Wipe them out if that is what they choose. But if you are ferocious in battle remember to be magnanimous in victory.

Iraq is steeped in history. It is the site of the Garden of Eden, of the Great Flood and the birthplace of Abraham. Tread lightly there. You will see things that no man could pay to see and you will have to go a long way to find a more decent, generous and upright people than the Iraqis. You will be embarrassed by their hospitality even though they have nothing. Don't treat them as refugees for they are in their own country. Their children will be poor; in years to come they will know that the light of liberation in their lives was brought by you. If there are casualties of war then remember that when they woke up and got dressed in the morning they did not plan to die this day. Allow them dignity in death. Bury them properly and mark their graves.

It is my foremost intention to bring every single one of you out alive but there may be people among us who will not see the end of this campaign. We will put them in their sleeping bags and send them back. There will be no time for sorrow.

The enemy should be in no doubt that we are his nemesis and that we are bringing about his rightful destruction. There are many regional commanders who have stains on their souls and they are stoking the fires of hell for Saddam. He and his forces will be destroyed by this coalition for what they have done. As they die they will know their deeds have brought them to this place. Show them no pity.

It is a big step to take another human life. It is not to be done lightly. I know of men who have taken life needlessly in other conflicts, I can assure you they live with the Mark of Cain upon them. If someone surrenders to you then remember they have that right in international law and ensure that one day they go home to their family.

The ones who wish to fight, well, we aim to please.

In a society that has grown tired of clipped, turgid and lifeless management speak, even within the military's officer class, accustomed to exchanges of bewildering acronyms, an injection of what almost amounts to poetry carried some meaning and an appropriate sense of drama for the conflict ahead. It put the conflict into an authentic context for all involved.

It's not difficult to find comparisons in *Henry V*:

> That he which hath no stomach to this fight,
> Let him depart; his passport shall be made,
> And crowns for convoy put into his purse;
> We would not die in that man's company
> That fears his fellowship to die with us.

This day is call'd the feast of Crispian.
He that outlives this day, and comes safe home,
Will stand a tip-toe when this day is nam'd,
And rouse him at the name of Crispian.
He that shall live this day, and see old age,
Will yearly on the vigil feast his neighbours,
And say "To-morrow is Saint Crispian."
Then will he strip his sleeve and show his scars,
And say "These wounds I had on Crispian's day."
Old men forget; yet all shall be forgot,
But he'll remember, with advantages,
What feats he did that day.

But Collins was speaking in 2003, at a time that the qualities of leadership had been subjected to more analysis in more books—mostly aimed at the corporate marketplace—than we could possibly read in a lifetime. Some of their lessons are conflicting and some are plain common sense. Yet the most stunning thing about this advice—even where it has merit—is that most of it seems to be studiously ignored.

This is why I was taken with Col Collins' reliance on Machiavelli. In spite of all of the modern thinking at his fingertips, he chose to carry with him the words of a medieval Italian diplomat and political philosopher. And he is not alone. Machiavelli is one of many historical theorists that continue to grab the attention of a modern audience. But does he have relevance to the future of leadership? And is there any need in contemporary society for Collins' oratorical skills? Certainly there were echoes of Collins in Barack Obama's presidential inauguration speech in January 2009.

"We go to liberate not to conquer," said Collins. "We will extend a hand if you are willing to unclench your fist," said Obama.

"We are entering Iraq to free a people and the only flag which will be flown in that ancient land is their own," said Collins.

"We will not apologize for our way of life, nor will we waver in its defence, and for those who seek to advance their aims by inducing terror and slaughtering innocents, we say to you now that our spirit is stronger and cannot be broken; you cannot outlast us, and we will defeat you," said Obama.

"If someone surrenders to you then remember they have that right in international law and ensure that one day they go home to their family. The ones who wish to fight, well, we aim to please," said Collins. This combination of steely resolution and purpose tempered by fairness and compassion seemed to underpin a new style of leadership drawing strength from humility. "I stand here today humbled by the task before us," said Obama.

Except that the style was not new. It was as old as the Bible since these sympathies are reflected in Christian values. We can see this ancient heritage in most forms of leadership. Leadership, like work, is as old as the soil. It is the styles that change to meet the circumstances.

In his influential 2001 book, *Good to Great*, Jim Collins presented evidence suggesting that great companies were not led by "gung-ho" or charismatic types. Instead, he wrote, the best companies were run by quiet, dogged people who put the business first and, above everything, combined a sense of humility with a will to succeed. The best companies, he argued, were led by unassuming types who preferred to avoid media recognition.

The late Robert Greenleaf was saying something similar in 1970 when he coined the term "servant-leadership" to describe people who put their workforce and their company before themselves. Collins added substance and context to the servant-leadership concept. It took a while for recruiters to digest this change in fashion. Company bosses, after all, had been reared in the 1980s and 1990s on the sayings and example of "Neutron" Jack Welch, one of the world's most influential chief executives when he was CEO of General Electric for two decades, between 1981 and 2001.

Like Napoleon Bonaparte, who valued the loyalty of his generals, Welch kept his senior executive team guessing about who he favored most. For Welch, choosing, withholding and sometimes changing the name of his successor was a tactic of management, ensuring that his top team remained on board, competitive, aggressive and focused on the top job. Anointing a successor too early would have deprived the company prematurely of some of its most formidable executives.

When the time came for Welch to step down he kept his immediate subordinates guessing right up to the day he announced his departure, knowing that headhunters were forever circling his top team, looking for any opportunity to poach a disgruntled executive.

Bob Nardelli, the man who lost out on the top job at GE to Jeff Immelt by the narrowest of margins, spent the subsequent five years running Home Depot, America's second largest retailer, taking annual profits from $2.8bn to $5.6bn in 2005. He was perceived, nevertheless, to have failed and forced to step down with a payoff worth $210m. Here we see both a modern definition of failure and the rewards available for those who fail.

Few of those who are feted for at least part of their time at the top survive in business unblemished. Sir Clive Thompson at Rentokil, Percy Barnevik at Asea Brown Boveri and Lord John Brown at BP, each suffered damage to their reputations either at the end of their terms or in subsequent controversies. Even Jack Welch later found himself defending all kinds of frills attached to his pension arrangements. It may be that leaders, as Tolstoy argued, are less important than they or we think they are. But we all seem to need a figurehead, the media particularly so. The Jim Collins philosophy is fine, but it does not sell newspapers. Newspapers need personalities.

It's difficult today to find a torch-holder for corporate leadership. Television has sought out entrepreneurs such as Sir Alan Sugar and the individuals who make up the panel of the Dragons' Den on the BBC. In the US there is Warren Buffet, nicknamed the Sage of Omaha. But most of these people are defined by their histories, not by the future. What about the new kids on the block—the bosses of the biggest Internet companies such as Jeff Bezos, founder of Amazon, the man described in *Time Magazine* as the "king of cybercommerce?" Successful as he is, visionary as he undoubtedly is, Bezos is a stereotypical entrepreneur, building his business in a garage, an inspiration to anyone seeking to start out in business. But Amazon ultimately became structured much as any other business. Amazon undoubtedly revolutionized retailing, but I'm not sure that it did the same for work. Nearly all Internet start-ups, even where they emphasize their egalitarian values, very quickly seek structure in their employment systems.

With structure comes process and with process comes the urge to separate planning and execution, promoting hierarchy and draining away personal autonomy and discretion.

If Bennis is right about the need for more collaboration in future—and I believe he is—then we must begin to look at more egalitarian figures in leadership today. It is not in the nature of business leaders, however, to be egalitarian. People are motivated by a few primary needs, according to Paul Lawrence and Nitin Nohria in their book, *Driven, How Human Nature Shapes Our Choices*. In what they present as a unified theory of human nature, they argued that everything that anyone does is based on four fundamental drives: to acquire, to bond, to learn and to defend.

Some of our acquisitiveness, they point out, does not make much sense other than in an evolutionary context. Our desire for more pay, for example, relies not on need but on relative status. They quote one experiment that gave people the chance to live in two worlds in which prices were the same. In one world they would earn $90,000 and their neighbors would earn $100,000. In the alternative world they would earn $110,000 but their neighbors would earn $200,000. Usually people took the first option because what they cared about most was their relative status.

Robert Frank, a promoter of evolutionary psychology, concedes that a "relentless focus on relative position seems more like a recipe for unhappiness than a useful motivational tool" but maintains that "the purpose of human motivation is not to make us happy but to make us more likely to succeed against the competition." So we are stuck with this drive to acquire, say Lawrence and Nohria. The need to bond with others, they say, is another fundamental feature of motivation. This one covers job fit and the attraction of teams. The drive to learn is apparent in the way people attempt to make sense of their world.

The drive to defend oneself may seem a surprising candidate for the list but experiments have shown how skilled people are in spotting sharp practice or cheating in others—a trait of defensive behavior. Equity is important in earnings structures. Consider this scenario: suppose you are told that you are going to share a £100 payout with another person you have never met or are ever likely to meet. The other person has the power to apportion the award how they see fit. They are told as you are, however, that if you refuse your share neither of you will receive anything.

In the past when researchers have run this experiment—called the ultimatum game—most people responsible for apportioning the award decide that the person sharing with them should get either £40 or £50. Sometimes they offer the lion's share as an added inducement. When a smaller share, say £10, is apportioned it tends to be refused, leaving neither participant with anything.

Refusal of any amount makes little sense when the alternative is to receive nothing at all. But such is the psychological need to feel a sense of equity that most people would rather go without than allow someone who they have never met to profit to a much greater degree than they do, even when the money they would receive has not been earned by either of them.

I tried the experiment on my wife, Gill, and one of my sons separately, suggesting a figure of £10. Gill said there was no way she was accepting £10 in the knowledge that someone else would be getting £90. My 19-year-old son, however, accepted the £10. "It's £10 I didn't have a minute ago and I don't know the other person," he said.

His reasoned response is not typical since most people, like my wife, hate to think that someone has taken advantage of their willingness to accept such a small share of the pay-out. Denying the offer is to exercise the only power they have: the power to get even. Getting even and being even in this case amount to the same thing. That the levels of wealth at which both participants will remain are lower than those that they would have enjoyed appears to be a sacrifice worth paying for the sake of equity.

Sandy Pepper, former human resource partner at Pricewaterhouse Coopers who introduced me to the exercise, ran it regularly among colleagues. "Whenever we play this game it provokes a fierce debate. People get terribly agitated about it," he says. In his book, *Senior Executive Reward: Key Models and Practices*, he writes that not only do most people possess a strong sense of fairness, but that responses to the experiment are influenced by culture. In the US smaller amounts are more frequently offered and more frequently accepted. The Japanese, on the other hand, tend to split the figure down the middle.[4]

Pepper says that most of his PWC partners adopt my wife's attitude. "I think that what drives PWC partners more than anything else is a sense of fairness and I think that this applies to other well paid people who tend to compare their earnings with those in competitor companies of a similar size," he says.

While this is certainly what happens in the boards of big public companies that use pay consultants to determine boardroom pay, comparisons have been introduced mainly by consultants in order to help them attribute pay awards equitably. The problem is that the use of pay data has exacerbated the ratcheting up of senior executive pay. This is because such data is usually assembled in quartiles. Since few executives want their pay to be in the lower quartile of their sector there is a constant move toward the median among the lower paid. But since the higher paid do not move to the median for the obvious reason that this would involve a pay cut, the data produces a constantly shifting upwards effect. Over years this has been considerable. What is often interpreted, therefore, as corporate greed, I suspect, is largely down to the mechanics of the executive pay system. Unconscious greed, however, is manifest in the disinclination among those at the top to redress this system.

If Lawrence and Nohria are correct in their interpretation of human needs, it is unlikely that we can expect those at the head of organizations to abandon their "drive to acquire" any time in future. But desires for equity and learning are likely to have a much deeper influence on leadership models in a society that is involved principally with the acquisition, exchange and distribution of knowledge.

Increasingly organizations in future will need to examine Mary Parker Follett's concept of *power with* discussed in chapter 5. For too long leaders have been accustomed only to exercising power over others.

For now, in business, as in politics and the military, the cult of the leader will remain. It sustains careers and organizations. It is a business in itself. But more than anything it preserves the myth of our significance in the world. As Thomas Carlyle wrote: "No sadder proof could be given by a man of his own littleness than disbelief in great men." The time is approaching, however, when those in power will need to listen much more to those around them.

None of the influences investigated in these chapters will be accommodated unless those in positions of leadership are open to new ideas and fresh thinking. Progressive management can only succeed in a spirit of experimentation and a willingness to adapt. Tomorrow's leaders will need to embody the spirit of those who succeeded in the past together with a broader reach, empowering more women, more minorities and greater diversity generally at senior levels. They will need to embrace new approaches to flexible working and home working, a more results-based approach to work and a willingness to source work in a greater variety of ways. This cannot happen freely in the organization silos and isolating hierarchies of most existing organizational structures.

When UK MPs elected a new speaker, John Bercow, to succeed speaker Martin, there were suggestions from one of the candidates, Labour MP Parmjit Dhanda that democracy might be taken out into the towns with votes outside parliament. His fellow MPs were not yet ready for such radical suggestions but government and corporations will need to accustom themselves to more democratic forms of control in future. Pressure from shareholders and the electorate, combined with ever-improving technologies for canvassing broader opinions are going to promote the *power with* agenda in future. This change will take time but it will be one more consequence of the communications revolution.

CHAPTER 10

No Accounting for People

We can never wholly separate the human from the mechanical sides.

Mary Parker Follett (1868–1933)

Lars Dalgaard is on stage in San Francisco, pouring bits of fruit in to a liquidizer. The fruit has been placed in various containers marked with "ingredients" such as engagement, collaboration, scalability and Web 2.0. Finally he pours in some yoghurt and presses the mix button.

The smoothie mixture doesn't quite happen, not then, not there on stage. Dalgaard shrugs. "You know what I mean," he says, and his audience nods in acknowledgement since the majority of them are drawn from some 2700 customer employers and 4.7m users of human resources software created by SuccessFactors, the company established by Danish-born Dalgaard, its chief executive officer.

SuccessFactors is the fastest growing software producer in the field of performance management. No matter how much information an employer seeks to gather on the skills and experience of its staff, SuccessFactors seems to have a program capable of slicing and dicing it almost any way managers need it.

Dalgaard introduces Stephen Woo, one of SuccessFactors' top programmers in order to demonstrate one of the company's latest systems that allows employees to award each other "badges" in the same way people can send each other virtual gifts on social networking websites. Woo has a lot of congratulatory badges from colleagues. One of them marvels at his pace of work, another thanks him for the quality of his work.

"It's gratifying to know I'm being valued every day in the community. I can give badges to others too. It's a great way of passing on thanks and recognition," he says. "People don't need to wait for their pay cheque, bonus or salary in the bank to know how they are contributing to a business. With this system people can give each other badges, just to show how much they value a colleague," says Dalgaard. "It's a really fun feature; it's not hokey; it motivates and makes people feel appreciated."

SuccessFactors has been spreading its reach in recent years beyond performance measuring and goal-setting software into other areas of what has come to be known as "software as a service." But it is in appraisal and employee skills monitoring systems that it has made its biggest impact among human resources professionals. The SuccessFactors systems are useful for team building in that they allow a manager seeking to set up a project, for example, to find who in the company possesses particular skills. "This smashes up the organisational chart, providing instead a complete picture of your employees wherever they are," says Dalgaard.

These software developments have proved attractive to HR professionals since they provide a tool that makes staff appraisal more transparent. Employees and managers can obtain a clear picture of performance against expectations. The system tracks where successes have been achieved and where some things may not have worked well, highlighting the need for any extra training. In the same way, HR managers are alerted to line managers who have been tardy in carrying out their appraisals. Where, in the past, the appraisal has often been viewed at best as bureaucratic and at worst a waste of time, the visibility and detail of the computerized system means that managers are more accountable.

A diligent employee is far less likely to be overlooked because the system can collect examples of the way every individual delivers work—or fails to do so—against a stated set of priorities (see Figure 10.1), thus making appraisal far more robust and less exposed to abuse. Managers cannot overlook the training needs of employees because those needs will have been recorded and monitored by HR staff. In the same way, employees cannot overlook the expectations of the job since there is nowhere to hide. But at least those expectations are outlined clearly. How many times have people felt demoralized because no one has explained or possibly even noticed how their work makes a difference within a business?

This kind of software is bringing the HR function out of the wilderness and into business planning because it delivers the kind

FIGURE 10.1 SuccessFactors stack ranker

New Module

SuccessFactors ☒

Welcome, Carla Grant Options Logout

Home Objectives **Performance** Compensation Development Succession Recruiting Company Info Employee Files Reports

Review Help & Tutorials

Stack Ranker Competency Assessment

⚠ Changes pending. You must click "Save" in order to keep your changes.

Save | Cancel | Print Preview

Stack Ranker

Summary ▾

1 Vik Stokes 3.67
2 Sid Mormony 3.56
2 Wilma Sown 3.56
4 Richard Maxx 3.11

	Richard Maxx	Sid Mormony	Wilma Sown	Vik Stokes
Communication				
Customer Focus				
Hiring				
Integrity/Ethics				
Job Knowledge				
Listening Skills				
Negotiation Skills				
Sense of Urgency				
Teamwork				
Summary	3.11	3.56	3.56	3.67

I'm Done

Visually rank talent | Go beyond performance reviews | Assess everyone at once

© 2009 SuccessFactors, Inc.

of information that chief executives need at their fingertips. Gaps in expertise, untapped skills and hidden talents can be exposed in a quick search. "How many times have people said: 'If only my bosses knew what I could do?' Well, now talent is going to be more visible," says Dalgaard.

As software improvements ease the process of measuring within employment, employers will need to concentrate more on the types of measures they should seek to be adopting in their workplaces. What are the best measures in employment? Research in performance management has been pursuing these questions for more than a century, possibly even as long as work has existed. Indeed some of our existing measurements for distance today are linked to human endeavor. Take the Roman mile, based originally on a thousand paces, *mille passus*, made by a Roman soldier. One pace measured two steps or five Roman feet. When the English decided to standardize the measurement in the reign of Queen Elizabeth I they chose to fix the length on multiples of the furlong which was 220 yards long. Thus the statute mile was established at 8 furlongs in length, or 5280ft (1760 yards).

The furlong itself derived from the old English meaning furrow length—the length of ground over which it was decided two oxen could pull a plough before they needed to rest. This measure, based on the workload of oxen, probably had more meaning than the mile itself within English agricultural society in the sixteenth century since it was used to establish the size of land holdings. Popular usage and recognition gives meaning to measurement in everyday life. While science strives for exactness in measurement, for most people in most situations, measurement is as emotional as it is scientific. In our language it is related to experience and recognizable form, hence our understanding of the rule of thumb.

Motorway drivers, for example, know that distance covered matters less in estimating journey times if roads are blocked with congestion. So traffic knowledge begins to influence their thinking and journey lengths are calculated in hours, a more meaningful estimate when there are known variables preventing a constant speed over distance. More than that, though, measurement is registered in the senses. While 50 mph is the same speed for someone on a bobsleigh plummeting down the Cresta Run in St Moritz as it is for the driver of a car slowed by repair work on a motorway, the car driver's sensation of speed is entirely different from that of the bobsleigh rider.

Differing human experiences, different strengths, different physiques and different attitudes, therefore, have continued to bedevil the best efforts at measuring work uniformly for more than a century, ever since 1899 when Frederick W. Taylor was engaged as a consultant at Bethlehem Steel works in Pennsylvania. He was asked to determine the most efficient and cost effective way of shifting a 10,000 ton batch of pig iron onto railway carts for delivery to a buyer.

To establish a piece rate for the labor, he carried out stopwatch timings on a work gang, added some time for rest periods, then set the pay rate and targets that, if achieved, would allow men to earn more than 50 percent above what they usually did on a flat rate for a day's work. The only catch was that the piece rate was beyond most workers. Few could sustain the pace for more than a day. One man who could, Henry Noll, was feted by Taylor as the perfect unit of production that could be regulated, measured and incentivized. His efforts excited a whole new breed of managers who became disciples of what came to be known as scientific management. The problem was that Noll was exceptional, not typical.

Scientific management on its own would most likely have died a death had it not been for its techniques—specifically breaking work down into its constituent parts and measuring these functions using a stopwatch, still a novel instrument at the time. The techniques were used by engineers at the Ford Motor Company to set up the first assembly line in 1913. Production efficiencies achieved by Ford were so remarkable and the profits from that first year of moving assembly so great that the company returned some of the surplus to employees in big pay rises leading to wages that dwarfed those in other industries at the time.

What became known as time and motion studies are still in widespread use today for the creation of production lines, and managers are still attempting to set new targets for workers using speed and efficiency-based timings. An example of just how arbitrary these timings can be was revealed in 2008 in a Royal Mail management document leaked to the Commercial Workers Union.[1] According to newspaper reports Royal Mail managers were using a software program to calculate how many houses a postal delivery worker could visit on a round. Walking speeds, it said, should be set at a target of four miles per hour. The Royal Mail itself said that the speed at which it asked its postmen and women to walk was around two miles per hour. But the evidence that managers were looking at efficiency savings and tougher targets only confirmed that scientific management is alive and kicking in the twenty-first century.

The postal targets are just one example of what has come to be known in business as Human Capital Management. Is HCM nothing more than scientific management in another guise? Or is it a trendy and relatively new name for human resources management that, after all, has a track record of shifting its job description? For decades before the 1990s HRM was known as personnel management. It has long aroused the suspicions of other business managers wary of its ambitions. Peter Drucker, the management theorist, was scathing in his criticism of personnel managers and what he called their constant search for gimmicks with which to impress their fellow managers. In a prescient comment, he said that "the constant worry of all personnel administrators is their inability to prove that they are making a contribution to the enterprise."[2] Drucker wrote those words more than 50 years ago yet they are as relevant to today's human capital movement as they were when he made them.

Amid such suspicion it is vital that human resources professionals, as they term themselves today, maintain an honest appraisal of their motives and concentrate on the principles of human capital rather than allowing themselves to be sucked in to a professional turf war for boardroom influence. Too much emphasis in recent HR literature—if this is not an oxymoron—has been placed on establishing the role at board level rather than concentrating on extracting maximum value from human capital.

This is a shame because the principles of human capital are worth pursuing if adopted in the shape understood by their originators. The first point that needs to be established is that human capital, as it was originally envisaged, is not a substitute term for either scientific management or human resources management. It is true that, like scientific management, it draws on metrics, but it is rooted in nobler aims than those of its human efficiency antecedent. The concept of human capital lies not in management theory but in the study of economics. Specifically it can be traced to the economic theories of Theodore Schultz, an agricultural economist at the University of Chicago who, with Sir Alfred Lewis of Princeton University, was awarded the Nobel Prize in economic sciences in 1979.

INVESTING IN PEOPLE

Schultz arrived at his theories on human capital in the early 1960s as a way of explaining the advantages of investing in education on a national scale to improve agricultural output. The next step was to explain this increase in productivity as a benefit for a national economy. In doing so he proved that the yield on human capital in the US economy was larger than that based on physical capital. This might not seem so surprising these days. But at the time the science of economics was based on physical capital. Trade statistics measured the movement and transport of goods—tangible products—not ideas. The realization that the creation of wealth was moving its emphasis from muscle to neuron would create new understandings in business management, but it did not happen overnight.

In the US the number of white-collar workers had only overtaken those in blue-collar jobs for the first time in 1956. Three years later Peter Drucker was exploring the role of the "knowledge worker" in his book, *Landmarks of Tomorrow*, but he did not use that term until 1969. In time accountants would discuss "intellectual capital," but this term could be applied to intangibles such as goodwill and brands. Human capital was something more specific that relied on the principles of investment or, to put it simpler still, input to get output where the value of that investment is the net difference between the two.

Schultz felt some discomfort with the terminology at first. "To treat human beings as wealth that can be augmented by investment runs counter to deeply held values," he wrote. But at the same time he acknowledged that "by investing in themselves, people can enlarge the range of choices available to them." In this way it could be appreciated that investment relating to employees could be channeled two ways: investment *in* people and investment *of* people in their work.

Gary Becker, the 1992 Nobel Prize winner for economics, who coined the term, "human capital," explained that expenditures on education, training and medical care could all be considered investments in human capital. He wrote: "They are called human capital because people cannot be separated from their knowledge, skills, health or values in the way they can be separated from their financial and physical assets."[3]

A machinist leaving a factory leaves behind his machine tool, an expensive physical asset owned by the company. But he takes with him his skills and his knowledge. Those skills and knowledge cannot be considered assets of the company. Traditional accounting methods would consider them only as a corporate cost in wages, benefits and pension. But the concept of human capital recognizes the inherent value of those skills that can be increased by investment. The value of this capital fluctuates depending on the usefulness and pay of an employee. It can also be changed by management interventions such as the provision of training.

If accounting practices were to list this floating human capital as part of the book value of a business, companies might be less cavalier in the way they cut their headcounts. But employees are not regarded this way in accounting; crazy, but true. They are a cost and therefore a risk to the business.

This is an uncomfortable truth because people, quite understandably, prefer that their contributions in the workplace are acknowledged as value adding (as they surely are, but not as an asset value in accounting practice). If companies are to appreciate fully the way they profit from human endeavor, then people must have a measurable value. Yet balance sheet accounting insists, by convention, that the costs of employees in wages and other overheads are listed as liabilities.

Today, as the net book value of an increasing number of information technology companies is measured far more in the intangible knowledge and skills of employees than it is in plant and machinery, the investment community has begun to seek better ways of capturing the value of so-called human capital in accounting systems.

As early as 1993 in the UK, the Accounting Standards Board (ASB) proposed the concept of an Operating and Financial Review (OFR) to improve methods of external corporate reporting. The board envisaged the addition in annual company reports of a statement by directors giving an idea of their future intentions. Plans for mandatory OFRs were summarily scrapped by the then UK chancellor, Gordon Brown in late 2005.

In retrospect the idea probably had more merit in its ideals than in its possible practical benefit. The swiftness of the economic decline of 2008 confounded most economic predictions and led managements in many companies to replace their best-made strategic plans with hastily revised survival measures. Any operating and financial review assembled a few months earlier would have been worthless.

The OFR had been welcomed, nevertheless, by proponents of human capital management as an opportunity to establish some meaningful measures of employment within the accounting sector. At last there seemed to be an opportunity for financial and HR specialists to work together in building new approaches to corporate accounting that recognized the contributions of people in organizations. The end of the mandatory OFR did not mean the end of human capital management. It did, however, derail efforts to bring some order and standardization to human capital reporting within the UK.

Earlier in 2005, before plans for mandatory OFRs were abandoned, I became involved in establishing a working party called the Human Capital Standards Group. The group convened a number of meetings during 2005/6 at the London headquarters of Investors in People, the training standards organization. It included some leading consultants, practitioners and investment specialists with expertise in human capital measuring. The meetings were held to try and build on the findings of *Accounting for People*, the 2003 report of a task force headed by Denise Kingsmill, now Baroness Kingsmill, then the deputy chairman of the Competition Commission. The task force was launched on a wave of optimism within the HR profession that at last the UK government and the accounting profession were recognizing the need to report formally on employment issues and measures.

In spite of its failure to influence government policy it is worth revisiting some of the findings of Accounting for People since they make as much sense today in trying to determine the future of human capital management, as they did at the time. While Accounting for People stressed that it did not seek to be over-prescriptive on the HCM content of the reports arising from operating and financial reviews, it identified five areas that it thought relevant for measuring in people management:

- the size and composition of the workforce

- retention and motivation of employees

- the skills and competencies necessary for business success and the training needed to achieve them

- pay and fair employment practices

- leadership and succession planning.

The report made a distinction between measures that companies would want to keep to themselves for strategic reasons in seeking to establish a competitive advantage and measures that could be shared among all companies. These shared measures would develop more meaning and value, it suggested, if they could settle around an agreed standard, thus establishing a generic status.

It was this status that we sought to pursue in the Human Capital Standards Group, drawing up terms of reference around five guiding aims and principles:

1. To provide a basic set of metrics that could be promoted as organizational standards for the purpose of external comparison by investors and other stakeholders in publicly quoted and private sector corporations.

2. To establish these standards as the underpinning of a wider understanding and use of human capital management in organizations.

3. To review and revise standards periodically in a process of continuous improvement.

4. To embed the practice of human capital management within all organizations around the principle of investing in people as a means of securing stronger individual and organizational performance.

5. To maintain the integrity of generic measurement in which measurements and their formulas are freely available to every organization that may seek to adopt them.

In a series of debates and information gathering exercises seeking expert opinion among various industry sources externally and internally from within the group, a consensus began to emerge around the areas of human capital most useful for information gathering and about the type of measurement that could provide the most significant results.

The group settled on seven areas of employment (very similar to those in Accounting for People) where measurement would be desirable:

- Overall performance
- Leadership and management

- Employee engagement

- Training and development

- Pay and reward structures

- Retention and recruitment

- Health and well-being.

Much of the debate centered on the ideal measurements that could be adopted in these areas. The debate fell into two camps that were not mutually exclusive, but related to the personal leanings of various individuals. One camp, what I would call the "scientific" group, was concerned with establishing proofs that measures were founded on valid principles. The other camp argued that measures work best when they are used universally so that they can develop common meanings and interpretations.

Concerns among the first camp might be compared with those of early railway pioneers seeking to establish gauges for running tracks. Those early engineers, such as Isambard Kingdom Brunel, held strong views about track gauge. Brunel believed that a broad gauge of 7 ft 0¼ in was most suitable for the track, offering higher running speeds. But not everyone agreed. The result was that different companies laid different gauges of track that even today, in some parts of the world, raise compatibility issues far more significant than arguments over the most suitable gauge. Does this sort of fragmentation happen today? Sadly, all too often. Mobile telephone manufacturers all produced telephones with brand-specific chargers until the Mobile World Congress, representing the five biggest manufacturers decided in 2009 that a universal plug would be adopted as standard by 2012. Hallelujah!

The same kind of obduracy exists in broader international measurement systems. In the UK we have reared a metrically confused generation, deriving much of their education in the metric system but living in a society that clings with a passion to islands of imperial measurement. As one of those raised on imperial measures I understand these passions. I have no desire to abandon the pint or the mile and I struggle to find meaning in liters and kilos. But there is a cost to this stubbornness as the US—another metrically confused nation—has discovered. In

1999 NASA lost the Mars Climate Orbiter because of a miscalculation involving metric and imperial measurements.[4] The total project costs topped $300m.

But, if natural human cussedness can be overcome in the early stages of measurement development, isn't the prize of generic harmony worth the struggle? This was the thinking behind the HCM standards group and its campaign that remains as valid today as it did at the time.

So what kind of metrics should employers be using in future? Should they be using them at all? After all, people are so unpredictable. But measuring nothing in human performance makes little sense since people are measuring themselves constantly against others. Our need to make comparisons is habitual, hence the success of the popular children's card game, Top Trumps, where anything from sports cars to mythical beasts are compared on a range of features in order for one card to trump the other.

Some companies, using the kind of software produced by SuccessFactors and its competitors have adopted similar kinds of "relative strengths" comparisons in their talent management systems, apportioning scores against a scale of factors drawn from those most prized by the company. The growth of this kind of measuring suggests that such employee metrics in large companies are going to become the norm. If so, three forces are going to influence their evolution—the need for simplicity and clarity, the need for relevance and the need for meaningful comparison.

FINDING THE RIGHT MEASURES

One big problem in employment measuring has been complexity. Another has been identifying the measures that matter most. During the 1920s at the Hawthorne works of Western Electric on the outskirts of Chicago, a series of experiments were carried out investigating the influences of various inputs on employment. The experiments started out as research into the influence of light intensity on productivity. But they were expanded to examine the influence of reward systems, staff recognition and staff feedback. After many years the scientists involved in the experiments came to the broad conclusion that maintaining staff morale and giving employees plenty of encouragement and recognition led to marked improvements in productivity. Today employers describe the willingness of employees to give of their best, without recourse to management coercion, as "engagement."

It was not just the Hawthorne conclusions that would influence the development of subsequent management theory, but the investigative methods, including the use of staff surveys, that continue to influence management–staff relations to this day. The philosophy behind staff surveys is simple enough: if you want to find how well people are being managed or how well they are led, ask them. In the same way if you want to know whether people are happy at work, satisfied with their pay or whether they are feeling well, you can ask these questions too.

What matters most about these exercises is the shape of the questions, consistency and frequency in running the exercise, the analysis of the results and, perhaps most of all, the management responses. Unfortunately (partly as a result of talent management regimes) the frequency with which managers move jobs within organizations today means that a continuity of purpose is rarely maintained. One manager's initiative is swept away, ignored or weighed differently by successors. This is why those working for companies with embedded, proven, work practices often perform consistently well since the underlying management and workplace culture is powerful enough to overcome the occasional management fad or break of habit.

In spite of what we know about good management, employers continue to repeat mistakes of the past, particularly during downturns when relationships become frayed and budgets are whittled away. Even Western Electric succeeded in destroying the goodwill it had built up over decades when the business was forced to make redundancies in the 1930s. A modern comparison, as we noted earlier, is the Royal Bank of Scotland. Here was an employer that had developed human capital management far beyond that of most of its competitors. The bank's failure proved that great people management alone cannot guarantee corporate success. That said, it is unlikely today that success will be sustained without it.

The case for strong performance management and its link to bottom-line success has been established in a number of studies. These include the 1995 research undertaken by US-based academic Mark Huselid, based on 968 responses to a survey of senior human resources managers in 3452 companies across a number of industry sectors. Allowing for various other factors and variables, it found that companies that applied a focused and systematic concentration on performance and human resources management produced, on average, an $18,000 increase in stock market value, per employee at the time. A later study reported even better improvements.

Over a five-year period from April 1996 to April 2001, a Watson Wyatt survey of 750 publicly traded companies in the US, Canada and Europe scored their employment practices against its Human Capital Index made up of a series of practices, including recruitment, reward, benefits, culture, service, technology and communications. It found that companies that scored poorly against the index had created little value for shareholders.

The same research found that practices in five specific areas of human resources management were associated with marked bottom-line improvements. These were:

Recruiting and retention

Total rewards and accountability

A collegiate flexible workplace

Strong workplace communications

Focused HR service technologies

A third study, this time in the UK among 3000 companies, carried out by the Work Foundation and published in 2005, found links between corporate share values and measures of employee performance.[5]

The Work Foundation had been working on a formula it could use to assess corporate performance and settled on something it called its Company Performance Index that evolved from consultations with chief executives aimed at selecting a combination of factors that underpin financial success.

To test the success of the index it was applied to predict the share returns of companies at either end of the scale in the 13 months of the study. Those that performed poorly against the index returned a 6 percent increase in share value against a 26 percent average gain among those at the top of the index. This was during a period when the average price gain for the UK stock market as a whole was 14 percent.

"Unfortunately we didn't actually invest in the shares or we would be rich," says Marc Cowling, the foundation's chief economist, who created the index. The index measures corporate effectiveness in five areas: customers and markets, shareholders and governance systems, stakeholder relationships, human resources practices and the management of innovation and creativity. Within these five measures, says Cowling, the indices covering people and innovation were the best predictors of operational performance. Unlike many other studies, the Work Foundation factored in other contributing areas to organizational success such as the relative impact of advertising, brand exposure and new products and markets, recognizing that employment measures alone cannot produce exceptional performance in business. This is why the balance scorecard approach of Robert Kaplan and David Norton has proved so popular in business.[6] The approach was refined specifically for human resources management in books by Mark Huselid, Brian Becker and Dave Ulrich.[7]

"With a properly developed strategic HR architecture, managers throughout the firm can understand exactly how people create value and how to measure the value-creation process," write Becker, Huselid and Ulrich in *The HR Scorecard*. More than eight years on I am still tempted to respond: easier said than done.

They are right to stress the point, however, that business managers must understand the interrelation of various factors that make an enterprise successful. "Most companies will have a board meeting and notice that their absenteeism levels are higher than the sector average, then tell their HR department to fix it," says Cowling. "But the real problem might have something to do with boredom because employees have too little opportunity to express their creativity," he adds.

One or two individual findings in the Work Foundation project caused some surprise. Many companies are forever working on their organizational structure, yet structure was found to be far less important than management style. Open communications, less formal processes, a value of quality over quantity in work and a concentration on long-term outcomes were highlighted for their positive impact.

This suggests that measuring should be used sparingly, qualitatively as much as quantitatively. It would be useful also if some measures could achieve some consistency across sectors, yet this continues to elude companies. It's right that HR departments should review and refine their measuring systems constantly, but as companies tipped into recession during 2008, information gathering was a clear target for cutbacks. Yet it is during a business downturn that information about employees can prove most useful. Imagine your company's employee engagement scores have improved steadily over six years of healthy trading, then plummet after a redundancy program forced by recession? Do you bury the bad news? Do you abandon your employee surveys? Shooting the messenger in this way is a typical response to a business downturn. Collecting employee feedback is a cost that can be pared from the system and it could be argued that few in management want to read yet more bad news.

But abandoning information-gathering simply because it is not projecting a rosy enough picture is a big mistake because such information is enriched by continuity. It may show, for example, that employee morale is holding up well in some parts of the business that could be explained by a series of factors. If factor x—a particular management style, for example—is working well in the widget distribution operation, perhaps it could be replicated in the assembly shop where morale and performance have dropped.

Another argument for collecting employee information consistently within a business is that a failure to do so leaves the task to outsiders. While several organizations run "best company to work for" rankings, often requiring companies to sign up if they want to participate, a growing number of employers are finding themselves subject to rankings by external bodies. The external ranking analysis invariably uses criteria determined by the ranking body, sometimes without the knowledge of the employer.

This happened to Enterprise Rent-A-Car when it was ranked negatively as an employer on a website called JobVent.com. Enterprise Rent-A-Car prides itself on a performance measuring system that it believes has been responsible for much of its growth in recent years. The company was celebrated by Fred Reichheld, the former Bain & Co director, in his 2001 book, *Loyalty Rules!* and in a later book, *The Ultimate Question: Driving Good Profits and True Growth.*

Reichheld's ultimate question is this: to what extent would you recommend this company as an employer to one of you friends? Used with other information this produces what he calls the "net promoter score." It's a good question to address to employees because it puts people on the spot. It is one thing to admire your employer and quite another to have the confidence to recommend it as a place of work for your friend. South West Airlines rely on such recommendations to such an extent that it uses its staff as recruiters, attracting applications through recommendations to family and friends.

Enterprise Rent-A-Car, the US car hire company, uses a similar performance measure of its company—based on questions to customers—to influence its staff management and rewards. Staff at Enterprise car-hire depots are not judged on their monthly sales figures alone but on responses to questions in just two areas of performance, measured against the company's service quality index. Customers are contacted by telephone each month and asked to rate their rental experience and their intentions to use Enterprise again. Branch scores on the index are posted alongside profit statements on management reports. Not only this; employees are reminded that no one whose branch has below average scores on the index will be promoted.

This kind of scoring raises the stakes for employee involvement in corporate decision making. As it is, individual branches of Enterprise Rent-A-Car have considerable autonomy in the way they choose to run their businesses. This suggests that a closer alignment of employee and corporate interests would create a more democratic organization. But it does not necessarily make for an entirely happy organization. The distinctive management style at Enterprise does not meet with the approval of everyone who works there if comments posted on JobVent.com are to be believed. At one time indeed—until the JobVent measuring system was amended—Enterprise was among the 10 most hated companies in its scoring from employee feedback. So, in this case at least, one employee's meat is another one's poison.

JobVent is just one of a number of external organizations that are ranking employers, as either good or poor places to work. These external rankings use whatever measures they choose and weight them as they wish. It might be a combination of pay, holiday entitlement, office conditions, perks and management systems. The point is that the rankers choose the criteria, not the employers. As this example in the box shows, media-based rankings can be popular among high-flying companies:

Topping the rankings

"We are a frugal company. But don't show up dog-tired to save a few bucks. Use your common sense." This is the travel policy of NetApp, voted by Fortune Magazine as the best company to work for in 2009, toppling Google from the top spot that it had held for the previous two years. Both companies are based in California, NetApp in San Franciso and Google in its futuristically named Googleplex, Mountain View. Both emphasize the value of their employees in the business and go to great lengths to ensure that people are happy in their work.

NetApp is a data storage and management company that has managed to build its business, recruiting new employees in the downturn. "We work in a collaborative environment, so an individual who wants mainly to work on their own probably isn't the right candidate here," says Grace Soriano-Abad, senior director for global staffing.[8]

"Our interview isn't just a process of going through the points of your resume. It's focused on asking questions that are for figuring out someone's values and how they operate. For instance, we might ask a candidate to share specific examples of a time when their values were perhaps challenged and what they did. That's how we try to figure out whether someone has the integrity we're looking for," she adds.

The most striking thing about her comments is that they could be replicated across almost any leading employer in the communications and information technology sector today. Collaboration is king and this applies to leadership roles as much as it does to other employees. Control, rigid parameters, single mindedness, politicking, overweaning ambition: few of these features of more conventional office environments have any place in the companies that continually vie for best employer awards.

Unlike Google, NetApp does not sell itself as a fun place to work but as a caring environment. Employees are given five paid days off a year to do something they care about. One group of staff spend time working for Feeding America, a relief charity that directs its aid at the millions of Americans who go hungry every day.

The company is strongly focused on energy saving, environmental issues and health, reflecting the concerns of its staff. There's a gym, yoga classes and volleyball. The working environment is not built on productivity formulas, says Dave Fitz, executive vice president, but on a belief system, what he calls "a leap of faith."

"I believe that when you have engaged people they will do 10 times more work for you. Your boss understands you and you understand your goals," he says, adding: "We want to build something that lasts; a company that's going to be here for the long term."

You don't hear things like that much in business any more, at least not uttered with any sense of conviction. But when I heard those remarks I was reminded of a remarkable speech made decades earlier by another American manager advising Japanese managers how they should rebuild their companies after the Second World War. The manager was Homer Sarasohn seconded from Western Electric. He said: "A business enterprise should be based on its responsibility to the public, upon service to its customers, and upon the realisation that it can and does exert some influence on the life of the community in which it is located."[9] He also spoke about a determination to stay in business in spite of adversity, to play the long game.

Such far sightedness in a business world that has become riddled with uncertainty is a virtue in any company. People in work are not looking simply at jobs today but jobs tomorrow.

Life in the Googleplex is portrayed as a campus atmosphere. The theme of fun at work is spread almost evangelistically. Employees see themselves as "hard core geeks" who work hard and play hard in the various ball courts around the grounds, partly to work-off the extra pounds gained from free lunches and dinners.

The role model for Google's employing structure was Genentech, the pharmaceuticals company, another former Fortune number one best company to work for. Art Levinson says: "What draws people to both companies is the environment—one where they have an ability to pursue things largely on their own terms."[10]

Large employers who do not digest these messages are not going to survive in the long term. The best employers today are built on respect for those who ensure they succeed. The best employers extend freedoms to their employees to engage in goal setting, work in their own time, find patterns of working that suit them best and work collegiately, directing their efforts for the good of the team.

The danger stalking each of these companies, and other companies like them, however, is structural. Even the whackiest, most eccentric garage start ups grow to build an HR department with all its attendant administration and employee policies, usually underpinned by employment laws and health and safety requirements. Is that the way things must be?

But wouldn't it be better if there was a single universal employer ranking system to which all employers could subscribe and thereby feed into? Governments operate such systems for schools, the places where we spend our formative years, but there is no single system for the places in which we spend the whole of our careers.

For the time being, however, companies must use what they can in measuring their staff, often calling on respectable proprietary systems, such as those developed by Saratoga, now part of PricewaterhouseCoopers and the Q12 engagement questionnaire developed by The Gallup Organization. Gallup's questionnaire arose in 1998 out of a feedback system for employers designed to identify and measure those elements of worker engagement that could be linked best with productivity and profitability.

Thousands of interviews and hundreds of focus groups later it came up with the Q12, a 12-question survey that identifies aspects of employee engagement. Results from the survey show a strong correlation between high scores and superior job performance, says Gallup. These are the questions:

- Do you know what is expected of you at work?

- Do you have the materials and equipment you need to do your work right?

- At work, do you have the opportunity to do what you do best everyday?

- In the last seven days, have you received recognition or praise for doing good work?

- Does your supervisor, or someone at work, seem to care about you as a person?

- Is there someone at work who encourages your development?

- At work, do your opinions seem to count?

- Does the mission/purpose of your company make you feel your job is important?

- Are your associates (fellow employees) committed to doing quality work?

- Do you have a best friend at work?

- In the last six months, has someone at work talked to you about your progress?

- In the last year, have you had opportunities at work to learn and grow?

The Q12 is only one measure of engagement. Research carried out by the Conference Board in 2008 came up with a set of eight statements that it says correlate with its own definition of employee engagement.

1. I am proud to work for (company name).

2. Overall, I am satisfied with my job.

3. Overall, I enjoy working for my immediate supervisor.

4. My job gives me a feeling of accomplishment.

5. My job is interesting.

6. I am motivated to contribute more than what is expected of me in my job.

7. I am not currently planning on leaving (company name).

8. I would feel comfortable referring a good friend to (company name) for employment.

Most of these measures focus on broadly similar themes so it is probably not too important which questions are used provided that companies use a consistent measure over time.

Standard Chartered Bank uses the Gallup Q12 measures, with a few additions of its own to gauge staff engagement in the bank. HR director Tim Miller has looked at the scores from engagement surveys among bank branches in different parts of the world. "No matter where they are in the world, the more engaged branches perform dramatically better than those with lower engagement scores," he says.

Analysis of management behaviors in better scoring branches produced some common factors. Managers in the best branches, he noted, tended to deal with poor performance by learning from mistakes whereas the worse managers spent too long analyzing why something went wrong. The best managers were good at providing feedback and had the ability to contextualize their work, often drawing on analogies and storytelling techniques to explain the workings of the bank. In this way employees understood the importance of their own contribution.

For the record, I have included at the end of this chapter a set of employment measures that were considered by the Human Capital Standards Group under various headings. Note that there is a mixture of qualitative and quantitative measures. This is because quantitative measures alone cannot hope to get at the substantive issues producing results. An absence record counts days off. It does not differentiate between days lost through illness and those lost through skiving.

Listed below are specific measures. For calculating quantitative measures, Saratoga has some well-documented formulae which it says it is happy to share without a fee. Statements or the strengths of agreement to questions could be measured on a five-point scale: Fully agree, partly agree, neutral, disagree, strongly disagree.

Overall performance (quantitative)

1. *Profit per employee*
Based on HR records of full time equivalents (FTE) and profit taken from published accounts

2. *Turnover per employee*
Based on turnover from published accounts and FTEs from HR records.

Leadership and management (qualitative)

1. *This organization is well managed.*
2. *I understand the aims of the organization.*
3. *I am well managed.*

Employee engagement (qualitative)

1. *I would recommend my employer to a friend as an excellent employer.*
2. *I am proud to work for my employer.*
3. *I believe in the aims of my employer.*
4. *I feel comfortable with the values of my employer.*
5. *I will do more than I'm asked to help this organization succeed.*
6. *I have a desire to do more.*
7. *I care about my job.*
8. *I enjoy my work.*
9. *I like the people I work with.*
10. *I want to continue working here.*

Training and development (qualitative)

1. *I receive the training and development I need to enable me to do my job well (including on-the-job training).*

Pay and reward structures (qualitative)

1. *I am satisfied with my pay and benefits.*
2. *My organization's reward and remuneration arrangements are fair.*

Retention and recruitment (quantitative)

1. *Percentage of vacancies unfilled within 3 months: Unfilled vacancies within 3 months/full-time employees or full-time employee equivalents.*
2. *Offers/acceptance ratio for advertised posts:*

Number of job offers made in last 12 months/number of acceptances in last 12 months.

Health and well-being (qualitative)

1. *I believe my employer cares about my health and well-being.*

The purpose of asking qualitative questions is to check the pulse of the organization. How do people feel about their work? How do they feel about how they are being managed? Responses could highlight parts of the business, such as a badly managed department that may need some attention. Profit per employee and turnover per employee provide feedback on profitability. But employers should be warned that aiming for ever-higher profitability figures could rebound on an organization as some law firms have discovered in the past.

In 2002 a request by Clifford Chance, the law firm, for its New York associates to bill 2420 hours a year backfired on the firm when associates complained that the target would be unattainable unless they were to engage in "padding" their hours—an outlawed form of overbilling. The firm abandoned the target, but not before one associate had complained: "The management cares exceedingly about hours billed, but gives no thought to the quality of my work." Another law firm, Allen & Overy received a similar backlash in 2003 when it asked its UK associates to work a minimum of 2200 office hours a year—the equivalent of 10-hour days, assuming five weeks of paid holiday a year. The Young Solicitors' Group, a UK body that has campaigned strenuously against the long-hours culture of legal practices, said at the time: "If you are tied to your desk for your 10 hours of recordable time every day, how are you going to fit in the rest of your life?" The law firms are in a difficult position because billed hours equate directly with partner profitability, and unless this can be maintained there is a risk that the best partners might defect to more profitable firms.

One avenue that all professional firms should consider in future is to focus less on billed hours and concentrate instead on the quality of work performed for a client, billing on outcomes rather than hours. This used to happen far more frequently before clients began insisting on seeing evidence of work accomplished in the form of billed hours. So the customer gets what the customer wants—evidence of work—even though what is really needed is simply a job well done. When pricing work, therefore, it still seems simpler for professional service firms to fall back on their time sheets.

Measuring productivity and the use of other work-related metrics will remain an imperfect science. When gathering feedback from employers during research for the Human Capital Standards Group it quickly became clear that work in this field is characterized by a wide variety of practices and opinions. There were strong areas of consensus around the need to measure the effectiveness of line management and employee engagement. But there were also fears that measurement could create distortions in a business from the point of view that "what gets measured gets managed."

In the detailed comments, most of the criticism of measures seemed to be centered on whether or not they were relevant. It was clear from the feedback that consensus over validity of measures will remain elusive. This should not, however, preclude some broad agreement that embraces the fundamental differences in measuring human rather than fixed capital.

Human capital measures must account for basic human differences. Every single employee in a workplace is an individual. No matter how neatly approximations of human behavior may be assembled to categorize people, every single one of us thinks, feels and behaves in different ways, sharing some qualities to differing degrees.

Just as Lars Dalgaard struggled to make his smoothie mix on that corporate platform, so employers will always struggle to make the people mix work. The theory of talent management suggests that it should be possible to put together elite teams, corporate versions of the so-called Galacticos of Real Madrid. But this is not always effective as too many egos and competing agendas gathered together in one team can lead to a dip in performance.[11] A careful matching of complementary skills makes much more sense.

While personality testing may grade people crudely into a big five of personality types—openness, conscientiousness, extraversion, agreeableness and neuroticism—life distributes its grading infinitely. The essential difference between accounting for people and accounting for other forms of capital is that to be human is the essential difference.

Qualitative measures, therefore, would probably afford the best means of collecting rich employee feedback, supported by a number of quantitative measures. The gathering of such qualitative information is particularly useful for year-on-year performance comparisons. For broader industry comparisons, however, there is a pressing need for some agreement on a range of generic measures. If generic measures are to have any meaning they must be usable for external comparison of businesses. Moreover they must carry meaning beyond the parameters of the individual companies in which they are used. But measuring alone is not enough. Measures can only deliver meaning in business if they are linked to good management. Good management bridges the gap between basic measurement and strategy. Good management establishes a working narrative around the measurement process so that results can be translated into learning, development and performance management. Albert Einstein was right when he said: "Not everything that can be counted counts, and not everything that counts can be counted."

I doubt if employers will ever find the perfect formula for consistent, sustainable performance excellence, but advances in measuring software, coupled with better understanding of human attributes will ensure that performance measurement has a strong future in workplace management. Like Frederick Taylor, some recruiters will never cease in the hunt for the perfect employee. That such perfection is unattainable is unlikely to present itself as a barrier to investigation. The search will go on.

CHAPTER 11

Time for Reflection

Working hours are never long enough. Each day is a holiday, and ordinary holidays are grudged as enforced interruptions in an absorbing vocation.

Winston Churchill (1874–1965)

When Sir John Lubbock introduced the Bank Holidays Act of 1871, he did so in recognition that the profit motive of industrialists had pared away leisure time to unacceptable degrees.

The act introduced four bank holidays in England, Wales and Northern Ireland and five in Scotland. But they were scant substitute for the 40 days a year, marking various saints' days that had been recognized by the Bank of England at the start of the century. These were pruned to 18 in 1830 then to four a few years later.

Lubbock, a banker, politician, naturalist and archaeologist (he introduced the terms Palaeolithic and Neolithic to differentiate the old and new stone ages) was a cricketing enthusiast and ensured that the days coincided with traditional village cricket matches.

It is with such whims, rather than economic arguments, that lasting arrangements in living patterns are made. If the wheels of industry fell silent for a few days on what, for a while at least, were called "St Lubbock's days," the beginnings of a leisure industry were taking root as the new railways took people to growing seaside resorts such as Blackpool, Brighton and Bournemouth.

Industrialization had swollen the cities, disrupting the fabric of village society and subsistence living where families had managed themselves, however meagerly. Poverty and overcrowding often forced people to lean on alcohol as one of the simplest forms of relief. This led to the temperance movement that was widely linked with notions of mutuality, self-help and worker organization.

Thomas Cook, the travel company, was established originally to organize railway excursions for temperance rallies in the English midlands. Working class people were yearning for cheap travel. The National Clarion Cycling Club, established in 1895, was used to spread the socialist ideas of Robert Blatchford as members delivered his pamphlets between the growing towns and cities. Glee clubs and sporting events all grew in response to a clamor for new communal support and social networks.

Today the workplace has reached another low ebb somewhat different in character to that of the newly industrialized society. In the West there has been no return to child exploitation, slum housing and filthy factory conditions, although such conditions remain a daily reality in much of the developing world. But while industrial nations have moved on in improved working conditions, health and safety laws, and better education, cheese-paring attitudes born from a focus on profit remain a drag on creating the kind of balanced society that is free from an unhealthy obsession with work.

One of the greatest impediments standing in the way of a healthier society is the tendency of employers' organizations to wield their political clout by reaching for the calculator and measuring the cost to industry of anything that might be perceived as workplace reform.

When the Scottish Nationalist Government proposed to make St Andrew's Day a national holiday the Scottish Chambers of Commerce estimated that an extra day off in Scotland would cost £400m in lost business.[1] In the same way the Institute for Public Policy Research asked for a holiday recognizing "community heroes" to be tagged on the day after Remembrance Sunday, but the Confederation of British Industry said it would cost the economy £6bn. The CBI comes up with such "cost to the economy" calculations at depressingly regular intervals in order to undermine almost any suggestion that it perceives as detrimental to business.

But business—or at least the financial sector—has not done too well at holding up its part of the bargain in the economic argument for the free market. Financial mismanagement has cost the global economy hundreds of billions of pounds and we can assume that transactions and decisions that led to this mismanagement transpired in the workplace.

This is what happens when people become focused myopically on financial gain. Unlike employers' organizations, governments are free to implement policies for the good of society. It is high time that they responded boldly in framing longer holidays, not so much for people to vegetate but to allow people more freedom to work or live as they wish.

David Macarov, a professor at the Paul Baerwald School of Social Work, Hebrew University, Jerusalem, argued for a restructuring of the workplace in an employment relations paper published in 2000.[2] The paper stated that in 1850 people used 13 percent of their energy at work. Some 150 years later this figure is less than one percent. "As technology continues to progress, fewer human workers and higher levels of productivity can be anticipated," he wrote.

Elsewhere in the same publication, Joseph Coates, president of Coates and Jarratt, a Washington-based policy research organization, argued that technology was enabling a restructuring of the employment market, taking many jobs out of the system while increasing gross domestic product. Efficiencies—such as direct data entry—created by technology were leading, he wrote, to "irreversible structural unemployment." Both authors agreed that there was a diminishing need for work. If the political imperative is to maintain spending power to keep the economy going, said Coates, "the role of human resources will be to look at strategies that would shorten work days, shorten work-weeks, provide sabbaticals and do this, in part, against the rising profit base of the economy."

One problem with these ideas is the psychological hurdle of paying people for working less. Another is to produce an equitable system for distributing wealth that engages wealth-creating businesses. The third problem is the source of the structural change in employment.

The first of these hurdles presented itself to British Airways in June 2009 when its chief executive, Willie Walsh, appealed to more than 30,000 of its employees in the UK for volunteers who would be prepared to work for between a week and a month for no pay, or to take the time as unpaid leave. Walsh had already agreed to forego a month's salary of £61,000 in July after the company had posted an annual loss the previous May of £401m, the worst slump in its history.

If Walsh thought the gesture would attract some solidarity with the rest of the workforce he was mistaken. As union leaders pointed out, Walsh could earn in a month more than four times the money that some of their members were earning in a year. Walsh portrayed the request as a fight for survival but most workers were unimpressed. "It's a big no. A very big no. Everyone is up in arms. We're not taking it. I'd love to take a month's unpaid leave but I can't afford to do that," said one baggage handler at Heathrow.[3]

Mick Rix, national officer for civil aviation at the GMB general union, said: "Most workers may consider this request if and when the company's executives take permanent and radical action to reduce their own remuneration packages."[4] It seemed a reasonable request, particularly if the company was in real danger of collapse. Suddenly no one was estimating the costs to business of people working less. Instead there were potential savings.

It may just be that airlines such as BA will have to get used to lower passenger rates. As spending and living patterns are changing, so are attitudes to travel. Flying is not so much fun as it used to be. Beyond recessionary factors, more broadly technology is not only changing the way we work, it is changing the consumer society. Mass industrialization is waning. Society is fragmenting into special interest groups. The mass market is splintering.

The idea of a diminishing need for work is based on demand in the conventional labor market. What about the other work that we do—housework, gardening, do-it-yourself? If this kind of work is increasingly important, perhaps governments may pay more attention to our domestic "subsistence" economy—the work we do outside the workplace. Another possibility would be to relax taxation scrutiny of the black economy where people are working at the margins. This is not to condone those who cheat the system, but to recognize that some entrepreneurism has its roots in low-taxed income.

All governments must work to free people from poverty and to encourage wage earning. Some seem to achieve their aims better than others. Southern European governments have sometimes admired but have been reluctant to support Scandinavian models of taxation-funded welfare. But Scandinavian countries run themselves with much narrower gaps between rich and poor.

The widening wealth gap between rich and poor in the US is a growing problem for the free market system, partly because it does not encourage the trickle-down phenomenon envisaged by Milton Friedman and his monetarist disciples.

Coates makes the point simply: "If you give a person who earns $100,000 a year another $1,000, he or she will probably salt it away. If you give that $1,000 to a person making $20,000 a year, the chances are he or she will spend it. As the rich get richer, they will tend to slow down the economy, depress wages, and in fact end up killing the goose that lays the golden eggs for them." In 2008 the goose was not only killed but trussed and stuffed and the golden egg exposed as rotten to its core.

First we experienced a downturn before economies, globally, plunged into recession. What happens in a downturn? Those who survive in work, work just as hard if not harder than before. But when profits begin to fall the idea of performance pay wears thin. We may be performing to the best of our abilities but business falls away. What can business do? Typically employers cut jobs, reduce their recruitment and leave vacant posts unfilled. Rising unemployment relieves pressure on pay inflation but also reduces government income from taxation and increases public spending on welfare and unemployment benefits. Little wonder that unemployment is considered a persistent drag on economies and potentially destabilizing to the social order.

Some companies in the UK, such as the car manufacturer, Honda, shut down for several weeks to reduce production in 2009. Wage freezes, even wage cuts are also popular responses. But paying people less does not stimulate economic activity. In 1914 Henry Ford surprised his competitors when he announced an unprecedented $5 day wage for shop floor employees. The average industrial wage in the US at that time was $11 a week. Ford was more than doubling it. At the same time he reduced the working day to eight hours by switching from two nine-hour shifts daily to a round-the-clock three-shift system.

Why did Ford raise wages so much? Because he could. Economies achieved by moving assembly were so great that he could afford to return some $10m of profits to employees. Thousands flocked to the company gates, but only for the money. Most people detested the new system but some would stick it

out for the wages. The deal for the workers looked too good
to be true and it was. The basic rate was less than half the $5
headline figure. The rest comprised a profit-sharing bonus.
To qualify for the bonus an employee had to have worked at
the company for six months and be classed as clean, sober and
industrious.

Exactly how industrious became clear after workers joined the
production line. They were timed by stopwatch while mastering
a rigorous production schedule. Then they were urged to speed
up. Labor turnover was so high that Ford needed to recruit 4000
people in the first year simply in order to maintain 1000 jobs.

But the rise in Ford earnings had a strong impact on the US
economy. Ford and other mass producers had created dispos-
able income to spend on ever-cheaper products of manufacturing industry. Mass industrialization had created a mass market
for goods. Another feature of the early twentieth-century that
contributed to mass consumerism was consumer debt—paying
on hire purchase or what some would call "the never never." In
his essay, *Shop Class as Soulcraft*, Matthew Crawford points out
that driving a new car bought in installments "became a sign that
one was trustworthy," what he calls "the moral legitimation of
spending."[5]

Keynesian economics would transfer this consumer ethic
into a creed and, finally, a duty after the job creation from mass
production hit the buffers in depression years. The interventionist
policies of Keynes demanded large-scale public works programs
to restore employment, earnings, buying power and thus, demand.
President Franklin D. Roosevelt instigated such a program under
his New Deal. But another plan to legislate for a 30-hour working
week was scrapped after resistance from employers.

Roosevelt's plan to shorten the working week should be
revisited by governments today. People should not be restricted
if they want to work more hours for a single employer but they
might be allowed to secure their jobs on the basis of a much
lower time commitment. This is not to suggest that the UK
should abandon its hard-won opt-out from the European Working
Time Directive that restricts employees to working no more than
48 hours a week. While 48 hours a week should be enough for
anyone, people should have the right to work however long they

wish provided that this does not disrupt or put at risk the lives of others, including other members of their families.

There should be scope in many jobs, however, for people to exercise more discretion in varying their hours. Why persist with the five-day week as the default system of working? Why not work from a new default that removes Friday from the working week and adds it to the weekend? I would go further and restore Sunday as a day of rest by protecting any full-time employee from demands to work unsocial hours unless an employer, such as a football club, for example, could establish that the nature of the business demanded high degrees of flexibility.

The establishment of stronger employee rights over working time would help to stimulate alternative growth in the economy. Some employees may choose to work a shorter working week for a principal employer, leaving them the opportunity to pursue a business interest or secondary job at other times.

Not everyone would rest on a Sunday, but more leisure time for more people at weekends would help to restore communal and family gatherings that have been lost in the long-hours culture that took hold in business toward the end of the twentieth century.

We already know that some days are more productive than others. A Manpower Human Resources report in 2007 found that Friday was the least productive day of the week.[6] Alex Bryson and John Forth, the report's authors, pointed out that working rhythms are influenced by the demands of different sectors. In the hotel and restaurant sectors, for example, weekends account for relatively large shares of working time.

In theory Mondays should be highly productive days, since most people have had the chance to rest, particularly if they treat Sunday as a special day. It is no coincidence perhaps that Roman Catholic–dominated southern European countries have maintained strong family affiliations where they have respected Sundays and the traditional rhythms that allow the working day to be broken by the extended lunches and the siesta.

In the UK the judiciary, teachers, lecturers and politicians all take prolonged summer breaks. Why are these breaks not available to the rest of the population? The announcement that the UK government would rise for a 12-week summer recess in the summer of 2009 led to concerns that MPs had too little legislation to keep them occupied.[7] But the law of the land should not be considered as some kind of bucket that needs to be filled. Work should be focused on need yet so much of what we do is tailored to expectations based on custom and practice. A news bulletin is created to fit a schedule. Even this book was commissioned to a set length, but why should a reader or a television viewer be exposed to any more reading or viewing than is strictly necessary or desirable?

Some, I know, will regard a shorter working week as a crazy idea but in the US university system the three-day weekend has become almost an institution. A *New York Times* article, How Thursday Became the New Friday, by Katie Hafner in November 2005 explored how Friday classes in US colleges and universities had been disappearing to such an extent that many senior students had come to view the three-day weekend as an entitlement.[8]

The custom appears to have evolved in the same way that the gap year emerged in the UK, informally at first, then, later, consolidated as custom and practice. Some have pointed to the need for faculty to find time for research, and meetings and what faculty wants, it usually gets. For students, however, as Hafner points out, Fridays are not all about relaxation since about 50 percent of undergraduates have part-time jobs. Some campuses, such as Duke University, have tried to buck the trend by restructuring schedules. College administrators have complained that billions of dollars of facilities are sitting idle for big chunks of the week.

Is this an example of generational resistance to systems of working that are no longer serving society? Dan L. King, general secretary of the American Association of University Administrators and vice president for academic affairs at Rhode Island College, concedes that Friday classes are "virtually disappearing." But should this be a cause for concern? If students can comfortably fit their studies in to four days, why should they be dragooned into a five-day working week? Don Tapscott, author of *Grown Up Digital*, says one of the most brilliant students he has met graduated without reading a course book or attending many lectures.[9] The vast majority of his research was undertaken on the Internet. Here again, is an example of the results justifying the means. Some may respond by arguing that cosseted students should be expected to complete their studies in shorter periods as happened in the UK during the Second World War. But this is to curtail one of life's most rewarding formative experiences. For many, student living is as fulfilling an experience as any that can be achieved through earning in work. This is not to make a case for life as a perpetual student, but the freedoms implicit in the undertaking of a university degree are as life enriching as the studies themselves.

Shorter working weeks should not be viewed as a retrograde step for business. Some companies have found advantages in running a four-day week. Frank Spicer, who founded Roundhay Metal Finishers, an anodizing company in Birstall, West Yorkshire, was hailed as something of a workplace visionary 30 years ago when he placed his workforce on a four-day week, making up their 40 hours from four 10-hour shifts. It saved him the fuel costs of keeping his anodizing vats heated five days. It also brought down worker turnover. People were happy with their three-day weekends.[10] But there was no stampede among other companies to follow suit. Perhaps the recession of 2009 will stimulate those companies that introduced short-time working to become more imaginative about how they use spare plant capacity.

Consolidating working patterns into optional four-day weeks could turn out be an economic good as people explore additional informal working opportunities alongside leisure and alternative activities. The last thing I would expect is that a three-day weekend would become an idlers' charter. That is simply not part of human nature. It may, however, lead to more people spending part of their earnings on leisure or learning, stimulating business opportunities in both the knowledge and leisure services sectors.

The suggestion is likely to be viewed as a reform too far among legislators hemmed in by the influential business lobby that has consistently opposed such moves. But some may agree that there is enough merit in the idea to at least begin a debate that could culminate possibly in a pilot experiment. Alternatively governments could introduce tax concessions for companies that pursue alternative uses of their premises during downtime, thus encouraging more diverse uses of business properties.

More time off should not be seen as a shirker's charter. On the contrary, the idea is to promote new relationships with the workplace and a shift from an historical obsession with the Protestant Work Ethic values that concentrate on work for work's sake.

Business must make a profit. But profit must be the successful and necessary by-product of the enterprise, not the enterprise itself. Enterprise must align itself with the interests of people. Unless it does this it will find itself in conflict with the very people it should be trying to help.

Shorter formal working hours should be viewed as a way of increasing the options of people to tailor their work around ever-busier lives. It would be handing more discretion to those in the workplace, while removing some power of compulsion from employers, but if employees care about the business in which they work the senior management should have nothing to fear. Ultimately there should be benefits on both sides of the bargain in happier, more secure and more contented employees.

CHAPTER 12

The Day Work Ended

Trying to predict the future is like trying to drive down a country road at night with no lights while looking out the back window.

Peter F. Drucker (1909–2005)

It's a wet day in late February 2059, and I'm looking out at the last withering blooms of the daffodils on our Scottish riverbank. I have just seen the biggest spring salmon—20 kilos at least, and no longer rare, jump in mid-stream. The light that filters on to the wooden desk that I made myself in craft class, is radiating through translucent energy-saving roof tiles designed to capture and convert thermal energy from the sun. A log fire is burning in the stove. I can afford the carbon offset.

I'm sitting in my fishing hut, writing some notes on recyclable intelligent Wallpaper™ that converts and translates sentences in a corrected format on to my personal log. The predictive phrasing has long ago learned my style, which is somewhat tiresome, to the extent that I change my words constantly to inject some unpredictability. But soon this too becomes predictable and the system tries to second-guess my diversions. Some of its second-guesses are far better than my first so I let them stay. There's an irritating smugness about this "app," a name that has stuck for any software application. I disabled its status update feature when on three days running it wrote, "Richard is feeling down" in my facelog. The mixture of impertinence and banality was too much to bear.

The log is divided into two sections: the first is a personal area where I store my living accounts, financial details, birth record, health data, academic and practical qualifications. It also includes my career history except that it is no longer called a CV or resume, merely "life details." People don't have careers now; they have lives. The second section is public—where I will be presenting my e-book *The Day Work Ended* when I'm ready to take outside input and feedback after draft publication.

Both sections are displayed on the Wall. The Wall, originally, was a video screen running the height and length of the room where we could interact with daily life globally. Conversations, meetings, games, reading, viewing, feeling, all take place on the Wall. Walls can be placed anywhere there is a surface, ideally flat. Some people run them in their ceilings and some—the fanatics—have rooms with multiple Walls bombarding their senses—but these are becoming rare because of the need to conserve energy. The great thing about the Wall, possibly its singled greatest redeeming feature, is that it can and must be switched off. The off button has become one of the most important interventions in daily life, where individuals can assert their independence at the flick of a switch.

Before the international transition laws associated with Peak Oil, health advisors—or, more accurately, their programs—recommend at least eight hours a day, beyond our sleeping hours, away from the Wall, even longer for young children. Longer periods could be spent on Wall time but this incurred surcharges to health premiums among insurers who monitor everyone's Wall use. They could do that because in 2039 we gave Admin the mandate to store our DNA identities through popular vote in the People's Parliament.

The Peak Oil transitions changed everything, however, leading to wall power reductions.[1] Walls grew, then shrank and in some homes disappeared all together as we tried to adjust to lower energy levels. Many people grab self-generated Wall time, using exercise bikes or communicate on the go. We're creating the fittest generation, mentally and physically that we have ever known. Who said that manual labor was dead? Today it's all the rage and we're loving it. Everyone is busy making things and repairing things. There's a wall slogan to deter consumerist tendencies: "think before you throw."

Some people—the obsessives—operate Wall banks, storing up Wall time through extended breaks, but health insurers will still penalize financially any Wall time of more than 10 hours at one stretch. Wall life is quite different from our "out hours" as we call them. The out hours are spent viewing and chatting, traveling, creating and fixing things, or doing whatever takes our fancy. The term "Social Walling" adopted in the early days has become meaningless. Social life is simply part of what happens on the Wall and beyond. Walling is fine but the advantages of the sustainability imperative and less long-haul travel means that there are so many people to meet in the local community. We have a blacksmith in our village and she's always busy.

Some, particularly the youth, will activate their Skin screens—skin-grafted video displays called Wallets, utilizing artificial digital flesh, powered by body movement—but mostly only for brief, casual use. You don't go outside and start Walling socially; it defeats the object. People do it and some people tolerate it, but it undermines social protocols that have grown in importance over the past 30 years.

I've given up real travel, apart from short journeys, preferring to go places on the Wall now. I still go shopping in the touch centers, supported by my artificial knees, but it's not quite the same as it used to be. There are advisors who tell you about the food and the weekly bargains and you can touch what you buy. In fact that's how you buy most mass-market foodstuff. Once touched it is removed robotically from display and packed for automatic delivery. I bought some interlocking starry tomatoes the other day by mistake, simply because I hadn't seen them before and wanted to feel one. In commerce it's called triggering a Midas-reaction. I call it underhand. There are no checkouts. A sweat-sensitive DNA sensor charges the purchase automatically to your account. I prefer the market stalls and local shops that can sell straight to your shopping basket if you wish. I try to support the local businesses, even though they lack the convenience of instant delivery. We retain physical shopping for its social, entertainment and local economic value and, goodness knows, that's still important.

The Walls—or today's energy-saving mini-walls (quaintly described as screens)—are where we get most things done. Almost every transactional function in society has a Wall component, centered on our individual homes. The sick are often treated at home apart from complex surgical routines that are handled in the local community hubs. Large hospitals were closed as health risks due to the way they were incubating diseases. Police, dentists, opticians, repairs people, service people, all operate from their homes, their journeys tracked by GPS devices in order to provide efficiency scores. Children still go to school but mostly to promote social interaction, recognized in social policy formation as a vital part of their upbringing. But they don't have school holidays. Holidaying as a concept has changed. It's just part of out-hours and there are plenty of those if we engineer them into chunks through our networks. Out-hour organization is a big market, far larger than the former travel market.

The first Walls were described suspiciously as Big Brothers until people began to install the technology in their homes by choice. They got their current name, somewhat pejoratively, from that Willie Russell play, *Shirley Valentine*. Many academic papers were written on the Wall's potential for isolation at the time of its introduction, or—to phrase it more accurately—its evolution from the Internet, building on the Milo technologies that revolutionized video-game interactions. These emerged from Peter Molyneux's Lionhead studios that introduced the X-Box 360 Project Nadal in 2009.[2] Lionhead was owned by Microsoft at the time. The Microsoft brand is no longer in use although the Gates protocols for monitoring diseases and virus mutations are named after the company's founder and Wall Windows are a nod to Microsoft's most successful innovation. Disease monitoring became vital in the 2020s after the second and most devastating of three twenty-first century global pandemics wiped out millions of mainly young people worldwide, accelerating developments in the world sustainability movement.

The Wall is run by GWC (Green Wall Corporation), one of the large UEs (united enterprises) that are supported by Global Admin. All of these ventures are virtual organizations although they are governed principally by video-meetings among their councillors—those elected as advisors within various areas of the Wall. The UEs are semi-permanent public/corporate amalgamations that began to emerge after the financial crisis of 2008. They can only be disbanded through popular voting that is also used to monitor councillor activity. Every human being on the planet is a shareholder of these organizations. Some have more shares than others, however, and shares and dividends are allocated based on the success of individual contributions within the Wall community. So it pays to get involved with the Wall.

For part of the time the Wall videos our lives but cloud access to video memory is strictly regulated and can only be achieved by what is left of our federal enforcement agencies, through a court process, subject to popular appeal. Popular appeals and popular voting take up a chunk of every citizen's lives beyond the age of 15. The Wall governs just about every part of our lives. People convicted of serious misdemeanors are incarcerated in their homes and living pods through Wall monitoring and security with off-switch rights withdrawn, until released through popular appeal.

Of course we have internal off-the-Wall activities—sex, eating, washing and toilet visits (if necessary), some conversations—and the Wall shuts down automatically when we're asleep or away to preserve energy. Off-the-Wall rights and on-Wall privacy protocols are zealously protected in tightly drafted privacy laws.

Popular Wall contributions are well rewarded and since most economic progression these days takes place on the Wall, the majority of academic studies are Wall-orientated too. We don't study for degrees today since continuing professional development, supported by Wall testing, monitoring and peer review, ensures up-to-date proficiency at whatever we are doing or seek to do at any stage of our lives. If I want to practice as a surgeon I must accept that my skills will be compared continually with a mean among hundreds of thousands of practitioners worldwide. Any new development or practice is evaluated by peers, some of whom, in collaboration (for which they are recognized), will build a learning module passed on to the medical community through alerts. Learning new procedures is not compulsory—no surgeon could be expected to know them all—and payment for proficiency is determined by demand. It is up to an individual to decide whether they want to broaden or narrow their expertise, or whether they want to concentrate on research or practice.

A surprising number of people still have jobs, including hairdressers, carpenters and window cleaners for older houses but not newer ones using nanotechnology-produced self-cleaning glass. Many services, including some professional services, however, have been automated. Just as water, sewage, electricity and refuse is piped, so are deliveries of most packaged goods. The system employs the same distribution pipes used for refuse disposal—a 50-year-old technology.[3] The jobs are where we can still find work and it's still called work, only hardly anyone thinks of it as we used to think of work. Most of us like to work in the same way that we like our exercise. Manual work is growing, partly as a way of saving energy, and partly because so many people enjoy making things with their hands. People cycle long distances between villages and the transition towns where most of the energy saving organization was pioneered.[4] The work is a healthy break from the Wall and health is important. My last job, before my health began to falter over the last three years, was ghillieing for people who come salmon fishing and I still hand out advice on the riverbank. It gets me out of the hut and I love it.

The professions have held together well and there remains a strong understanding of vocation, but corporate careers have dissipated in the last 50 years. There are no highly paid stewards in The Wall community. Hierarchical structures headed by chief executives became ultimately unsustainable and unnecessary You could say that almost everyone today, certainly in Wall contributions, is involved in management of some kind and the councillors are elected and respected because of their knowledge and influence and, yes, political skills. Affiliations still exist. As support for individuals begins to wane in popularity testing, their continued status is put to a vote, but only after an agreed period of time, otherwise people would be continuingly courting popularity. It happens enough as it is.

But the councillors don't run things. In England we still have MPs and they still congregate in Westminster, as do senators in the US Congress but this is following historical patterns. In reality they are powerless without the popular mandate that must be consulted in all significant votes. Most of us take our Wall involvement seriously as it's the way we earn our livings, the way we are rewarded and appraised and the way we exercise what we call total democracy. Much of our Wall earnings and Wall bills are determined through so-called involvement metrics. Additionally I have my individual niche on the Wall and part of my income is determined by popularity ratings and advertising income. Some teachers earn a lot that way. My earnings are also supplemented by self-sustaining efforts achieved through permaculture.[5]

Leadership, decision making, just about everything that could be described as government, whether corporate or public sector (the distinctions grow increasingly vague), is achieved through mandate. Power and influence are wielded through great ideas and everyone who lives with the Wall—70 percent of the global population—decide what constitutes a great idea. Millions of special interest groups maintain minority interests and cult status for ideas that are out of the mainstream and some of these pass into the mainstream, usually through viral reactions on the Wall. The thing to understand is that for most purposes there is no centralized administration. Society has devolved most of its functions into community or state administrations called Hubs and Cantons respectively. But some things such as oil society transition, carbon, sustainability, sea farming, disease management, resource management, climate, space exploration and international military policing are governed through global mandate.

Most small everyday decisions are made through emotion sampling—Milo testing. The Wall monitors our facial reactions to various proposals and ideas. I've tried to fool it but it can pick up the smallest reactions, including pupil dilation. Performance measurement is built into almost every Wall activity and this has been a focus of dissent in recent years.

The commercial side of the Wall can be irritating. Before the decline from Peak Oil began to bite, retailers and manufacturers would pay to find out what clothes we were wearing and what nano-creams we used. They even took our vital statistics—including the ever-controversial body mass index—and monitored our brain patterns (by consent). These activities are dwindling today as we learn to live with less of the materials and power sources that relied on oil. Even before Peak Oil, however, we could switch off the commercial inputs if we chose to do so. People were getting sick of the "have you tried ...?" spanks. Spanks are instant Wall-based interjections that happen as we do any daily ritual. Take dental work: most people go for expensive coatings these days but I still use toothpaste and I have my favorite brand. I got sick of the toothpaste spanks so "boxed" them. The boxes—we used to call them tick boxes—are long lists of personal preferences built in to every Wall. They fail to deter the commercial search sensors that think they know us anyway and a stimulating part of my life these days is spent outwitting them. But the spanks survive because they're fun—always different and always original. The best ones go viral. "Hey did you hear the spank about …?" is a common opening line down the pub. Yes, pubs have also survived. The best ones have no Walls. It's where the older generation go to recall their childhoods and memories of television.

My great grandchildren—I don't have many—are always bombarding me with questions:

"What are those things around your eyes?"

"Spectacles, I like wearing them."

"What was television like?"

"Very like the screen that replaced our Wall, only you just sat down and watched it."

"Why do you go to the toilet?"

"Because I never got used to nutritional balancing and do not like the unpleasant side-effect (or smells) of excessive sweating when you don't get it quite right. Besides, I like peanuts."

Their parents are more trying still. One of my granddaughters has just been learning about e-mails. "How did you ever get anything done? There were so many," she said, "And what was that Twitter fad all about? Did people really bother to write down how they felt?" Other grandchildren are questioning and somewhat dismissive of our life without the Wall. "No Walls?" they say. "What about Berlin? Your generation didn't know the meaning of walls." They're right. We thought walls were for keeping people in, or keeping people out. Today they are gateways.

This year, Gill and I are celebrating our Oak Wedding anniversary—80 years. I'm 101 and would have died years ago had I been dependent on twentieth-century health care. But health support has moved on rapidly in the past 60 years. People are living routinely beyond 100 these days, apart from the *Pures* and I'll come on to them—in fact I'm heading that way now; just a year to go before I will be designated pure. Gill has come to terms with it. I've had at least three potentially fatal conditions in the past 30 years and the next, I have decided, will be the last. The prostate was sorted quite early, in the 2020s. Then they caught the Alzheimer's in time with regenerative brain treatments. I've still lost a lot of memories from my first 70 years but most of the stuff in recent years is pretty sharp. It's not the brain that's tiring me now, it's treatment fatigue, a common medical syndrome that has no cure. People simply get tired of all the chemical, surgical and genetic modifications. They are taking away what it is to be human and it's the source of a big debate in all age groups.

That's how *purism* started. It began in sport when they decided ahead of the Delhi Olympics in 2036 that all events would be unrestricted with a "laurel" category for those who could establish their purity from drug or physical assistance. To be categorized pure you need to have been drug free for five years. I'm approaching my fifth year and I'm not sure I'm going to make it. My grandchildren and some of their children encouraged it. I suppose it was part of the backlash against the boomers that started quietly in the 2020s and triggered the age conflicts of those years when many governments introduced voluntary euthanasia. Only in some countries it didn't seem so voluntary. In the worst atrocities care homes were bombed. A few countries came close to generational war during the pandemics when the young came on to the streets in protest at the environmental legacy of their elders. There was a lot of anger back then. It was the time of cause-related insurgency and the dirty bombs that ravaged city living.[6]

But much of this unrest has subsided with the death or dehumanization of most of the boomers. It was only a willingness to work longer that saved my generation from what could have been far uglier consequences; that and the sustainability and environmental struggle that kept us all occupied for so long. Only technological interventions prevented what was heading for a water war in the Middle East as the oil supplies were running down. Another factor I almost forgot: some of our older leaders, when we had them, held on to the nuclear trigger and that concentrated a few minds. Today, however, nuclear power is ubiquitous. Nimbyism has gone. It's the reverse now. Everyone wants a mini-nuclear facility in their back yard so that they may enjoy the accompanying residence concessions, subsidies and, most of all, electrical power.

We still have oil reserves, remarkably, but since Peak Oil the world has been switching through necessity from oil to other forms of energy where it can. Oil is so expensive that it's used sparingly and mostly to supplement the power needed to run the worldwide wall. Petrol-engined cars and motorcycles are no longer manufactured in large numbers, but the latest are exceptionally efficient and they're still using the reduced road system, although mostly for leisure. Today we use alternative resources—wind, sun, waves. Fast sail boats and kite boats are crossing the oceans at speed. Bicycles and tricycles are smooth, light, fast and easily propelled using frictionless bearings and super-gearing. They allow us to maintain our rechargeable batteries that are used almost everywhere. Even my great-granddaughter's pet hamster has its wheel hooked up to a battery. Solar panels, personal windmills, intelligent flooring—we cannot move, hardly, without some kinetic energy conversion feeding our power-hungry homes.[7]

I took the pure route, medically, partly to ease the generational resentment that I could feel, even when it wasn't plainly stated, and partly because I wanted my life back, or should I say death. I want to die with my boots on so I've planned a round-the-world voyage with some old friends and I doubt if we shall all make it back. I don't want to end up wasting away in bed or taking the "planned option" in a dying center, euphemistically named "dream hubs." It's hard to describe them but, obviously, they make the most of Wall and Milo technology. If you ever saw that feature film *Soylent Green*, with Charlton Heston and Edward G. Robinson, you will get the drift. Not that dead people are packaged as food, but we are converted into fertilizer if that is our choice. Fast decomposition chemicals can be infused shortly after death for those—most people these days—who wish to nourish a tree. I've opted for an oak here by the river in Scotland if I come back from the sailing trip—oaks don't grow in the south anymore, even though woodlands are expanding everywhere. Some still choose cremation but that has become prohibitively expensive because of the carbon laws.[8]

A lot of young people are choosing to be pure today. It can be expensive in the activity insurance surcharges for those who take part in sport and adventure pursuits, and the purists tend to earn less than fully committed Wallers, although it is possible to wave all surcharges and many are doing so. They organize their own rescues and emergency services where they need them. Generally, however, they simply live with risk. "It's what living's all about," says my eldest grandson, a committed purist who is a proficient skier and alpinist. He reminds me that it's no longer possible to climb Everest with supplementary oxygen. That was banned by the Nepalese, under pressure from purist groups, in the mid twenties. All other 8000m peaks followed suit. Anyone seeking to visit the poles now must do so unsupported with no prospect of mechanical rescue if they fail. Overflying has been abandoned by popular agreement. Besides, long-haul flying is restricted and too expensive for most people now. Most flights are short self-propelled journeys using hyper-light materials.

The smoking and drinking debates were heated ones in purism, and still are. Some purists tried to claim that both should be acceptable as pure, taking the retro view that highlights their historical significance socially. There was also the argument that alcohol and tobacco were drawn from natural ingredients and processes. Again popular vote prevailed and the purists won with a few exemptions. Some commentators have noted that technically it would be possible to win an Olympic laurel today while intoxicated, but no one has tested it yet.

Purism, however, has been severely tested in swimming competitions. It was easy to rule against artificial aids such as plastic fins but when fast genetic skin modifications enabled web-footed and web-fingered competitors to enter events in the 2030s it provoked a ban. So all Olympic swimming now is purist and that has upset some disabled swimmers. It has meant that skin-web measurements are taken ahead of every event. Professional swimming, however, condones genetic modifications and the latest free-diving champion, nicknamed *the Shark*, uses a surgically implanted gill arrangement that has made him semi-aquatic. I hope he gets eaten. He is a designated *Dee*, as I will explain. In a similar development a new branch of genetics research is pursuing the human wing project but a muscle-powered flying human, without mechanical assistance, has yet to appear. Among the *Dees*, where some have established feather-growth on their bodies in pursuit of fashion, anything is possible. But then they are not human and that's official.

The *Dees* were originally knows as Mods because of their willingness to indulge in and benefit from genetic modification, biomedical engineering and cellular prosthetics. Enthusiasm for such extreme transformational change was concentrated among the aging boomer generation—an 80-year-old woman gave birth to a child in 2039, for example.[9] Widespread distaste for such aberrations led to a prolonged global debate and the first Human Modification Directive in 2051. It was Section D that caused all the trouble. This section classified the extent of modifications permitted to retain human status. The concessions were substantial but did not go far enough for some, including those who, under the new definition, were already living outside the code. These—I'm not sure I can call them people anymore—were called Section Ds, quickly shortened to *Ds or Dees* as it is usually represented in print today.

Prejudice against Dees is rife off the Wall although anti-discrimination codes forbid any pejorative terms in Wall society. My sister-in-law became a Dee after her husband died. She had maintained a sub-D, although highly modified status up to her ninetieth year until she said "to Hell with it" and ordered a full body makeover with Youthjuice™ implants. That tipped her outside the code but her children are all comfortably off and she argues that she's not going to suffer with the loss of her human rights. "I don't care about that stuff anyway as long as I can go on shopping," she says. "So I can't vote, so what? I'll shop till I drop." And that event, it seems, could be well into the future, possibly beyond the life spans of some of her purist grandchildren.

Of course the brand merchants are thrilled about the growing worldwide Dee community because it's one of the few areas where old economic theories still apply. It has revived corporatism and the pursuit of wealth, creating many Dee billionaires. One Dee entrepreneur, controversially, is restoring a motor yacht he saved from recycling and has plans to revive formula one motor racing using expensive biofuels, and in Monaco of all places, one of the bastions of Dee society. The story is all over the Wall.

So how do we earn a living today? How are we paid? Well we collect Wall units for various activities, including visitor traffic within our niches and from winning ideas that are exchange-able for food and other goods, often through local currencies. In practice incomings and outgoings are moving across the Wall constantly so I take a weekly audit. Some do it daily. In spite of the road reduction program, arising from higher costs and lower levels of travel, much of the twentieth-century infrastructure and heritage remains and there is a healthy property market although most green spaces are protected now in various categories, including the giant African bio reserves.

All members of the worldwide Wall community have basic support within the system but some live in nothing much bigger than a large cubicle about the size of a shipping container (on which they were based), or in composites of boxed communi-ties. Mumbai has the biggest boxed community in the world supporting 20m people, but at least they have clean water and sanitation, and most of them have their screens since Wall tech-nology is cheap. Wall units are convertible into cash for those who prefer to express their wealth this way. Money is still important for national identity although some federally minded Europeans continue to attach themselves to the Euro. Any currency is valid so long as it's registered with the Wall, a result of currency priva-tization after the great banking collapse of 2028. Conversions are instant and there is a thriving market in currencies with fluctuat-ing exchange rates.

The most popular and stable currency is the *Green*, since this is carbon-backed and the carbon laws are the most powerful in the world with deep popular support. Religious currencies remain strong with many people choosing to convert to the Islamic *Salam*. The Second Life currency has survived, as has Monopoly money and the Totnes pound.[10] A very few corporate brands have survived from the early-twenty-first century—Coca Cola is one and that does not have its own currency. But some of the biggest brands do. WallUts, the company that runs Wall-based utilities has the *Wally* and that is very popular because of its rising value, although most people these days know how to hedge. The biggest retailer is WallMart, an EU, named after the takeover of Walmart by PDD Corp (formerly Pipeline Daily Deliveries), a company that pioneered piped distribution of goods and two-way garbage retrieval.

A few people still use pounds sterling but the pound only circulates in a minority of ultra purist communities and sects although the Pall Mall clubs still accept them. The most patriotic Americans—and there remain many millions—have stayed faithful to the dollar that has become closely associated with— some would say tainted by—fundamentalist Christianity and beliefs in intelligent design. They teach that God built the first Wall and most of them refer to it as the Firmament although theologians debate whether the Firmament existed before God or whether it was contemporaneous with Him, rather than something He created. Naturally the Americans had to rename Wall Street when it fell into disuse and became confused with the global communications network. Today it's colloquially called The Folly and only assumes its former name in history texts.

The world still has its poor, unfortunately, but in the vast majority of societies the gulf between the highest and lowest paid has narrowed considerably. There are Green and Wally billionaires but most of the wealthy have signed up to philanthropy. The big motor yachts of the early twentieth century—with the one controversial exception, mentioned earlier—were recycled decades ago, but some big sailing ships are still independently owned and large populations have become sea-based today in giant floating pod communities that journey the world as they choose, by popular mandate, as always. Some Royalty has survived, including the British Royal Family that had a big influence in the roots of the global sustainability movement through King Charles III. The King lost his battle against genetic modification, however, going to his tree a somewhat bitter purist to the last.

I can't remember when it was that we stopped talking about work or retirement and that's what has been absorbing most of my research in the past four years. Work wasn't abolished. The words just fell out of use, although people still use the terms in their former context in some parts of the world such as the Outer Hebrides, the Appalachians and in many East Coast US communities. I even caught my 74-year-old son saying he was tired of work, the other day. That's the way it's normally used now, when you realize that what you're doing feels like a chore, almost like a curse. In that sense work really has become a four-letter word. Perhaps it always was.

We all still talk about jobs. We love our jobs, down the allotments, in the garden, on the market stalls, hobby farming (permaculture) in the fields, doing the admin (a specialism of the left brainers). In fact there is a big demand for jobs and there are simply not enough to go around (which means that some will pay to do them, trading on the unofficial job market). But people are always thinking of new jobs on the Wall. No one talks about, understands or measures unemployment in the newer generation. Jobs, however, are regulated. They must be deemed purposeful for approval in the mandate. Today the buzz word for human economic deficiency is unfulfilment and at the last count global unfulfilment was running at about 100m worldwide, even within the Wall. Outside the Wall no one knows and probably no one cares.

Are we happier now that we have consolidated our place in a biodiverse world, still threatened by disease and climate change (that has not been quite so fearsome as some predicted in the 2000s)? I wouldn't say that life is any better than it was in my forties. It's longer now than it was for some people at that time, but there has been a cost. The world population seems to have peaked and the debate today is all about the threat of population shrinkage. Birth rates everywhere have decreased. Much of Africa is still a mess, but China, the world's biggest economy has proved itself a stabilizing influence, politically, particularly since it agreed (after much resistance in the popular vote) to accept English as a world language. It doesn't matter much since there is instant translation on the Wall and communities are engaged all over the world in preserving their distinctive cultures and languages in resistance to the Wall's potential for uniformity that has been acknowledged. Popular cultural protocols have been established to reduce the threat of homogeneity.

Economics, as a discipline has been turned on its head, mainly as a result of the decline from Peak Oil, following a familiar Bell curve trajectory that has led to all kinds of new theories dealing with the war on debt and de-growth societies, including, I'm pleased to record, the economics of enough. Emotional growth and spiritual growth have become economic topics, underpinned by various happiness indexes, studied avidly within the Wall community.

One of the big exceptions to this summary is the swelling Dee community. In spite of their human deficiencies many Dees betray endearingly human traits. A lot of them, like the Shark, are popular in the media and entertainment and some are quite freakish, as might be imagined. Some are international institutions and game stars and we have found that we need them. Among a number of Section D exemptions are those permitted for our space pioneers who are traveling ever-lengthier journeys across the solar system. Those undertaking the longest-traveled crewed-Voyagers are ten years out and will live out the rest of their lives in space. They all predate the Human Modification Directive but a new so-called Hawking crew has been recruited entirely among the Dee community and modified for deep space travel and regeneration; new Dees (human initially) will be born on the self-sustaining journey. There is even a chance they may return one day in the distant future. If they do achieve their primary goal of contacting extraterrestrial intelligent life, it is ironic that the meeting will not involve humans, but a semi-artificial species that is very like us.

Someone at NASA, now one of the global united enterprises, had chosen to call the space probe the Integral but it was renamed Enterprise XII, under pressure from NASA councillors.[11] When the name-change leaked out it stimulated a lot of Wall debate about the potential among Dees to create a dystopian society. That led to a fierce Dee backlash from one of their most popular members, the self-styled D-503 who claims to represent what he calls a Dee "trade union," the Charter. Provocatively he argues that the Charter is a product of "out of the box" innovative thinking and discussion. He questions how much any of us can trust the Wall and points to the voting scandal of 2052. Systems applications needed a thorough overall after it was discovered that a virus program was deliberately destroying hefty chunks of popular voting, thereby fraudulently sustaining a number of Admin councillors and MPs in their positions of influence. Some of these disgraced councillors are still serving long-term home incarcerations.

The Wall, says D-503, is the real dystopia, but I don't see it that way. These swift interventions highlight the strength of the Wall to my mind. The Wall is here to stay. Its influence in transforming capitalism, politics, the judiciary and governmental institutions has been pervasive as a catalyst for trends that were already emerging early in the twenty-first century. But I do think The Charter, and its outline of Dee demands, makes some valid points about the proliferation and systemizing effects of human performance metrics. The Dees are redrafting their own bill of rights as I write and it will be interesting to see how it progresses in the general popular vote. A first draft was rejected by a substantial margin.

The Dees, I will admit, seem to have a lot of fun among themselves. Tattooing, body piercing and the wearing of tweeds fell out of favor in most Wall communities but remain popular among the Dees who have something of a laissez-faire attitude to life. Surprisingly they get on well with most of the pures, but are held in broad contempt by many in the Wall population who simply do not understand the persistent Dee obsession with the 1970s. Still topping the Dee music plays is that evergreen Led Zeppelin anthem, *Stairway to Heaven*.

One final word of warning: please remember that the whole of this chapter was composed using Wall-predictive phrasing. So it's entirely possible that you are reading a modification of my thoughts, processed by artificial intelligence. I knew I should have used a pencil.

CHAPTER 13

Toward a Better Society

There are known knowns. There are things we know that
we know. There are known unknowns. That is to say, there
are things that we now know we don't know. But there are
also unknown unknowns. There are things we do not know
we don't know.

Donald Rumsfeld (1932–)

If the previous chapter seemed fanciful, I should point out that I am not predicting *the end of work* in the way that was envisaged by Jeremy Rifkin in his book of the same name. Rifkin's analysis of a third industrial revolution was sound in many respects, but his assumption that machines would increasingly replace labor in future is flawed. Machines create labor. Our knowledge machines—computers—create more knowledge, more analysis, more debate and more mashing and slicing of what we know. But we can't see it all, not even with the sifting skills of the search engine. Today we have unknown knowns—things we know but don't know we know, just to add another facet to Donald Rumsfeld's abstruse explanation of US military thinking in Iraq.[1]

The Internet has become a kind of knowledge soup with some of the latest technologies designed to separate the ingredients. Much of the new work is flavoring the soup and creating new recipes in a world hungry for novelty. But how shall we find the flavors and how shall we separate the real insights from the growing trash-heaps of Internet knowledge (if that is not too grand a word)—the known knowns that we simply don't need to know or care to know? That's a big job for the future although the rankers and the list-makers are already at work. The website, Stumbleupon.com has reduced the lottery of web surfing by concentrating on the stated interest and preference patterns of users.

Work is here to stay. It's part of who we are. So we should not even be contemplating the end of work. But work isn't working very well. The ideas of scientific management that reduced the knowledge of the artisan to a mechanical process are alive and kicking today, distilling what we do into manageable chunks, then apportioning a rate for the job, thereby creating a visible commodity. People deserve better than that. It is why work needs to adopt new definitions that make it more agreeable as a way of life. But this will not happen without some radical rethinking around the structure of work and the way that people are employed and paid.

This is why I have concentrated as much in this book on what needs to happen as I have on what will or what might happen. Some of the developments outlined in the previous chapters will not transform working life without a will among employers and governments to change the way people learn, earn and contribute to society.

In summarizing the chapters I am aware of issues I might have covered more thoroughly. Globalization, the environment, education, the trade unions and pay reform are all substantial topics that have not been subjected to any detailed input here. Work is such a big subject and so intrinsic to our lives that one could argue that it is influenced by almost everything, even the weather. If global warming is happening, and most of the evidence I have seen from official sources suggests that it is, we cannot know how it will change our lives. I have tried therefore to avoid speculating too much around what Rumsfeld described as the *known unknowns*, not to mention the *unknown unknowns*. I have tried instead to focus on the themes and trends that are visible today and which are already shaping the future.

Probably the most fascinating of these for me, as one of the baby boomers past his half-century and with inadequate pension provision to live as he would wish to become accustomed, is demographics. What will a world look like where the old outnumber the young? Bournemouth? The place that has so many pensioners it is nicknamed "God's waiting room" was found to be the happiest town in Britain in a 2007 poll.[2] But I cannot envision a world of care homes and bathchairs. My generation was simply not raised to think in any other way than remaining positive and doing things as long as we could. We simply will not "go gently into that good night".

Look at Sir Ranulph Fiennes, the man who the BBC described as "the explorer who refuses to grow old." At the age of 65 he climbed Mount Everest. "People are not growing old like they used to," wrote Andrew North, reporting for the BBC from Everest base camp.[3] Fiennes, the first man to cross both polar ice caps, overcame heart problems in his determination to reach the top. He had a heart attack near the summit during an earlier attempt. Fiennes would be a remarkable man in any generation. After one polar expedition he sawed off his frostbitten finger ends, using a jigsaw, simply because they were getting in the way. "The surgeon said it was a neat job," he recalled later.[4] Just months after recovering from his first heart attack in 2003 he recuperated by running seven marathons on seven continents in seven days.

He described his strategy for reaching the summit as to "Plod forever, but never believe you are going to get there." It could almost be a philosophy of life, certainly for those who are looking to work beyond what we still regard, but surely not for much longer, as retirement age.

Demographics and the end of retirement as we know it, therefore, had to be central themes in any analysis of the future of work. But the book couldn't ignore technology either, particularly information and communications technology and the way it is creating new perspectives on work among the younger generation. What did surprise me was that there should be any dispute that young people were benefiting from their learning relationship with the Internet. I hope the strongly evidence-based observations of Don Tapscott, highlighted in his many books, will have been sufficient to silence the naysayers. Technology brings great benefits and with them, accompanying problems, particularly when the technology itself begins to dominate the stage and the spotlight when really it should be making music in the orchestra pit. We must learn in future how to make technology work for us rather than the other way round.

What about women? This is such a difficult subject. Women themselves don't seem to know the answer, but the evidence suggests that more and more of them are either choosing career over family or struggling to manage career and family. The implications of these choices will be profound in two ways—first, in the growth of future populations and second, in the feminization of the workplace. What of the low-paid and low-value jobs that seem to be the lot of so many women, often working part-time? I fear that we shall be stuck with this work for many years to come. It would be refreshing to see more of those in higher-paid jobs undertaking some of this work—bosses cleaning their own offices, for example. Some of the more elitist-minded would argue that highly paid people are far too valuable to undertake menial work. I disagree. Menial work enables all of us to stay grounded. Jesus taught us this lesson when washing the feet of his disciples.

There are signs that people are beginning to revise their thinking about physical work. Matthew Crawford's *Shop Class and Soulcraft: An Inquiry in to the Value of Work*, was an unlikely best seller in the spring of 2009, when it questioned the way manual skilled labor had been devalued in the US. Shop Class is an American term for technical classes in secondary schools, the sort of practical education undertaken that can be found in skills academies and tertiary colleges that mix academic and vocational work in the UK.

The book was developed from an essay written in 2006 where Crawford lamented the demise of practical tuition in US schools and colleges. "It appears shop class is becoming a thing of the past, as educators prepare students to become 'knowledge workers,'" he wrote.[5] Warehouses were full of machine tools discarded from schools, he noticed, at the very time that people were beginning to reconsider the way that manual work could add meaning and a sense of satisfaction to their lives. I can see why so many Americans could be attracted to such sentiments. Historically America has been a practical society, underpinned by values of thrift and durability. Consumer society it may be today, but it has never shaken off the mantle of the artisan and that should be a source of pride.

Perhaps we shall see a renewal of the spirit that informed the arts and crafts movements of the nineteenth century when so many people became disillusioned with the ugliness of industrialization and the factory system. Today we are experiencing a new form of ugliness—the ugliness of process-driven modern management; ugliness in the jargon it has adopted; ugliness in its reporting structures and pettiness; ugliness in its physical structure—its cubicles, screens and sterile, cold and boxy plate-glass offices. Much of modern work lacks beauty and that's such a shame. But there is no place for beauty on a balance sheet. "Beauty is in the eye of the beholder, get it out with Optrex," wrote the late Spike Milligan, in his own unique style of social comment.

But are we brave enough to guide our children to a vocation that involves learning a craft? Are we strong enough to emphasize the value of intrinsic satisfaction in work over the reward of a City salary and bonus? I'm not sure that we are, and that is why our children must find their own way. The only message on vocation I passed on to my own children was to find something at which they excelled and which they enjoyed, then to find how they might make a living at it—the more specialist the better. George, our youngest, is still at school so who knows where his muse will take him? John graduated in economics and promptly turned his back on a career in the City in favor of working in the film industry. He studied for an MSc in film industry management and entered the industry at ground level, working for little pay but learning all the while. It is still too early to say whether he has found his vocation, but extra responsibilities and a little more pay have come his way in recent months so he may yet find that he has found his true calling.

Robert, the middle son, is still working at his degree in Maths and French, but in the meantime has created himself a business that is returning regular income equivalent to a well-paid graduate traineeship. He seems to spend much of his spare time on his games website and game innovation and draws great satisfaction from the feedback he receives from those who play his games.[6] Robert is not alone. There are thousands more like him all over the world. All of them are truly engaged in what can only be described as the new work. They use social networks, forums, texting, any freely available technology they can lay their hands on for furthering their work. But there is no great loyalty to the medium. Facebook and Twitter are popular communications platforms. Will their popularity last? Who knows? Something better may be just around the corner.

The trend for more young people to attend university is likely to continue in future. "Education, education and education," said Tony Blair, when outlining his priorities for the government to the Labour Party conference in October 1996. But is education simply a matter of passing exams, degrees and yet more degrees? And is the system preparing young people suitably for working lives? It might not have seemed so for the estimated 1m young people aged between 16 and 24 who were expected to be without either work or a college place in the summer of 2009.[7] Would some of them have been better advised to find a marketable skill?

Crawford describes college education as "the ticket to an *open* future." He writes: "Craftsmanship entails learning to do one thing really well, while the ideal of the new economy is to be able to learn new things, celebrating potential rather than achievement." Is it sensible to be preparing Jacks of all trades? Or should young people begin concentrating early on a specific skill? There are shades here of the deliberate practice argument advanced by Geoff Colvin in his book, *Talent is Overrated*.

The pursuit of excellence in a single speciality is to be admired, but most people must decide for themselves just how far they want to go. The late Ustad Ali Akbar Khan, the Indian classical musician and the world's leading exponent of the 25-stringed instrument called the sarod described the mastery of his art thus: "If you practise for 10 years, you may begin to please yourself. After 20 years you may become a performer and please the audience. After 30 years you may please even your guru. But you must practise for many more years before you finally become a true artist—then you may please even God."

Excellence lies in hard work and stretching hard work at that. That said, some people are capable of stretching themselves in ways that others don't. This was observed by David McClelland, the social psychologist, more than 50 years ago. McClelland devised a "ring toss" experiment that involved children competing with each other in throwing hoops over wooden pegs. They were told they could stand as close to, or as far away from the pegs as they wished.

Before the experiment the children had completed a test that marked them on their urge to do well, or what McClelland called their "need for achievement." The children with the highest scores in the test tended to stand at a distance that required a challenging throw—but not so challenging that they had no hope of succeeding. As they improved, they extended the throwing distance. The low scorers would either stand far back or get so close that they could not miss the peg.

McClelland believed that Western industrialized societies had built their economic success by encouraging those, as with the high-scoring children, who created challenges for themselves. Reviewing the experiment in 2001, Professor Richard Easterlin of the University of Southern California concluded that the satisfaction of any particular desire led inexorably to the creation of a new one.[8] No matter how we progress throughout our lives, general levels of happiness across the population tend to remain constant, he observed. More than this, he said, our desire to buy things increases in proportion to our income. So the more we earn, the more we want. Unfortunately these desires cannot be sated since we are never able to sustain anything more than some short-term gratification as a result of material gain. I suppose this explains why entrepreneurs find it difficult to call a halt to their quest for further acquisitions. The word "enough" is missing from their vocabulary.

This basis for economic progression was questioned by John Kenneth Galbraith in *The Affluent Society*, his 1958 critique of the US economy in the aftermath of the Second World War. Galbraith was using the term in the book's title ironically since he argued that the affluence—derived from a concentration on private enterprise—ignored the need for better public services. Too much industrial effort, he suggested, was concentrated on satisfying trivial consumer desires when there was a more pressing need for improved public services in the form of better schools, social services and infrastructure. Rifkin was pursuing a similar argument, urging more work to be directed into community life and the third or charity sector.

But capitalism has stood in the way of this, and triumphantly so. The banks that grew like cuckoos in the 1990s and beyond, are growing again today, establishing an almost divine right to dominate the nest, fed as they have been by anxious administrations that know no better, finding the money where they could when there was a real danger that the cosy financial nest could collapse in 2008. Hopes of stronger regulation were fading in the summer of 2009 as the banks once again began hiring and poaching staff with the promise of new bonuses from trading profits.

Even the Royal Bank of Scotland had a new boss, Stephen Hester, with a £9.6m pay package, justified by incentives that would be paid if he could turn a profit for the taxpayer's substantial investment in the bailed-out bank. The bankers, concluded John Plender, writing in the *Financial Times*, were "off the hook", adding: "Against the background of unresolved global imbalances, there must be a possibility that with bankers once again at play, the financial system will return to chaos in the not too distant future."[9] As baseball legend, Yogi Berra once remarked: "It's like déjà vu all over again."

It's difficult to see how our consumerist urges can be controlled. Crawford raises sociologist Richard Sennett's argument that the craftsman cherishes what he has made while the consumerist discards serviceable goods in a restless pursuit of new things. Who could argue with the evidence of the new Sunday worship at car boot sales up and down the land? Crawford goes on to argue that "the craftsman's habitual deference is not toward the New, but toward the distinction between the Right Way and the Wrong Way."

He is right to insist that much of the manual work that was not sterilized by scientific management is ennobled by intellectual content. This is why it is no longer satisfactory, if ever it was, to make white-collar and blue-collar distinctions that assume a superiority of white-collar work. Hundreds of blue-collar jobs today are highly skilled. If we must insist on collar-type in considering the new work it is better to describe it as *no collar work*. They don't have dress codes at Google.

In the same way it is no longer sensible to complain of the degradation of blue-collar work alone. Degradation of work, whatever shirt we wear, is a modern malaise in the process-focused workplace. What price the old experienced hand, striving to stay afloat in what Crawford calls a "rising sea of clerkdom" toeing the company line, following company procedures? His case for respecting the crafts recalls Robert Persig's reverence for quality and good work, embodied in the spiritual and explained in his seminal work, *Zen and the Art of Motorcycle Maintenance*. The Work Foundation is researching these aspects of work in its Good Work Commission, but seems to be struggling to find full-blooded support in business beyond a widespread interest in employee engagement—the one trick pony of modern management.

This book was never intended as a starry-eyed vision of the future. The way we are employed will continue to feature good and bad practice. The bad news is that so much drudge work will remain if we let it and so will poverty in future years if we continue to treat it like the beggar we pass on the street. I can see no end, either, to the salary-fueled war for talent that will continue to enrich the fortunate few at the expense of the many. I would dearly love to see more job ownership in tomorrow's society, but where is the political and commercial will for such systems? It simply isn't there just now even though we know that employee-owned businesses can be successful and sustainable models of enterprise.

The forces of change will not be applied universally or with equal strength across the labor market. In 50 years time I have no doubt there will still be communities with their butchers and bakers and—who knows?—possibly with their candlestick makers too if soaring energy costs have forced people to adopt more frugal ways of living.

While some people will continue to work much as before there will be far more opportunities in future for people to engage in fulfilling vocations, sometimes as self-employed artisans, marketing themselves as an *organization of one* through the world wide web or its evolved inheritor. Here search engines exploiting the long tale of distribution allow the ultra specialist to reach a small and globally dispersed market. Today our key word search really can find the needle in the haystack.

If companies do embrace the idea of shorter working weeks—and I have deep reservations about their willingness to make that step—it could liberate more people to do other work, what could become for some a labor of love—their true vocation. I fear, however, that suggestions for shorter working weeks will be interpreted crudely as a shirkers' charter with accompanying "loss to business" estimates in their billions. Just as there is a greed for money in today's society, there is a greed for people. Business must learn to share their people. Companies do not own the lives of their employees. If they need any confirmation they need only look at their balance sheets. People may be regarded as assets by HR directors but, without a radical change to the accounting system, finance directors will always book them as a cost.

There simply is no accounting for people, but there is performance management and that is bound to grow more sophisticated in future, given the availability of software tracking systems such as those developed by SuccessFactors and other providers of HR software. I am not optimistic of wholesale adoption of generic human capital measurements although consensus around engagement questionnaires is more likely, given the mutual respect among people involved in creating these measures. It's important, however, that HR software is not abused by power-hungry managers more concerned to control rather than nurture talent.

If HR is to behave strategically in future it must focus its efforts around performance management—ensuring the right people are in the right place doing their best work with all the support they need. Tim Miller, HR director at Standard Chartered Bank warns against HR associating itself too closely with employee welfare. "HR has to earn its corn by demonstrating that it can add value through improved productivity. It's there to drive business performance. If it's doing anything else then it should stop it," he says.[10]

Another imperative for HR professionals and their management colleagues in traditionally structured employers in the immediate future must be to establish diverse employment pools, both vertically integrated across all age cohorts, including the over-sixties and even the over-seventies, and broadly based in gender, ethnic composition and the disabled. Diversity must also extend to the employment contract so that full-time staff are augmented by part-time and contractual staff who should be made to feel as much a part of the team as those recruited in permanent posts. The second-class status of so much temporary and contract work at present is undermining the flexible ideal.

It is difficult to predict the type of work that will expand in future. For individuals, sector expansion is not the real consideration anyway. The route to relative prosperity and satisfaction in future will be found in developing a niche of expertise. Environmental change and the sustainability agenda is offering many prospective career avenues. But there are too many variables—the rate at which oil will run out and the progress of alternative energy sources, for example—to be definitive about the physical developments in the future of our planet. This is why I have concentrated on trends and themes rather than on scenarios.

Furthermore I have taken an optimistic view of global warming and of society in general. I do not envisage a Third World War but I do think that many countries will be riven by internal conflicts and insurgency in the near future (just as they are in Afghanistan and in parts of Pakistan today) as ideologies and religions (specifically Islamic fundamentalism but possibly also Christian fundamentalism) battle for influence. A dirty bomb that spreads nuclear or bacterial contamination could be a future weapon in such conflict and this could possibly reverse the influx of populations into the great cities, for a time. If this could be avoided, however, cities will grow in strength as centers of human excellence and collaboration, as discussed in Chapter 2.

Much of the work in the coming 50 years will need to focus on making society more sustainable: reducing waste, reducing carbon output, conserving water and improving food production. Part of this work and some of the impetus for this work will arise from mass organization exploiting the global communications revolution that is transforming our world today. But that will not prevent communities from both thinking and acting locally in more devolved societies.

Social historians may argue about the causes and the precise beginning, but I have no doubt that they will look back in 50 years' time to the decades preceding and following the year 2000 as a watershed in working practices as significant as any described during the period of Britain's industrial revolution. Unlike the industrial revolution, however, this latest watershed will not be characterized as sector specific or confined to a defined locality. It is worldwide and delivered largely through broadband networks.

If we look back at the nineteenth century as the steam age and think, as we should, of the twentieth century as the age of the internal combustion engine, I wonder if our grandchildren will view the early part of the twenty-first century as the age of the search engine? It would be a fitting epithet since the power and ubiquity of information retrieval is as formidable as any that multiplies the combined energy of harnessed horses.

Revolutions are visible in the way they transform society. Some, such as the French, American and Russian revolutions, were replacing monarchical rule with new systems of government. Others, more benign in their nature, may be just as transformational but can take longer to consolidate their impact on living patterns and social attitudes. Sometimes an event such as a war, a recession or financial boom can appear more transformational, but the impact may be short term, possibly involving regressive behaviors as people employ recognizable responses to a familiar threat, such as falling sales.

The history of the way we live and work is more evolutionary than revolutionary in nature, but there have been discernible watersheds and milestones in the past. The one we are experiencing today is multifaceted, drawing influences from a series of trends that cumulatively add up to a shift in attitudes, straining to find a more comfortable environment.

Some of these trends can be expressed as migrations of practices and habits shifting from one norm to another. Among the migrations we have explored in this book are:

- Industry to knowledge services

- Office to home

- Collective to individual

- Process to project

- Formal working hours to discretionary time

- Work across boundaries.

Each of these migrations are factors contributing to the changing face of work but each will be experienced in different strengths across different sectors, industries and workplaces. Most working people today will have felt the impact of at least one and almost certainly more of these trends. One last possible addition to that list of migrations, although it is still early days in gauging the undercurrents, is a movement from sedentary work to physical labor. The screen has come to dominate our lives and sooner or later some will say: "enough."

Some of these migratory forces are causing real discomfort in workplaces struggling to maintain classical controlling management patterns. Like hermit crabs seeking larger shells, people today are yearning for more accommodating arrangements in which to undertake their work.

Their quibble is not with work itself. We all understand the need to undertake work in order to improve our lives and provide for our dependents. No, the underlying source of anguish for many people in work today is an antiquated system of employment and management designed for an industrial age.

Previous forecasters such as Bill Bridges and Daniel Pink have identified the job itself as the problem. Bridges described the job as a 200-year-old social artefact.[11] I have some sympathy with his frustration that organizing work into packages called jobs is failing to meet the demands of swiftly changing businesses. Sadly the alternative of freelance employment has yet to create a stable enough framework to ensure that people can expand their working horizons in conditions of relative security.

There is little evidence that people are clamoring to abandon their jobs, and many who have opted for temporary working do so out of necessity, occupying these flexible roles in the hope that it will lead to more permanent employment. A minority of executives, such as those pursuing careers in interim management, have succeeded in establishing themselves as "permanent temps." But, as yet, they have not formed the vanguard of a free agency conversion in the traditional employment market.

One reason for this is the merry-go-round in permanent jobs. The peripatetic nature of so many so-called permanent jobs today is undermining relationship building in the workplace and destroying goodwill in transactional contract work.

What is needed to accommodate the new work, therefore, is nothing less than a root-and-branch reform of employment, pensions, savings and taxation systems that must allow people to exercise much greater choice over their working, earning and learning patterns from cradle to grave. While governments could and should be leading this reform, employers can influence change through their own approaches.

This book has featured a number of examples where employers are pursuing change in specific fields: British Telecommunications and its approaches to health monitoring and home working; B&Q and its enlightened attitude to older workers; Best Buy and results-based working; Microsoft in its understanding of the desire for internet-based collaboration among young people; Standard Chartered bank in the way it links engagement measures to people management; John Lewis in job ownership.

But these changes are piecemeal, often specific to pioneering companies and rarely supported by enlightened government policies. This should surprise no one considering that the government is an institution supported by a civil service steeped in job-for-life principles. I'm writing here of the UK government but the same observations apply to almost any governmental system in the world.

The John Lewis Partnership has pursued a successful model of job ownership for more than 80 years that has created an involved, respected and well-paid workforce. It has maintained significant pay differentials across its hierarchy without the kind of ratchetting up of senior executive pay that has distorted reward systems and encouraged excessive risk taking in the financial sector. Yet where in any government legislation since the partnership's inception in 1928 can we discern any attempt to promote this form of business ownership? Job ownership may not be the answer for all enterprise, but it deserves a better chance to thrive than it has enjoyed hitherto.

While I'm confident this book has assembled the most influential trends influencing the future of work, it is difficult to gauge their relative strengths in shaping the future. Nor can this analysis prepare employers for the kind of sudden shift in trading conditions arising from unexpected events such as the 2008 financial crisis or the 2009 swine flu outbreak and pandemic. All it can do is to agree with the argument of Nicholas Taleb in his book *Black Swans* that unlikely disruptive events do happen with an all too alarming frequency. Those who survive them combine long-term contingencies with short-term adaptability.

We should expect periodic disruptions that can not be accommodated in business plans, but they should not divert employers and governments from responding imaginatively to attritional change resulting from demographic trends and shifting attitudes. Young people, in particular, are rejecting some of the lifestyle options of their parents, sometimes out of choice in a growing preference for cohabitation, for example, and sometimes out of economic necessity.

When discussing the trends featured in this book among a round table of senior executives from among the UK's biggest companies, I was asked to predict the likelihood of their influencing change in a fundamental way. The question underpinned the importance of outlining a series of policy considerations. While I believe that fundamental changes in working practices are inevitable, the duration of the watershed and the economic success of a new tier of knowledge industries could be eased by more progressive employment policies designed to accommodate the new work and changing attitudes.

Finally I want to stress that nowhere am I arguing in this book that work is the enemy of society. Work, on the contrary, is essential for a happy society but it is important that we are masters of rather than slaves to our work. Even where we try to define good work, however, we must face the irreconcilable truth that great performance in almost anything that we do requires practice and determination. Geoff Colvin made as convincing an argument for this as I have heard anywhere in his book, *Talent is Overrated*. Nevertheless I am troubled by his argument that what he calls "deliberate practice" cannot be fun .Fun is probably the wrong word to use in the context of work. Instead I would choose to use the word "satisfaction." A job well done after many hours of sweat or stressful intellectual input can be immensely satisfying. Admiral Lord Nelson in his dying breath spoke with some comfort of having done his duty. A sense of duty has become outmoded in the workplace today. It needs to be revived. We all have a duty in our work to perform to the best of our ability. We contract to do so when we take on a job. It is something that has underpinned the reign of Queen Elizabeth II and it is this understanding that maintains respect for her office in an increasingly cynical world.

If I'm arguing for anything in these pages it is for people in work to have more discretion and more latitude to do their work as they know it should be done. People need to have more ownership of their work and more choices. Not everyone wants to run a company or to be a TV star although sometimes they think they do. Not everyone wants to be a millionaire although, again, too often this is promoted as a badge of success. The more we can remove the distortions of planted desires the more we can discover and pursue our true ambitions, which surely must be to live fulfilling lives.

Outlined here is a list of key imperatives for employers and policymakers preparing for the future of work:

CHARTER FOR THE NEW WORK—A POLICY AGENDA

1. Understand that the home is interchangeable with the office for thousands of people working with information and communications technology who need to be supported, trusted and measured by their results.

2. Retire the concept of retirement and remove default retirement ages for all, while enabling those approaching their later years in employment to move toward more experience-tapping work. Embrace the concept of age management.

3. Encourage progression among employers and employees to view Friday as part of the weekend—a default day off—and not part of the working week, shifting discretion and autonomy among people to choose how they want to spend more of their time, including working longer hours for a single employer if they so wish.

4. Promote qualitative measuring in employment and generic measures for comparison in the sharing of results within public company annual reports. But build in safeguards and employee rights to avoid a workplace ruled by metrics.

5. Focus on results, not time spent on a task.

6. Introduce more practical, context-related learning and collaborative teamwork into the school curriculum.

7. Make all professions more accessible and break down professional "closed shop" protectionism, while encouraging

meaningful continuing professional development linked to internationally agreed standards.

8. Insist on relationship experience and empathy (or emotional intelligence) in management in addition to technical mastery.

9. Promote and incentivize employee ownership of companies.

10. Promote employee health and well-being with well-designed interventions and workplace monitoring and reporting of metrics.

11. Broaden recruitment criteria wherever possible in order to create truly diverse workplaces, reflecting disabilities, ethnicity, gender, age and cultural differences.

12. Create conditions for employees to exercise discretion and concentrate on work within their job parameters that is relevant, meaningful and ethical.

13. Understand and accommodate different attitudes and approaches to work among the Internet generation. Learn from their collaborative experiences.

14. Publish the gap between top and bottom pay in every public company report, expressed as a ratio. Treat high ratios as a governance issue.

15. Scrutinize all work for job enrichment and purpose, recognizing the detrimental effects of repetitive work, lacking discretionary behavior. Accept claims of drudge work as a contributory factor in industrial tribunal claims against employers.

16. Restore dignity to the manual trades and how they are perceived, particularly in the education system.

17. View leadership as a generic competency that should be practiced among all employees in taking greater responsibility for their work, career development and project initiatives.

18. Make Sunday special again. A day of rest is as valuable in secular society as it is to those who preserve the day of worship.

Notes

Introduction

1. *US Now*, Banyak Films, screened at the Royal Society for the Encouragement of Arts Manufactures and Commerce, London. December 8, 2008.
2. http://uk.zopa.com.
3. Jack Welch with John A. Byrne, *Jack, What I've Learned Leading a Great Company and Great People*, Headline, 2001, pp. 162–7.
4. The Work Foundation launched a Good Work program in 2008 to examine what is meant by good work and how it can be encouraged among employers.
5. Jim Webber, obituary, *The Guardian*, December 15, 2008.

1 A watershed in life and work

1. *Anna Karenina*, Penguin Classics, 1978, p. 275.
2. British Gas share sale advertising slogan, 1986.
3. "Mid-Level Morale at All Time Low," *Financial Times*, December 9, 2004.
4. Interview with author.
5. Andrew Holmes, *Commoditization and the Strategic Response*, Gower, 2008, p. 208.
6. "General Motors Goes Bust," *The Week*, June 6, 2009.
7. "ILO Jobs Crisis Observatory," www.ilo.org. ILO's Global Employment Trends 2009 report.
8. *What Matters: 10 Questions that Will Shape our Future*, McKinsey & Co., March 2009.
9. "Companies have to Understand the Value of Values," *Financial Times*, November 30, 2006.
10. This observation and those in the previous paragraph are drawn from my earlier book, *Blood, Sweat and Tears: The Evolution of Work*, Texere, 2001.
11. "Kalahari Bushmen Thrown Off their Land," *The Ecologist*, September 2003. A second report in March 2007 outlined the

struggle of the bushmen to return to their lands in spite of a court ruling upholding their challenge against eviction.

12. "Goodbye Gucci: It's the Age of Co-Op Capitalism," *The Times*, February 25, 2009.
13. A series of stories on MPs' allowances ran in the *Daily Telegraph* throughout May 2008.
14. Interview with author, June 2007.

2 Demographics—an underlying force for change

1. *What Matters: Ten Questions that Will Shape our Future*, p. 52.
2. "Women Put Careers before Raising a Family," *Daily Telegraph*, June 26, 2009.
3. "The US Broadband Battle," bbc.co.uk, May 27, 2009.
4. "UK Broadband 'notspots' Revealed," bbc.co.uk, May 26, 2009.
5. "Night Jack Blog Loses Fight for Anonymity," *Financial Times*, June 16, 2009.
6. "Baby Boom Britain won't Retire Quietly," *The Observer*, March 22, 2009.
7. "Survive the Baby Boomer Exodus," Official Board Markets, www. packaging-online.com, January 3, 2009.
8. At least 20 million children under the age of 5 years were overweight globally in 2005, according to the World Health Organization. "Obesity: In Statistics," bbc.co.uk, January 2, 2008.
9. Author's interview with Tom Kochan, *Financial Times*, June 15, 2006.
10. *The Washington Times*, February 6, 2009.
11. "Middle-Class Poles Leave Britain for the Greener Grass of Home," *Sunday Telegraph*, February 22, 2009.
12. "More Flexible EU Labour Laws will Create Jobs," *Financial Times*, December 6, 2007.
13. *The Guardian*, February 16, 2009.
14. Interview with author for Recruitment and Employment Confederation, Future of Employment Working Group.

3 Goodbye retirement, hello living

1. "Sullenberger Describes Emergency Landing in Hudson River," *Los Angeles Times*, June 9, 2009.

2. "Loyalty Bonus Should Not Be Devalued," *Financial Times*, July 27, 1994.
3. "Redundancy Reigns in Metroland," *Financial Times*, May 18, 1994.
4. *The Straits Times*, January 10, 2009.
5. "Join The Queue," *Management Today*, June, 2009.
6. "Patrick J. Purcell, Older Workers: Employment and Retirement Trends," *Journal of Deferred Compensation*, March 22, 2006.
7. *Daily Telegraph* obituary, August 17, 2007.
8. "Wealth," *North American Review*, June, 1889.
9. "Older Workers have Healthier Habits," Community Banker, January, 2009.

4 Whatever happened to lunch?

1. "Visible Measures that Help Reduce Absenteeism," *Financial Times*, April 17, 2008.
2. "When Going to Work is a Walk in the Park," *Financial Times*, July 15, 2004.
3. "Why Health is Good for your Bottom Line," *Financial Times*, February 26, 2004.
4. "How Unhealthy Work Stops us Doing our Jobs," *Financial Times*, November 10, 2005.
5. http://www.hcp.med.harvard.edu/hpq/.
6. "The Benefits of Investing in Employee Health," *Financial Times*, February 14, 2008.
7. *Facing Europe's Demographic Challenge: The Demographic Fitness Survey 2007*, Adecco Institute.

5 Women or children first?

1. caissierenofutur.over-blog.com.
2. I. La Valle, L. Giles, and S. Perryman, "A New Deal for Secretaries?" Report 313, Institute for Employment Studies, September 1996.
3. "Women Soar Ahead at University," *Sunday Times*, p. 7, June 7, 2009.
4. "Women are Victors in 'mancession,'" *Sunday Times*, p. 25, June 7, 2009.
5. Catherine Hakim, *Work-Lifestyle Choices in the 21st Century: Preference Theory*, Oxford University Press, 2000, p. 3.

6. Avivah Wittenberg-Cox and Alison Maitland, *Why Women Mean Business*, Jossey-Bass, 2008, p. 31.
7. Ibid., p. 32.
8. "Davos 2009: Where are the Women?" *Businessweek*, January 26, 2009.
9. *Why Women Mean Business*, p. 1.
10. *Daily Telegraph*, January 31, 2009.
11. *Daily Telegraph*, December 29, 2008.
12. *The Guardian*, September 22, 2004.
13. Richard Layard and Judith Dunn, *A Good Childhood: Searching for Values in a Competitive Age*, Penguin, 2009.
14. "My New Guilt as a Selfish Working Mother," *Financial Times*, February 8, 2009.
15. "Parents—Pull your Socks Up," *Sunday Times*, February 1, 2009.
16. "Women Put Careers before Raising a Family," *Daily Telegraph*, June 26, 2009.
17. *Blood, Sweat and Tears*, p. 230.

6 Technology—scourge or savior of work?

1. "Has Obama's BlackBerry Got the Edge?" *Daily Telegraph*, January 30, 2009.
2. In 2006 an Australian computer programmer claimed to have found evidence for the missing "a." In 2009 other linguists said they had proved otherwise, *Daily Mail*, June 4, 2009.
3. "Beauty of Simplicity," *Financial Times*, May 6, 1998.
4. Carol Kennedy, *Guide to the Management Gurus*, Century Business, 1991, p. 105.
5. "Sometimes Cash Rewards are not up to the Task," *Financial Times*, July 3, 2008.

7 Making sense of social networking

1. www.senseworldwide.com.
2. "Global Faces and Networked Places," Nielsen Online, March 9, 2009.
3. "2009 Global Interviewing Practices and Perceptions," DDI, based on feedback from 1900 interviewers and 3500 jobseekers worldwide.
4. A survey of 200 employers carried out by Challenger Gray & Christmas, HR consultants, Network World, July 21, 2008.

5. *The Independent*, November 1, 2008.
6. David Bolchover, *The Living Dead: Switched Off, Zoned Out—The Shocking Truth About Office Life*, Capstone, 2005, p. 3.
7. Global Secure Systems poll of 776 UK office workers, January, 2008.
8. Quoted by the author in "Employers Must Test the Strength of Weak Ties," *Financial Times*, June 19, 2008.
9. ComScore.com, "Twitter traffic explodes ... and not being driven by the usual suspects!" Sarah Radwanick, April 7, 2009.
10. Michel Delon (ed.), *Encyclopedia of the Enlightenment*, Fitzroy Dearborn, 2001, p. 3.
11. *Blood, Sweat and Tears*, pp. 108–9.
12. Delon, p. 3.
13. Ibid, p. 5.
14. Michael Moynagh and Richard Worsley, *Working in the Twenty-First Century*, Economic and Social Research Council, 2005, p. 122.

8 The inheritors

1. www.cmu.edu/randyslecture.
2. Jon Krakauer, *Into the Wild*, Anchor, 1996. The book was made into a film of the same title in 2007.
3. Seattletimes.com.
4. "Escape the System for Something More Challenging—Today's Graduates are Becoming Entrepreneurial Because of a Curriculum that Suffocates Creativity," *Financial Times*, October 19, 2006.
5. Ibid.
6. "Young People Facing the Future," Fondation Pour L'innovation Politique, 2008.
7. *Daily Telegraph*, October 7, 2008.
8. "Graduate Milk Round Dries Up," *The Independent*, May 26, 2009.
9. Don Tapscott, *Grown Up Digital*, McGraw Hill, 2009, p. 75.
10. Ibid., p. 74.
11. Mark Bauerlein, *The Dumbest Generation: How the Digital Age Stupefies Young Americans and Jeopardizes our Future*, Tarcher/Penguin, 2008.
12. "Google CEO urges grads: 'Turn off your computer,'" Associated Press, May 18, 2009.

9 Leadership, teamwork and collaboration

1. *Daily Mirror*, May 27, 2009.
2. *Daily Telegraph* (Sports Section), June 12, 2009.
3. Laurie Beth Jones, *Jesus CEO: Using Ancient Wisdom for Visionary Leadership*, Hyperion.
4. Sandy Pepper, *Senior Executive Reward, Key Models and Practices*, Gower 2006, p. 30. Pepper, in turn, sourced the experiment to James Surowiecki's *The Wisdom of Crowds: Why so Many are Smarter than the Few and How Collective Wisdom Shapes Business, Economies, Societies and Nations*, Little, Brown, 2004.

10 No accounting for people

1. *Daily Telegraph*, December 11, 2008.
2. *Blood, Sweat and Tears*, p. 284.
3. Gary S. Becker, *Human Capital: A Theoretical and Empirical Analysis, with Special Reference to Education*, 2nd edn. New York: Columbia University Press for NBER, 1975.
4. CNN.com, September 30, 1999.
5. "Cracking The Performance Code: How Firms Succeed," The Work Foundation, July, 2005.
6. The balanced scorecard emerged in 1992. It's usually described as a performance management tool for comparing and aligning various operational activities with the strategic objectives of the organization, to ensure that no single activity is dominating management concerns or distorting business results.
7. Brian E. Becker, Mark A. Huselid, and Dave Ulrich, *The HR Scorecard: Linking People, Strategy and Performance*, Harvard Business School Press, 2001, and *The Workforce Scorecard: Managing Human Capital to Execute Strategy*, Harvard Business School Press, 2005.
8. Best Companies, *Fortune*, January 29, 2009.
9. *Blood, Sweat and Tears*, p. 205.
10. "100 Best Companies to Work For," *Fortune*, 2007.
11. Geoff Colvin, *Talent is Overrated*, Nicholas Brealey, 2008, pp. 137–44.

11 Time for reflection

1. "Secret Ingredients of an Efficient Workplace," *Financial Times*, September 13, 2007.

2. "The Future of Work," *Employment Relations Today*, Special Millennium Issue, Winter 2000, Volume 26, Number 4. John Wiley & Sons.
3. "BA Asks Staff to Work for Nothing," bbc.co.uk, June 16, 2009.
4. "BA Staff Anger at Call for Pay-Free Month," *Financial Times*, June 16, 2009.
5. Matthew B. Crawford, "Shop Class as Soulcraft," *The New Atlantis*, Number 13, Summer 2006.
6. Alex Bryson and John Forth, "Bad Timing: Are Workers More Productive on Certain Days of the Week?" Manpower Human Resources Lab Briefing Paper.
7. "MPs to enjoy a 12-week summer holiday," *Daily Telegraph*, April 21, 2009.
8. "How Thursday Became The New Friday," *New York Times*, November 6, 2005.
9. Don Tapscott, presentation, Canada House, London, November 25, 2008.
10. Traditional Industries Benefit From Turning Japanese.

12 The day work ended

1. Peak Oil—the point at which the world reaches maximum petroleum production—was first discussed by M. King Hubbert in 1956. Predictions of oil exhaustion and rates of use vary widely, but a 2005 US Energy Department Report, the Hirsch report, concluded that Peak Oil is a future reality and that the world will need to prepare for transitions to lower levels of production.
2. The first Miol presentation can be viewed at http://www.youtube.com/watch?v=yDvHlwNvXaM&feature=related.
3. The Swedish-made Envac waste recycling system sucks rubbish from homes to a central collection point via underground tubes. A system was installed in a mixed used housing development at Wembley in 2008.
4. Transition towns emerged from a concept developed in Kinsale, Ireland and adopted as an experiment in urban development Totnes, Devon, where the council has introduced the Totnes Pound, redeemable in local shops. Lampeter, a town planning to follow suit was featured in the *Guardian* article, "Pioneering Welsh Town Begins the Transition to a Life without Oil," April 7, 2007.

5. An approach to designing settlements that leans on natural ecological design and plant symbiosis, www.permaculture.org.uk.

6. Military consensus was developing in 2009 around internal insurgency as a model of future warfare. "Armed Forces Must Change or Risk Failure, Warns Next Chief," *Daily Telegraph*, June 25, 2009.

7. "Japan harnesses energy from footsteps," *Daily Telegraph*, December 12, 2008. Experimental "power generation flooring" in two Tokyo railway stations is converting the energy of commuters into electricity.

8. In 2009 West Yorkshire's Kirklees Council banned relatives from dressing the deceased in favorite outfits, asking them instead to pay £60 for an eco-friendly council-approved shroud. *Daily Telegraph*, June 16, 2009.

9. A 67-year-old Spanish woman gave birth to twins in 2006 after fertility treatment.

10. www.totnes.transitionnetwork.org.

11. The Integral is a space ship featured in a science fiction novel, *We*, completed by Yevgeny Zamyatin in 1921. The fictional space ship designer and the novel's protagonist, is known by his serial number, D-503. *We* was the book that inspired George Orwell to write *1984*.

13 Toward a better society

1. The remark was made at a news conference in February 2002, quoted in "Rum Remark Wins Rumsfeld an Award," bbc.co.uk, December 2, 2003.

2. This was based on a poll of 6000 people carried out for First Direct Bank, "Bournemouth Happiest Town in the UK," bbc.co.uk, March 8, 2007.

3. "The Explorer who Refuses to Grow Old," bbc.co.uk, May 21, 2009.

4. Interview with the author, quoted in "Been There, Done That," *FT Weekend*, July 23, 2005.

5. Matthew B. Crawford, "Shop Class as Soulcraft," *The New Atlantis*, Number 13, Summer, 2006.

6. www.BadViking.com

7. "Neets (not in education employment or training) Figures to Top One Million for the First Time," *Daily Telegraph*, June 30, 2009.

8. Richard A. Easterlin, "Subjective Well-Being and Economic Analysis: A Brief Introduction," *Journal of Economic Behaviour and Organization*, Volume 45, Issue 3, July 2001, pp. 225–6.

9. John Plender, "How Fading Political will has Let Banks off the Hook," *Financial Times*, June 27, 2009.

10. "Your Mission, Should you Choose to Accept it," *Financial Times*, February 9, 2006

11. Interview with the author, 1995.

ABN Amro, (bank), 170–1
  Volvo yacht, 162–3
Absenteeism, 77–8, 198, 256
Accounting for People, 192–3,
  208
Aconcagua, 111
Adams, Scott, 10
Adecco Institute, 91, 256
Agarwalla, Rajat and Jayant:
  Scrabulous and Lexulous,
  24–5
Age Management, 68–9
Agency Workers Directive, 52
AIG and Edward Liddy, 31
Aiken, Howard, 21
Airbus Industries, 52
Alliance Boots, 90
Al Qaeda, 32
Amazon, 179
American Association of
  University Administrators,
  217
Amiel, Henri Frederic, 77
Antigua and slavery, 35
Aon Consulting, 65
Apprentice, The, 11,123
Arkwright, Richard, 21
Armstrong, Neil, 113
Arts and Crafts movement and
  Robert Thompson, 27
Asea Brown Boveri, 179
AstraZenica, 88
Atkinson, Richard, 21

Attention Deficit Hyperactivity
  Disorder (ADHD), 5
Axelrod, Beth, 9

B & Q, 73–4, 250
Baden Powell, Lord Robert:
  Scouting for Boys, 4
Ball, Chris, 65–9
Barnevik, Percy, 179
Barry, Dave, 125
Bauerlein, Mark, 159
Becker, Brian, 198, 259
Becker, Gary, 190
Bell, Daniel:
  *The Coming of Post-Industrial
  Society,* 21
Bennis, Warren, 171, 174, 180
Bercow, John, 183
Berra, Yogi, 1, 244
Betjeman, John, 58
Bezos, Jeff, 179
Bhutto, Benazir, 98
Biaji, Marco, 53
Biederman, Patricia Ward, 174
Big Brother, 11
BlackBerry, 1, 5, 95, **113–19,**
  257
Black, Carol, 78–9
Blair, Tony, 71, 241
Blatchford, Robert, 211
Bluetooth, 119
BMW, 52–3,
Bohemian–Gay Index, 41

Bolchover, David, 131
Bonaparte, Napoleon, 178
Boyle, Susan,
   Britain's Got Talent, 143
Branding, personal, 126–7
Bridges, William: 249
   Jobshift, 10
British Airways, 212–13
   and Nadia Eweida, 33
British Broadcasting Corporation,
   Bang Goes the Theory, 164
   Desert Island Discs, 128
   Dragons' Den, 155, 179
   Great Britons, 172
   Today programme, 45
   University Challenge, 18
British Gas, 25
British Petroleum, 179
British Telecommunications,
   86–7, 118, 163–4, 250
Broadband communications, 24,
   43, 117, 118, 120, 122, 247, 255
Brown, Gordon, 66, 191
Brown, John, 179
Bruce, Fiona, 99
Brunel, Isambard Kingdom, 172,
   194
Buffet, Warren, 72, 179
Burbank, John, 128
Burns, George, 56
Business in the Community,
   Business Action on Health, 90

Caesar, Julius, 173
Careers, 54, 60, 63–4, 72, 74–5,
   137, 203, 220, 225, 249
   alternative, 148,
   of women, 98, 100–2, 105–7
   of young people, 153, 155
Carlyle, Thomas, 35, 172, 182

Carnegie, Andrew, 21, 72
Carnegie Mellon University,
   145
Carson, Rachel:
   Silent Spring, 38
Cass Business School, 159
Chambers, John, 121
Champy, James, 9, 58
Chartered Institute of Personnel
   and Development, 156
Chasten, Kay, 84
Check-out culture, 148–150
Children's Society, The, **104–5**
Chiswick Park, 83–4
Churchill, Winston, 20, 172, 210
Cisco Telepresence, 121–2
Civitas, 106
Clarke, Arthur C., 114
Clifford Chance, 207
Climate change, 15, 34, 234
Clinton, Hilary, 98
Coates and Jarratt, 212
Collins, Jim, 175, 178–9
Collins, Lt. Col. Tim, **174–8**
Colvin, Geoff, 173, 242, 251
Competencies, 154, 192
ComPsych Corporation, 75
Computer games, 143–7
   Club Penguin, 146–7
   *Massively multi-player online
      role-playing,* 146
Confederation of British Industry
   (CBI), 66, 77, 211
Conran, Shirley, 92
Countdown, 63
Courtice, Polly, 38
Crawford, Matthew:
   Shop Class as Soulcraft, 215,
      240, 242, 244, 260, 261
Credit crunch, 7, 171

Creelman, David, and Creelman Research, 134–5
Customs and Revenue Service, 89

d'Antona, Massimo, 53
Daily Mail, 18, 257
Daily Telegraph, 17, 70, 99, 106, 167, 175, 255–61
Dalgaard, Lars, **184–6,** 208
Dee, river, 71
Deedes, Bill, 70
Demographic impact on work, 12, 38, **41–55,** 68, 73, 96, 238, 239, 255, 256
Desert Island Discs, 128
Development Dimensions International (DDI), 128–9
De Wall, Anastasia, 106
Dey, Rajeev, 154
Dhanda, Parmjit, 183
Diana, Princess of Wales, 172
Dilbert, 10
Discrimination:
 age, 60, 63, 99–100
 sex, 97, 99–100
Disraeli, Benjamin, 141
Donkin, George, 5, 143, 241
Donkin, Gillian, 181, 227
Donkin, John, 241
Donkin, Robert, 5, 143, 241
Dragons' Den, 155, 179
Drucker, Peter, 22, 132, **188–190,** 220
 Landmarks of tomorrow, 21
Duke University, 217
Dunn, Judith, **104–6,** 257

Easterlin, Richard, 243
Ebsfleet United, 3
Economics of enough, 36, 38, 234

Edwards, Ifan, 133
Einstein, Albert, 209
Elevated Leadership International, 47
Elizabeth I, 186
Elizabeth II, 251
Emory University, 148
Employee engagement, 19, 26, 62, 90, 184, 194, 196, 199, **203–8,** 245–6, 250
Employment policy recommendations, **252–3**
Employment Policy Institute, 49
Enterprise Rent-A-Car, **199–200**
Environmental change, 8, 16, **38,** 160, 228, 238
Eurociett, 51–4
European Union 42, 51, 54, 55
European Working Time Directive, 215

Facebook, 6, 24,116,125,128–131, 135, 141–2, 147, 241
Family friendly policies, 102–3
Fayol, Henri, 115
Financial Times, The , 14, 29, 33, 36, 59, 81, 93,115,133, 164, 244, **254–262**
Fiennes, Ranulph, 238–9
Fitbug, 77
Flash games, 143–5
 Bloons and Harris brothers, 145
Florida, Richard:
 Who's Your City?, 41–4
Follett, Mary Parker, 108, 182, 184
Fondation Pour L'Innovation Politique, 153
Ford, Henry, 21, 214
Ford Motor Company, 3, 22, 188, 214–15

Foxtons estate agents, 130
France Telecom, 85
Frank, Robert, 180
Free agency, 10, 15, 34, 249
Friedman, Milton, 24, 214
Friends Reunited, 137

Galbraith, John Kenneth, 110, 243
Gallup Organization, The, 203
    Q12 Engagement
        questionnaire, 203, 205
Gap years, 150–1, 217
Garmin Global Positioning
    System, 111–12
Gates, Bill, 24, 72, 223
General Electric, 11,178
General Motors, 28, 254
Genghis Khan, 172
Gervais, Ricky:
    The Office, 10–11
Generational groupings, 47
    Baby boomers, 47, 58, 63, 161,
        228, 238
    Millenials, 47, 160
Ghosn, Carlos, 99
Ghoshal, Sumantra, 17
Gibbs, Robert, 113
Gilligan, Andrew, 45
Gladwell, Malcolm, 114, 138, 142
Globalization, 12, 28–30, 32, 39, 238
Global warming, 238, 247
GMB General Union, 213
Godden, Charles, 111
Goldman Sachs, 98
Goodwin, Fred, **169–171**
Goody, Jade, 18
Google, 24,147,160, 201–2, 244,
    258
Gourlay, Alex, 90
Graduate, The, 148

Granovetter, Mark,
    The Strength of Weak Ties, 139
Gutenberg, Johannes, 8, 140

Hadfield-Jones, Helen, 9
Hakim, Catherine, 97, **100–4,**
    109, 256
Hammer, Michael, 9, 58
Handy, Charles, 10, 61, 72
Hanks, Tom,
    Forrest Gump, 19
Harding, Matt,
    WherethehellisMatt.com, 155
Harper, Professor Sarah, 61
Harvard Business Review, 9
Harvard Medical School, 89
HBOS, 31
Headhunters, 169–170, 179
Healthy work places, 12, 14, 28,
    36, 47, 65, 68, **77–91,** 104,
    111, 194, 207, 211, 220, 250,
    253, 256,
Hebrew University, Paul
    Baerwald School of Social
    Work, 212
Heckscher, Charles,
    White Collar Blues, 58
Henley Centre HeadlightVision,
    151–4
Hertz, Noreena, 37
Hester, Stephen, 244
Hewlett Packard, Halo system, 121
Higher Education Policy Institute,
    96–7
Hitler, Adolf, 172
Hoffer, Eric, 162
Hoolihan, Anne, 47
Holmes, Andrew:
    Commoditization and the
        Strategic Response, 27–8, 254

Home Depot, 179
Honda, 214
Horton, Richard, 46
Hot-desking, 22
House of Commons, 69, 167
House of Lords, 69
Hudson Solutions, 150
Human Capital, 9, 13, 39,
    188–197, 205, 208, 246, 259
    Metrics, 89, 189, 193, 195, 208,
    225, 236, **252–3**
Human Capital Management,
    188, **192–3,** 196
Human Capital Standards Group,
    192–3, 195, 205, 208
Human motivation, 180, 192
Human Resources Management,
    9, 26, 84, 92, 188–9, 197–8,
    212
Huselid, Mark, 197–8, 259
Hutton Inquiry, The , 45
Huxley, T. H., 8

Immelt, Jeff, 179
Immigration laws, 50
Incomes Data Services, 29
Infosys Technologies, 28–9
Institute of Ageing, Oxford
    University, 61
Institute of Directors, 129
Institute for Employment Studies,
    95, 256
Institute for Public Policy
    Research, 211
Interim Management, 10, **61,** 249
International Labour
    Organization (ILO), 30–1
    World of Work Report 2008, 30
Internet,
    Wi-Fi networks, 67, 120

Investors in People (IIP), 192
iPhone, 5, 117

Jackson, Samuel L., 168
Job ownership, 245, **250**
JobVent.com, 200–1
John Lewis Partnership, 36, 250
Jones, Peter, 155
Jordan, Vernon, 138
Josse, Sebastien, 163–5
JP Morgan Asset Management, 164
Judge Business School, University
    of Cambridge, 37

Kaplan, Robert, and Norton,
    David, 198
Kaplinsky, Natasha, 100
Keen, Andrew:
    The Cult of the Amateur, 7–8
Kellaway, Lucy, 105, 115
Kelly, David, 45
Kennedy, John F., 16
Keynes, John Maynard, 34
Khan, Ustad Ali Akbar, 242
King, Martin Luther, 13, 149
Kingsmill, Denise, 192
Kipling, Rudyard:
    If, 14
Kirkbride, Julie, 167
Kochan, Tom, 48
KPMG, 156
Kutuzov, Mikhial Illarionovich,
    165

Larkin, Philip, 2
Lawrence, Paul, 180, 182
Layard, Richard, **104–6,** 257
Leadership, 9–10, 39, 47, 101,
    162–183, 201, 225, 253
    metrics, 192–3, 206

League of Nations, 32
Leary, Timothy, 58
Led Zeppelin, 236
Lee, Richard, 35
Lewis, Alfred, 189
Lincoln, Abraham, 76, 166
LinkedIn, 138–9
Lionhead studios, 223
Litchfield, Paul, 86–8
Lloyds Bank, 31
London School of Economics, 26,
    78, 97
Lovelock, James:
    Gaia hypothesis, 16
Loyalty in the workplace, 9, 58,
    62, 157, 178, 200
Lubbock, John, 210
    And St Lubbock's Days 210
Lunch breaks, 81–2

Macarov, David, 212
MacArthur, Ellen, **163–5**
Machiavelli, Niccolo, 173,
    175, 177
Machlup, Fritz, 21
Macmillan, Harold, 63, 166
Macri, Joe, 110
Maita, Aki, 5
Maitland, Alison, **98–9,** 101,
    107, 257
Management Today, 64, 246
Manchester United, 168
Manpower, 216, 260
Marat, Jean-Paul, 137
Marcos, Imelda, 37
Martin, Michael, 167, 183
Maslow, Abraham:
    Hierarchy of Needs, 39
McCain, John, 141–2
McCandless, Christopher, 148

McClelland, David, 242
McDonald's McCareers, 130
McKellen, Ian, 168
McKinsey & Co, 9, 32, 124, 154
McKnight, William,
    3M, 24
McLuhan, Marshall, 140
Meaney, Mary, 124
Mellander, Charlotta, 41–4
Members of Parliament,
    Expenses scandal, 140, **167–8,**
    173
Merkel, Angela, 98
Metropolitan Police, 45, 54
Microsoft, 24, 72, **110–11,** 117,
    122, 133, 158, 223, 250
    Windows operating system,
    111, 117, 223
Michaels, Ed, 9
Michigan, University of, Business
    School, 138
Michener, James A., 41
Milgram, Stanley and Small
    Worlds (six degrees of
    separation), 137–8
Miller, Arthur, 118
Miller, Tim, 205, 246
Milligan, Spike 241
Mintzberg, Henry, 115
Mobile telephones,
    early use, 114
    curbs on, **119–120**
Molyneux, Peter, 223
Mondragon, 36
Moran, Margaret, 167
Morgan Stanley Asia
    and Stephen Roach, 32
Morecambe Bay cockle pickers, 51
Moynagh, Michael and Worsley,
    Richard,

Working in the Twenty-First Century, 140
MIT Sloan School of Management, 48
MySpace, 128, 147
Muntz, Annemarie, 52

Nardelli, Bob, 179
NASA, 159, 195, 235
National Clarion Cycling Club, 211
National Health Service, 85
National Enterprise Academy, 155
Nationwide Building Society, 73–4
Nelson, Horatio, 173, 251
NetApp, 201–3
Net generation, 6, 12–13, **158–160,** 253
New work, charter for, **252–3**
New York Times, 217
Nielsen Online, 127–8, 257
Nissan, 94, 99
Nohria, Nitin, 180, 182
Noll, Henry, 187–8

Obama, Barack, 3, 13, 31, 113, 141, 143, 149, 177
Offshore Challenges, 164
Olduvai Gorge, 20
Oliver Twist, 67
Omlet.com, 147–8
Oracle of Bacon, the, and Albright College, 138
Orwell George, 5, 58, 261
Owen, Robert, 79
Oxford Entrepreneurs, 154
Oxford University, 18, 61, 154

Pausch, Randy, 145
Pay and reward:

attitudes towards, 22
consultants, **182**
executive pay, **31,** 169, 179, 182, 184, 244
freezes, **29,** 214
gender pay differences, 102
low pay, 108
metrics, 192, 194, 206,
pressure on, 27, 29, 212
redundancy pay, 53, 62
sick pay, 78, 83, 88
theory, 25–6, 108, 187, 188, 190, 214, 250
top to bottom ratios, 31, 253
Peak oil, 8, 221, 226, 229, 234, 260
Pensions:
final salary, 63–4
Heyday, 66
reduced, 48
reform, 75, 249
US, 74
Pepper, Sandy, 181–2, 259
Performance Management, 11, 184, 186, 196, 209, 246, 259
Performance Measurement, 12, 89, 185, **193–4,** 197–200, 203, 205, 209, 226, 236
Persig, Robert, 244
Personnel management, 9, 188
Peston, Robert, 8
Pew Internet and American Life project, The , 43
Philanthropic work, 72–3
Pink, Daniel: 249
Free Agent Nation, 10
Plender, John, 244
Portfolio work, 10, 33, 61, 72
Preference Theory, **100–1,** 108, 256

Pricewaterhouse Coopers, 181,
    203
PRIME, 69
Prince of Wales's Business
    and the Environment
    Programme, 38
Protestant work ethic, 2, 35, 149,
    219

Quakers, 79

Ratner, Gerald, 129
Real Madrid, 168, 208
Recruitment, 9, 54, 59, 88, 143,
    157, 214, 253
  metrics, 194, 197, 206,
  of graduates, 150, 151,156
  online, 154
Reichheld, Fred, 200
Red Brigades, 53
Reformation, 8, 23, 136
  Work place reformation, 8, 25
Renaissance, The, 136
Rentokil, 179
Ressler, Cali and Thompson, Jodi,
  Why work sucks and how to fix
    it, 132–3
Retirement, 13–14, 44, 46–7,
    56–76, 233, 239, 252, 255,
    256
Richard Rogers Partnership, 83
Richer, Julian, 114
Rifkin, Jeremy, 237
Riley, Rachel, 63
Rix, Mick, 213
Robinson, Anne:
  The Weakest Link, 11
Ronaldo, Cristiano, 168
Roosevelt, Eleanor, 75
Roosevelt, Franklin D., 172, 215

Roundhay Metal Finishers, 218
Royal Bank of Scotland, 31,
    170–1, 196, 244
Royal College of Art, 147
Royal Irish Regiment, 174–5
Royal Mail, 78, 188
Rumsfeld, Donald, 237, 238, 261
Russell, Willie, 223

Sahlins, Marshall, 35
Sail Races,
  Isle of Wight, 162–4
  Round Britain and Ireland,
    162–4
  Sevenstar, 162–4
  Vendee Globe, 162–4
  Volvo Ocean, 162–4
Sam, Anna,
  The Tribulations of a Check-
    Out Girl, 92
Sarkozy, Nicholas, 18
Sanderson, Mike, 162
Saratoga, 203, 205
Schumacher, Ernst:
  Small is Beautiful, 34
Scientific management, 26, 188,
    189, 237, 244
Scott Bader Commonwealth, 36
Scott, Selina, 99–100
Scottish Chambers of Commerce,
    211
Scouting movement, 4
Sense Worldwide, 125
Seguela, Jacques, 18–19
Sellers, Peter,
  Being There, 19
Shierholz, Heidi, 49
Shirley Valentine, 223
Shorter working weeks, 216–19,
    245

Shultz, Theodore, 189
Skype, 118, **121–2**
Slumdog Millionaire,
  and Ayush Mahesh Khedekar,
  17–18
Smith, Adam, 21, 36
Social networks, 3, 24, 39, 125,
  128, 133, 139, 211, 241
Somavia, Juan, 30
Soresen, Carsten, 26
South, Laurie, 69
South West Airlines, 200
Soylent Green, 229
Stalin, Joseph, 172
Standard Chartered Bank, 205,
  246
Standard Life Health Care, 88
Stellinger, Anna, 153
SuccessFactors, **184–6,** 195,
  246
  Stack ranker, 186
Sugar, Alan, 11, 123, 179
Sullenberger, Captain Chesley,
  56–7
Sun Tzu, 173
Sustainable living, 8, 15, 34, 38,
  164, 247
  Sustainable companies, 245

TAEN (Third Age Employment
  Network), 65–8
Taleb, Nicholas, 250
Talent Management, 123, 128,
  195, 208
Tamagotchi, 5
Tandberg, 121
Tapscott, Don: 239
  Growing up Digital, 13
  Grown up Digital, 157–160,
  217, 258, 260

Taylor, Frederick Winslow, 26,
  187, 209
Taylor, Robert, 29, 32
Teamwork, **162–183,** 252
Teletext, 85
Tele-working, 22
Teliris, 21
Temporary working, **51–3,** 61,
  158, 249
Thor, Bragi, **141–3**
Thomas Cook, 211
Thompson, Clive, 179
Tiplady, Martin, 54
Toffler, Alvin, 21
Tolstoy, Leo:
  Anna Karenina, 20–21, 40
  War and Peace, 165–6, 179
Tomlinson, Ian, 45
Torres, Raymond, 30
Toynbee, Polly:
  Hard Work, 92–4
Toyota, 29
Training and development, 26,
  185, 190, 192
  metrics, 192, 194, 206
Trimble, Gail, 18
Trump, Donald, 11
Tsar Alexander I, 165
Turner, Mark, 164
Twain, Mark:
  Tom Sawyer, 25
Twitter.com, 23, **134–5,** 227, 241,
  258
  Founders, 134

Uden, Stephen, 158
Ulrich, Dave, 198, 259
Unemployment, 29–30, 46, 49,
  58, 60, 73, 97, 214, 234
Unite Union, 53

University of Southern California,
  243
Us Now, 3, 254

Values, human in employment,
  8, **18–19,** 35, 113, 179, 190,
  201, 240
  metrics, 206
Vatican, 8
Veblen, Thorstein, *on conspicuous
  consumption,* 37
Vedior, 52
Video conferencing, 121
VieLife, 85, 89
Vietnam War, 7
Viggers, Peter, 167
Virgin Atlantic, 129
Virtanen, Marianna, 36
Voluntary Services Overseas, 72
Volvo Ocean Racing, 162–163
Vorderman, Carol, 63

Wal-Mart, 28, 130
Walsh, Willie, 212–3
Walt Disney Company, 85, 147
Walters, Robert, 151
War for Talent, The , 9, 64, 84, 245
Warhol, Andy, 128
Watson Wyatt, 197
Wayn.com, 149
Webber, Jim, 13
Welch, Jack, 11, 178–9, 254
Western Electric,
  Hawthorne experiments, 195–6
Westminster, Palace of, 82, 166, 225
Wheretowork.com, 108
Wikipedia, 4, 25
Wittenberg-Cox, Avivah, **98–9,**
  101, 107, 257

Woodley, Tony, 53
Work:
  and contraception in women,
    58, 97
  Commoditization of, **26–8,** 94,
    254
  Enjoy-Work concept, 84
  Freelance, 10, 61, 140, 164, 249
  Home working, 15, **117–18,** 133
  Long hours culture, **35–6,** 131,
    216, 252
  Migrations, 248
  *Results Only Work
    Environment,* 132–3
  Work-fit at BT, 86
Work Foundation, The, 197–8, 259
  Good Work Commission,
    244–5, 254
Work houses, 66–67
World Economic Forum, Davos,
  98
World Health Organisation, 89,
  255
World War I, 32, 165
World War II, 57, 65, 81, 172,
  202, 218, 243
World Wide Web, 4, 245

Xerox, 140

Young People Facing The Future
  report, 152–3
YouTube, 6, 118, 142, 145, 155, 260
Yuppie, (Young upwardly mobile
  professionals), 64

Zamyatin, Yevgeny, 261
Zappos.com, 134
Zopa.com, 3, 254